MW00800731

CRISTIANO LEONE

ATLAS OF PERFORMING CULTURE

CRISTIANO LEONE

ATLAS OF PERFORMING CULTURE

New York · Paris · London · Milan

.2

. 3

.4

MUSIC FESTIVALS .313

In the 1990 documentary *Un sentiment de bonheur* directed by Edgardo Cozarinsky, the art historian André Chastel recalls his memories of a distant morning on the Palatine Hill in Rome. That day, those ruins shrouded in prunus, evergreen laurel, and oleander, evoked a sensation different from the customary intellectualized approach. What he was experiencing was happiness.

In that synesthetic moment, his happiness was not evoked by dates or information—it was his imagination that had stripped the vision down to its very core, laying bare the foundation below. A prodigious performance was unraveling, something that gathered long past times, the individual, collectivity, nature, and the work of humankind.

Being constantly founded on interaction, culture is eminently relational and participatory, and therefore, at the same time, ephemeral, subjective, and unrepeatable. In this sense, culture has a profound performative power. This vision allows those who embrace culture to feel a specific kind of enjoyment associated with the intuition of an elusive aesthetic, which is inseparable both from the audience it relates to and the historical, cultural, and spatial context in which it is manifested.

The cultural creations explored in this *Atlas of Performing Culture* are the result of a subjective artistic sensitivity. However, all those leafing through these pages are invited to reactivate them with their own memories, knowledge, desires, and feelings. In this way, readers will help transform this volume into something potentially infinite through the memories it inspires.

However volatile and fleeting it may seem, every performance is indeed capable of imprinting indelible traces in the spirit of the world, like a force that simultaneously embraces, impinges, unites, and aggregates, with the aim of creating a community. Therefore, if understood as performance, culture is capable of satisfying humankind's ancestral need to observe and be observed, to move in synchrony with the pulsating breath of others, to seek and elicit a tear or a smile on a nearby face, and to generate new rituals and mythologies.

Performing culture is simultaneously body, symbol, research, commitment, creation, form, entertainment, matter, sacredness, revolution, and emotion. Most importantly, it is the act of love that binds the artist, the work, and the audience together.

The final result is not only greater than the sum of its parts but is rewritten from scratch every single time.

CULTURE THAT TRANSFORMS

What links a Japanese island-museum, the Rio Carnival, a live stream on Instagram, a debut performance in a Brussels theater, a twenty-four-hour party in the English countryside, and a cultural center in the former public funeral home on the outskirts of Paris? Apparently not much, except for one thing—they all help create a stage for one of the most profoundly rooted experiences in human existence: performance.

What do we mean by Performing Culture?

To perform is a verb meaning "to execute," "to carry out," "to accomplish." The word *performance* is one of those terms that today has taken on a multitude of meanings. In artistic contexts, the word performance defines a genre that lies somewhere between theater, dance, and visual art and involves an artist executing actions in public.

But *performance* also means a simple action carried out by a device or machine such as a car or a smartphone. *To perform* is a notion we can associate with people when they demonstrate certain abilities or achieve results in an assigned task, thus it's synonymous with traits such as "to be bright" and "on the ball," either in work contexts or in social and personal relations.

Performance, however, is not merely an attribute pertaining to effectiveness, but also a philosophical concept that incorporates a specific linguistic function and the human tendency for self-theatricalization, fundamental axes in structuring mechanisms by which people create and experience collectivity. Many philosophers have elaborated on performativity applied to diverse fields of knowledge—from linguistics and gender studies to sociology and political science—but this is neither the time nor place to explore the conceptual development of this complex and elusive term. What we will do is focus on something that has always represented a key element in human experience. That "intangible and almost nothing" connecting the disparate contexts cited in the opening lines of this text is the attitude toward performance. If it's capable of linking such a variety of realities, then we must be dealing with something very powerful indeed. Performance is a human attribute that requires no specific environmental, geographical, social, or temporal conditions to occur, as it is more a kind of anthropological pulsation. It is a function that is activated when language becomes action: when one "stops talking" about something to accomplish it, transforming both the surrounding reality and the subjects involved. A "narrative" that, by the very fact of being realized, becomes the very reality it conveys.

←
Yves Klein's performance *Anthropometry*, artist's studio, 14 Rue Campagne-Première, Paris, February 1960.

Here we refer to John L. Austin's notion of "Performativity." A linguist by profession, in the post–World War II period Austin proposed a Theory of Linguistic Acts, postulating the concept of the "performative act," whereby he demonstrated how words are not only used to describe or indicate things in the world, but are themselves things in the world that we use to perform actions. The most obvious examples to demonstrate this linguistic function are phrases such as "I baptize you," "I declare you innocent," "I pronounce you husband and wife," which have a formal value, but this same phenomenon occurs when we bet, thank, forgive, forbid, and so on. The ability to simultaneously be a vehicle of expression and an instrument of action does not pertain to spoken or written languages only, but is something that runs through all of humankind's expressive forms. What happens, then, when this process is initiated by art?

If the performance act defines the subject as much as the practices and actions it introduces, then art is the main vehicle for this pulsation to unfold and find some form of awareness; it takes on its role by unveiling itself in that very same moment. The work of art is simultaneously an act and an expression, a deed and a statement. It is the union of form and content, empowering human beings to reformulate their personal and collective experiences, highlighting the significance we attribute to things, without having to retell their story but merely attributing to them a means of direct existence.

The examples cited in the opening lines are useful to give a sense of the range to which this "anthropological pulsation," as we named it, can manifest itself. Artistic experience represents one of its manifestations, but performance is also found in other human domains as it encroaches into the realms of sociality, ritual, politics, and law.

It is not by chance that performance—through the impetus of the historical European avant-gardes—contributed to the birth of the true artistic current of "Performance Art" in the twentieth century. This term refers to an art form that was codified in the 1970s and has continued to develop to the present day, intertwining sometimes haphazardly with a wide range of performing arts.

While Performance Art was born from the historical European avant-gardes, it was in the United States between the 1950s and 1960s that it began to take on a more defined form. This is when the first use of the term "happening" was heard. It was only in the 1970s—the decade in which "performance art" made its appearance in dictionaries—that this creative movement was first theorized and most probably reached its apogee.

In that period, the movement received negative connotations that underlined the difference between Performance and other performing arts, emphasizing the apparent antithesis between performance art and the theatrical experience. When compared to traditional theatrical stagings, performance lacked a rigid narrative structure and tried to engage the spectators by eliminating any demarcation between stage and audience. This opposition between "performance" and "performing arts," particularly in the theater, is now vigorously defended by many artists, such as Marina Abramović, as reported by *The Guardian* on October 3, 2010:

> To be a performance artist, you have to hate theater. Theater is fake; there is a black box, you pay for a ticket, and you sit in the dark and see somebody playing somebody else's life. The knife is not real, the blood is not real, and the emotions are not real. Performance is just the opposite: the knife is real, the blood is real, and the emotions are real. It's a very different concept. It's about true reality.

This vision of performance art in opposition to theater is shared by many academics. The cultural anthropologist Victor Turner clearly expressed the distinction between performing arts and performance art by indicating that the latter is "making, not faking."

Yet, performance has a deeply theatrical nature, even when it is conceived as anti-theatrical. Abramović's recent work *The Seven Deaths of Maria Callas*, which was presented in the world's leading opera houses, shows how the opposition between performance art and theater is in reality much more articulated than the dichotomy would lead us to believe.

This is why this book will discuss a range of contexts in which different elements are considered as belonging to the worlds of performance art, performing arts, and through their interaction, also to the realm of architecture and visual arts. After all, the term "Performance Art" was used precisely to denote a narrow field of performance practices adopted mainly by visual artists and characterized by meticulous experimental research. Today, performance is a particularly fecund artistic discipline and ideal terrain for exploration and confrontation for artists who wish to establish a direct relationship with the audience using the body as the preferred instrument to create dialogue that can be engaging, disturbing, frivolous, or even unsettling.

This art form has always positioned itself as a synthesis of diverse media, as demonstrated by the now-historicized experiments of the last few decades. An excellent example is the landmark experience of Black Mountain College. In the 1950s and 1960s, in North Carolina, the composer John Cage, the visual artist Robert Rauschenberg, and the choreographer Merce Cunningham conducted their first

←
Marina Abramović, *The Seven Deaths of Maria Callas*, Teatro di San Carlo, Naples, 2022.

experiments by blending minimalist musical language, painting, and dance. Cage incorporated the unpredictability of experience in his compositions. Influenced by Cage's aesthetics, Cunningham revolutionized the parameters of his dance, focusing on the potential of the individual body and, like Cage in his music, on randomness. Cunningham established the order of the steps by tossing a coin and communicated only the duration of each choreographic phrase, leaving the composer complete independence. They were later joined by Rauschenberg, who collaborated on the sets for many of the Cunningham troupe shows.

The collaboration between Cage, Cunningham, and Rauschenberg undermined the traditional frontiers of the arts from the ground up, precisely through indeterminacy, improvisation, and the encroachment of dance, music, and visual arts. In August 1952, the Black Mountain College dining hall hosted an event conceived by Cage, Rauschenberg, Cunningham, and the poets Charles Olson and Mary Caroline Richards, in which the simultaneous combination of music, dance, and art gave birth to a performance destined to go down in history: *Theater Piece no. 1*. Performers had an interval of time to express themselves independently, without submitting to any predetermined musical score, choreography, or lyrics. The only constraint was the duration of each phrase of the performance, which Cage had indicated to his colleagues.

It is important to note that the very people who were considered by the early critics and theorists of the genre as the "fathers" of Performance Art called one of their performances precisely *Theater Piece no. 1*! This experience, which would impact significantly on so many other performance artists, testified early on to the intimate connection between Performance Art and Performing Arts.

Over the decades, performances have taken on countless forms, depending on the historical context and the artists who devised them. With Allan Kaprow, the conventions of pictorial representation were abandoned in favor of the interactive dimension of people in action. His performances became known as "happenings": unprecedented event-actions in which randomness played a decisive structural role. The focus on the body and dance in Anna Halprin's New Dance and the experience of George Maciunas's Fluxus group also contributed to the evolution of Performance Art. Fluxus involved artists who were active in both music and visual arts, such as La Monte Young, Yoko Ono, and Terry Riley. The artistic practices that were developing in North America would later become established in Europe, where other renowned artistic personalities such as Joseph Beuys embodied their philosophy and modes of expression.

Beginning in the 1970s, Performance began to take on a more distinct form, and proved to be a valuable instrument to reflect the cultural climate of those years.

pp. → 14 | 15

↑
Isadora Duncan dancing on the seaside, 1910s.

→
Martha Graham with Bertram Ross, *Visionary Recital*, 1961.

North American performers started to appear in Northern California in 1967. These were the years of the Peace March and the People's Park demonstrations in Berkeley, a prelude to San Francisco's Summer of Love and the birth of the psychedelic (counter)culture. In Southern California, however, performance art was characterized by profound political engagement: Judy Chicago's Feminist Art Program and the feminist movement in general appropriated this artistic medium to assert the autonomy of the body and its fundamental role in society.

Even on the East Coast in New York, performance was tinged with a political hue. Many artists rallied to the Art Workers' Coalition by taking a stand against New York's major art institutions that were guilty of not openly opposing the Vietnam War.

Performance in those years presented itself as a supreme act of opposition to the commodification of art: it was not reducible to an object, and as such could not be collected or sold as it was ephemeral and immaterial. Of course, much has changed today: performance has been fully integrated not only by the *intelligentsia* but by the market too. In the process of dematerialization of artistic creativity, performances are routinely musealized, commercialized, and collected.

The normalization of such practices undoubtedly favored their opening to a mass audience, but they never abandoned the provocative nature of their themes and content. Performance rarely lost its outrageous character, which was skillfully exploited by various artists who used it to raise heated debates about the rights of minorities, the undocumented, and the marginalized, and as such they received support from other activists and academia.

Increasingly, performers themselves became the core element of their artistic action, their own absolute protagonists. From time to time, they risked their lives, tore down taboos, and prefigured new paradigms, and they did so with their own bodies, making them mythical and instantly recognizable. Chris Burden had himself shot, Joseph Beuys conversed with a coyote, Gina Pane cut off body parts with a blade, Marina Abramović offered herself to the public's mercy surrounded by objects of pleasure or death, Hermann Nitsch slit a bull's throat, ORLAN surgically transformed her own body. Trivialized and taken out of context, these actions were enough to consecrate their authors to mass fame, raising them to the status of true icons and even commercial commodities. Today, the frontier between artistic research and showmanship is even more blurred, so much so that even some pop stars do not hesitate to propose elements of performance art to the mainstream. Figures such as Madonna or Lady Gaga come to mind.

Truth or fiction? Theater or anti-theater? Performance is neither one nor the other—yet it is both. Consider the works of Robert Wilson, such as his twelve-hour show, *The Life and Times of Sigmund Freud* (1969), or his famous *Einstein on*

→ ORLAN, *The Kiss of the Artist*, Grand Palais, Paris, 1977.

→→ Niki de Saint Phalle, *Les Tirs*, Paris, 1961.

INTRODUIRE
5F
LE BAISER DE L ARTISTE
Doublé Peau
Très pratique
Combien Féminin
Grand Luxe
MERCI

← ←
The Woodstock Music and Art Festival, Bethel, New York, August 1969.

←
Buzz Aldrin's bootprint from the Apollo 11 mission, July 1969.

↑
Philippe Petit walking across a tightrope suspended between the World Trade Center's Twin Towers, New York, August 7, 1974.

the Beach (1976). So, what is this new performance about? Theater or Performance Art? Visual art and dance converge in a powerful mélange in Wilson's work (his cast always included many visual artists and dancers). Wilson had studied art and architecture before becoming one of the century's most distinguished playwrights and theater directors. His theater united the American experimental movements of The Living Theater and The Bread and Puppet Theater, but also Antonin Artaud's Theater of Cruelty, Richard Wagner's idea of total opera, not to mention the influence of Cage, Cunningham, and New Dance. The same can be said of other theater directors such as Nekrosius, Romeo Castellucci, and Thomas Jolly to name but three.

It is time to take a break from this brief excursus, whose sole purpose was to emphasize how deeply Performance Art and Performing Arts are interconnected and well beyond our present attempt to catalog them. Experiments in the artistic fusion of theater, literature, visual arts, dance, and music in a performance dimension certainly did not begin with the US art experiences of the 1950s. Before being writers, painters, or sculptors, the Futurists, Dadaists, and Surrealists were performers. The medium of the performance allowed them to manifest their ideas, to make them concrete, and to create interaction with the audience. Many Futurist actions were not conceived as artistic expressions in and of themselves, but were created or undertaken for their provocative significance. They were gestures of social, political, and cultural rupture. Only later—when artists finally defined and connoted their movements—did their production adapt to more conventional modes of expression and eventually reach the stage of producing material objects.

In reality, the culture of performance has its roots in the nature of humanity, in its need to reconcile body and idea, to belong to a community, thus allowing the individual not only to survive, but to find a deeper meaning than mere material existence.

Therefore, culture is indeed performance, because it entails a living and unbroken relationship with its creators, with those who enjoy it, with the city, with history, and with the historical context in which it was born. The indissoluble relationship between space—whether urban, natural, or even digital—and its inhabitants gives rise to pulsating and ever-changing configurations; vital intensities and accents are intercepted by art to trigger a complex dialogue with different spaces, architectures, and communities. In the past few decades, we have seen decisive public investment in this relationship between art, culture, and urban spaces. Governments recognize its potential to regenerate the fabric of the city, which is the most common form in which contemporary human societies have chosen to aggregate. By virtue of their nature, art forms with a prevalent performance component seem

→

Romeo Castellucci, *Sul concetto di volto nel figlio di Dio*, Theater der Welt festival, Essen, June 2010.

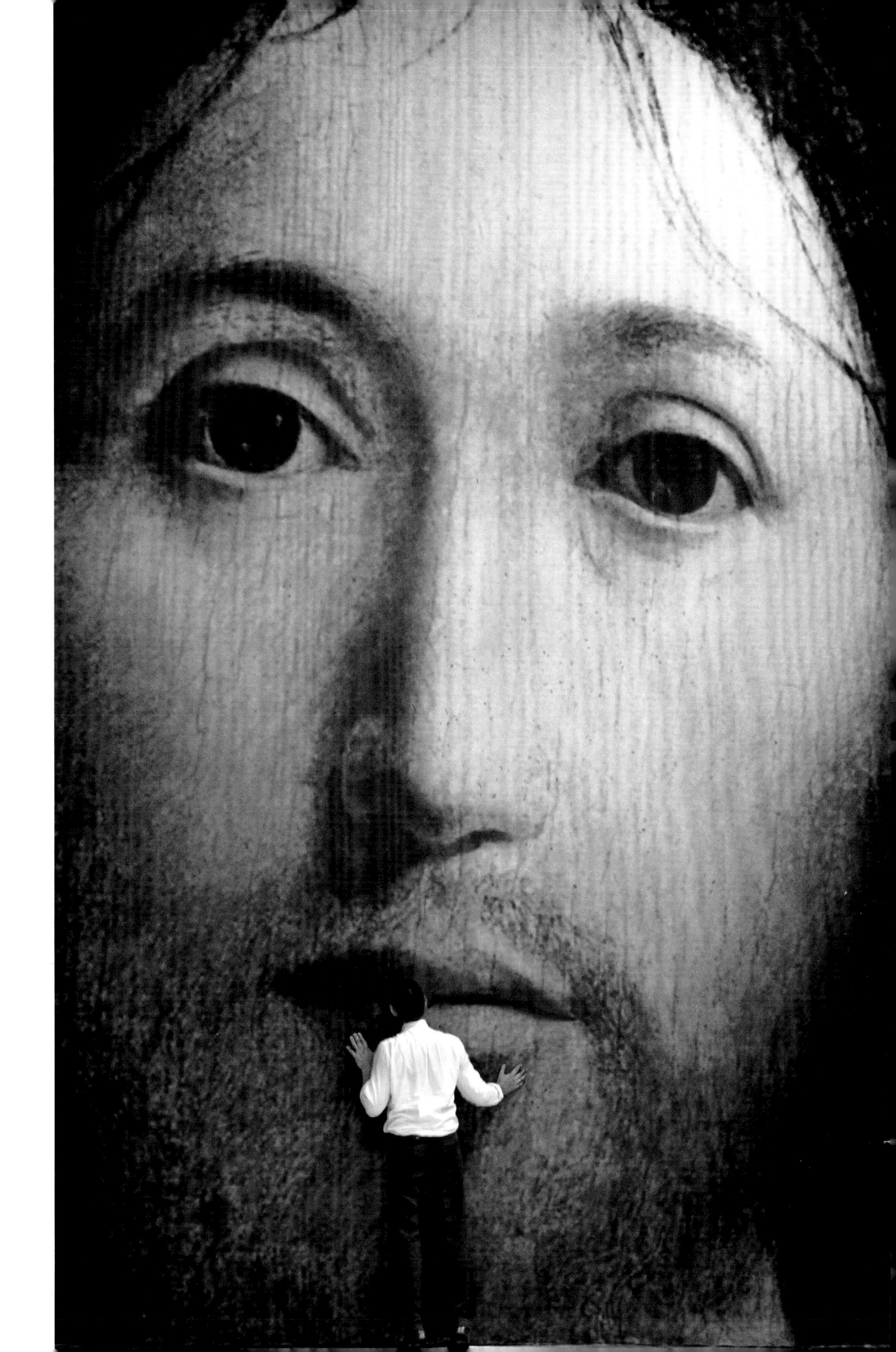

to be ideal allies of local governments and are an important contribution not only in redefining cultural policies, but also play a role within essential social functions such as fostering aggregation, education, inclusion, and empowerment.

They do so through hybrid languages, by drawing on the tensions of contemporaneity, by questioning the environment and its manifestations by placing the body and gesture at the center, for the performer as well as for the observer. Therefore, the performance element is usually the chosen art form to impact on collective political, social, and aesthetic processes. The mechanisms they exploit, however, are the same found elsewhere: in archaic rituals, contemporary forms of aggregation, the dynamics of social networks—all with varying degrees of awareness and organization.

If history has shown us the centrality of art in the development of human societies, the present time obliges us to make an important reflection. The pandemic marked a potent pause, which touched this pulsation at the very core, radically challenging the way people work, how they experience the city, how they aggregate, talk, and greet each other. There is a pre- and a post-pandemic time, which affects our social lives as much as our political, professional, and cultural lives. What was before, and what is going to be after? This is where this book starts, from the need to examine what has existed so far and how it existed in order to create a fixed image of something constantly in motion, something that projects itself and has been projected into something else. A partial and inevitably rarefied image, sure, but one that nonetheless proposes new pathways worthy of further exploration.

In these chapters, we will depart on a journey into the countless possibilities through which culture morphs into a collective performance, exploring places where it comes alive and the mechanisms it follows. This is a potentially endless journey, which will proceed in two steps: first, delving into some specific cases used as examples, no matter how ephemeral and flexible; and then, offering short focuses to demonstrate how inextricably culture is linked to performance. A sort of storytelling carried out through snapshots and evocative images in an attempt to reveal the variety and complexity in which our cultural system operates.

This is an incomplete, provisional, and volatile atlas born from a specific and subjective vision, namely the personal experience of the author, whose gaze is inevitably influenced by the social and cultural context in which he belongs. Without claiming to be complete and exhaustive but attempting to present as many geographical contexts as possible, this book was imagined with the purpose of sharing a personal journey through the many forms by which culture manifests itself and how it impacts on reality. As such, it starts from the creative language of art that is closest to the author to then reach out to other dimensions pertaining to a more diffuse and everyday sociality. We will explore various situations and contexts worldwide, ranging from institutional to independent and commercial entities, to discover that they are far more connected than the "almost nothing" we assumed at the beginning. We will demonstrate how public space is indeed expanding and dematerializing. At the conclusion of our wanderings through art centers, museums, theaters, foundations, festivals, etc., we will understand how in the post-pandemic cultural system, the frontiers of the digital dimension have definitely widened; the digital is now considered a "public" place for all intents and purposes, whose specificity and criticality we are still trying to comprehend. We use the adjective "public" in quotation marks because although the platforms through which the digital dimension operates are primarily private, having an online presence has become a necessity for many public cultural institutions, and above all for individuals. There is a growing need to be visible and perform in the collective space, where many of the phenomena that are important to our existence take place.

Among other things, the dichotomy between public and private has always greatly influenced the dynamics of the cultural system, involving the flow of funds, modes of action, and the aesthetic and ethical developments of cultural production in a complex intertwining of political vision and economic interests, which together determine the role and function of art within society. As we shall see in more detail, there are several possible configurations involving public function, economic sustainability, and artistic vision, which give rise to a multiplicity of models and highly diverse forms that in the end can be very distant from the notion of cultural action. Shifting between public funding, business plans, local governments, and the utopias of visionary entrepreneurs, we will observe how the very concept of "artistic direction" is in a state of flux and is implementable in different ways each time.

The cases we deal with in the following chapters show different ways in which a cultural project comes to life. In many of these cases, what is essential is the willingness of an individual—whether an artist, operator, or entrepreneur—to follow up on a personal idea or desire (which at times can be backed by public administrations), around which a network of support and collaboration is created. There are, however, other cases in which politics is the driver behind a particular project that is considered to be aligned with certain political and electoral goals, relying on established figures active in the artistic field as well as associations and entities from the region. These examples demonstrate how the intuition of the single person, however fundamental it may be, is not

←
Masayoshi Sukita, *David Bowie: Watch That Man III*, 1973.

→
Diana Ross performing on stage in Central Park, New York, July 1983.

←

Fernanda Oliveira and Fabian Reimair performing in Jiří Kylián's *Petite Mort*, produced by the English National Ballet, Sadler's Wells, London, 2015.

→

Zhang Huan performing *12 Square Meters*, Beijing, 1994.

sufficient to implement a cultural project but acts as a catalyst to activate a "movement"—a group of people coming together as a team, a specific art scene, or the inhabitants of a specific place—to intercept certain preexisting needs, desires, and tensions. Once again, culture is performative because it always involves relationships and triggers transformation.

The classification used to distinguish and group together the different case studies is often artificial, but at the same time it is instrumental in highlighting the similarities and diversities of the various forms in which the cultural system is structured. We will follow a trajectory useful in reconnecting the contemporary arts to that anthropological pulsation referred to earlier. The goal is to concretely demonstrate how the performative process intervenes to transform the experience of everyone by merely interacting with their imagery and everyday life.

We will start by examining multipurpose cultural centers, physical places where artistic and cultural activities manifest their relationship with architecture, the urban fabric, and the natural environment. After all, the relationship between human beings and nature, artistic artifacts, architectural spaces, or historical and archaeological traces of the past is also profoundly performative. We will then move on to other specific spaces designated for live performance activities, namely theaters. Then we will abandon the idea of physical space and adopt a space/time approach by exploring the panorama of multidisciplinary festivals (that is, ephemeral and temporary events that make uniqueness their salient characteristic), considering those that choose only one or more performing arts as their focal activity. We will then deal with the great music festivals, moving closer to the idea of gathering, ritual, and collective celebration that has punctuated human history from its earliest forms of existence. This itinerary will debunk the detestable cliché whereby contemporary art, and particularly performance art, is incomprehensible, self-referential, and infinitely distant from people's concrete lives; something ephemeral that has nothing to do with the issues facing humanity over time. Wandering from city to city to explore these places and realities will give us insight into the infinite variety with which different cultures can mold something inescapable and constantly present in our lives. We will trace the lines that connect high-brow art to more popular forms of entertainment, countercultures, civil and religious rituals, and finally, social networks, in a wide flow of images, gestures, sensations, emotions, and concepts where nothing is ever detached from or unrelated to its surroundings, where everything is bound together in a single and constantly unfolding web. This is our understanding of Performing Culture.

↑
Yuval Avital, *Foreign Bodies no. 1 / Icon no. 91*, Blenio Valley, Switzerland, 2017.

CULTURE THAT TRANSFORMS SPACE

CULTURE THAT TRANSFORMS SPACE

Just as the present time is ever more taking the form of a kaleidoscope of possibilities, so are the artistic languages that encompass it, thus promoting a porous relationship with the host space, urban communities, and not least, the natural environment. The first chapter focuses on the realities that highlight how culture transforms space and consequently enters into a close relationship with the local communities. While on the one hand we will be looking at abandoned constructions—old disused factories, former neighborhood markets or public morgues—which, since the post-war period and increasingly so during the 1990s and 2000s, have been renovated and used as cultural centers, on the other we will discover some "hidden corners of paradise," where natural elements are linked to artistic and architectural interventions to show their intrinsic relationship, connecting the enhancement of the region to that of cultural heritage. This, too, is part of Performing Culture, far more than one can imagine.

The model these cultural centers adopt is often multifunctional, multidisciplinary, and experiential. Their purpose is to house under a single roof a heterogeneous cultural mission able to channel different target audiences toward the enjoyment of multiple formats, satisfy the productive needs of the artistic community, and offer the general public a place that can fulfill different social functions, ensuring a specific and pleasurable experience. These venues offer the possibility of a direct, intimate, and deep relationship with the artworks—from interactive projects to insightful meetings and guided tours, from sensory experiences to side activities, such as drinking, eating, and shopping. By changing the frame in which art is enjoyed, its meanings are enriched; furthermore, a sort of ripple effect is created that transforms the very context where all this takes place.

Therefore, these are places devoted on the one hand to artistic production, on the other to the demands of contemporary society, in which meetings and exchanges between different lifestyles can happen. These places help generate a broader awareness of the meaning of "artwork," demonstrating that it is not only the product of the artist's creativity, but anything that, placed in a certain frame, can help us discover new sensations and readdress the significance of our everyday lives, leading us to rethink the meanings and codes shared by the community. If we acknowledge art as an alteration in language that becomes an expression and affects the observer or participant by inducing some form of transformation, we will discover that these places act in the same way as an artwork, not only providing the viewer/visitor with objects to admire, but also acting as devices capable of triggering this transformation. As we shall see in detail, performance is an intrinsic feature of the very existence of these places, requiring the conscious activation of a connection between time, space, subjectivity, and collectivity.

One of the planes where this lively and energetic dynamic is most visible is its relationship with architecture. We shall see that the reassessment of spatial organization, the manipulation of materials, and the elaboration of meanings (historical as well as symbolic) associated with forms, structures of space, and environmental elements are central to the reactivation and refunctionalization of these venues. Here, high-brow culture is offered to new audiences and devises new frameworks in which to express itself. Dialogue with the communities—both urban and rural—that inhabit the places where these centers are installed is of primary importance for the definition of goals, possibilities, and responsibilities. In any case, it is worth realizing that these processes almost never occur spontaneously and are often the result of a specific political will or of the emergence of more general trends, which intertwine and stimulate phenomena that reverberate in urban contexts and their communities. These are trends and phenomena that should be monitored, supported, and governed. Consider how "urban redevelopment" is associated with the gentrification of contemporary cities, a process that undoubtedly reflects a potential for development and improvement of the living conditions in certain areas of the city, but at the same time implies the risk of speculation and the exacerbation of phenomena such as marginalization and the radicalization of social conflict. And also consider how mass tourism is affecting—often positively, sometimes negatively—the development of certain geographical areas: previously distant from cultural trajectories, now they are global tourist destinations that have to face issues such as the protection of local communities, exploitation of environmental heritage, and the redistribution of resources.

By relating themselves to the site's historical heritage and meaning, these cultural centers manage to change the feeling that certain places embody but without losing track of them. Thus, the culture they produce narrates a new idea of the city, re-elaborates the relationship between city center and periphery, as well as between city and rurality; it rethinks its own function, and offers insight into new possible articulations between human beings and the natural environment. This, too, is part of performing culture.

104 CENTQUATRE–PARIS

104.FR

— *From undertakers to the heart of life*

↑

104 Centquatre–Paris.

Located in the 19th arrondissement of Paris, at 104 Rue d'Aubervilliers, Centquatre–Paris is a space for artistic residency, production, and dissemination, hosting a wide range of cultural activities for the most diverse audiences.

Conceived by its director José-Manuel Gonçalvès and his team as a collaborative artistic platform, 104–Paris brings together a vocation for inclusion and a focus on the most innovative contemporary production.

Once inside, the center offers many possibilities to experience its different programs: shops, restaurants, free spaces for artistic practices also including activities for children, a hub for urban and cultural planning, and coworking for startups, in a crossover of art and innovation. The 104–Paris experience is an example of cultural planning in which a project of urban regeneration resulted in a composite space in which all strata of the city can converge.

COMING BACK TO LIFE

In 1870, the archbishopric of Paris, which was in charge of the city's burials, established the municipal funeral home in these buildings, which then came under the management of the City of Paris in 1905 and remained in operation until the late 1990s, when the Municipality's monopoly on funeral services ended.

In 2003, the then-mayor of Paris, Bertrand Delanoë, decided to renovate the site, continuing his policy of cultural revitalization and architectural renewal of the city. In 2006, this initiative would be incorporated into the "Grand Paris" project, an intervention plan aimed at transforming the Parisian conurbation into a global and European metropolis, while at the same time integrating the suburbs into the life of the city. Delanoë is also credited with the construction of the Gaîté Lyrique, the restoration of the Théâtre du Rond-Point, and the conception of the Cité de la Mode et du Design. He is also considered the inventor of the Nuit Blanche, later exported to other European cities, and finally Paris Plage, a summer initiative whereby the Seine riverbanks are lined with sand to create temporary city beaches.

The intention was also to sustain social development at a neighborhood level. Thus, 104–Paris was designed to become an internationally relevant cultural hub but with a pivotal national role, while enhancing the local heritage and offering a model of social cohesion and cultural inclusion.

→→
Centquatre–Paris, the Nef Curial.

A public tender was launched, which was won by Atelier Novembre, an architectural firm specializing in public buildings, whose design best respected

étition
Oppenheim

POUSSER

the authenticity of the site. 104–Paris was to be a place of circulation open to the neighborhood, an artery, a place of aggregation and discovery. Atelier Novembre envisaged the central entrance to become a "public thoroughfare," connecting 104 Rue d'Aubervilliers and 5 Rue Curial.

In 2005, Mayor Delanoë appointed two figures from the theater sector as directors of 104: Robert Cantarella, actor, director, and playwright, and Fréderic Fisbach, director and theater and opera actor, proving how from the earliest stages the theatrical matrix would characterize the development of these hybrid venues in which the performing arts flourish today. Cantarella and Fisbach envisioned an "anti-museum," with the ambition to revolutionize the relationship between the public and artists by hosting creative activities representing all disciplines and opening these to the public. Thus, visitors could watch art "in progress" in a micro-neighborhood within a working-class area that was capable of attracting a sophisticated audience, on a par with more institutional venues such as the Palais de Tokyo, by offering an original mélange of culture and society.

Fisbach recalls that they rewarded the architects' idea of crossing, of this artist-occupied "street" where one could walk, sit, discuss, and eat. They believed in social inclusion through culture, and their hope was that this venue would cultivate it.

On completion of the renovation works, the 39,000 square meters of usable space housed sixteen production workshops, two performance auditoriums, five ateliers open to amateur associations, thirteen ateliers for artists-in-residence, rooms adaptable in size and setup for working groups, and spaces from 22 to over 300 square meters to rent for events.

The center was opened on October 11, 2008, and criticism was not long in coming. The City of Paris was the sole public funder, with an initial investment of 100 million euros and annual grants of eight million euros: a decidedly high cost for the municipal coffers, which did not correspond to an equally high rate of public participation. The cultural program was considered too elitist with the center being perceived as an alien object, detached from the social fabric of the neighborhood. To address this criticism, the mayor appointed a new director through a public call in June 2010. The choice was made for a figure with solid experience in managing suburban cultural spaces and José-Manuel Gonçalvès, former director of the Ferme du Buisson (an old nineteenth-century farm converted into a cultural center in the 1980s), was selected.

→

Centquatre–Paris, Halle Aubervilliers.

Gonçalvès's strategy moved toward rethinking the spatial logic of the venue, and what was formerly perceived as a static museum became more of a living structure, thanks to the promotion of actions aimed to revitalize its cultural and artistic mission in an attempt to reconnect it with the city.

THE PLATFORM OF THE ARTS — In order for 104–Paris to effectively become a center of national importance without losing its strong regional heritage, it was given the legal status that could take into account this dual identity. Thus it was made an EPCC, a public institution of cultural cooperation. José-Manuel Gonçalvès reimagined the center as an artistic and collaborative platform open to all arts and offering an accessible, contemporary, and engaged program. 104–Paris's mission was oriented toward fostering contemporary art creation through artistic residencies and support for cultural facilities, but also toward economic development, thanks to the participation of businesses, with halls available for conferences, events, fairs, etc., and partnerships with institutions such as Gaumont and the BNP Paribas Foundation. At the same time, it proposed itself as a focal point for social development in the neighborhood, providing citizens with a lively place of cultural empowerment involving the active engagement of the neighborhood. Finally, it set down its blueprint for the development of research and innovation through the "104factory," a startup incubator offering workspace, meeting rooms, and access to entrepreneurial training and one-on-one support.

The homepage of the 104–Paris website is a useful starting point to get a sense of the life and activities that take place here. Photo exhibitions, jazz concerts, live electronic music, hip-hop sessions, Qi Gong classes, workshops for children, guided tours, emerging theater festivals, a bookstore, and an organic market. One of the main features of this space is precisely its ability to organize its own strong, centralized, and coherent plan, while acting on different levels through alternative uses of the space and different approaches to user engagement. Without being able to examine in detail the vast number of events, reviews, projects, and initiatives that have transited here, let us schematically mention the project lines that have animated the cultural offer of 104–Paris in recent years.

↓
Centquatre–Paris, Cour de l'Horloge.

SUPPORTING CREATIVITY — 104–Paris plays an important role in supporting artistic creativity by providing a production space for established and emerging international artists and offering to the general public different ways to engage with artistic practices. In addition to rented rehearsal rooms and workspaces, each year 104–Paris identifies some national and international artists who are invited to work on their own creations for a significant period of time to establish solid and lasting links with the center and the neighborhood, while also providing production support. Some names involved in this initiative are Olivier Dubois, Alessandro Sciarroni, Lia Rodrigues, and Bertrand Bossard. Then, there is a more open form of artistic residency known as *résidence d'essai*, aimed at national and international professional artists, as well as art school students of all disciplines, which is accessed through a selection process by submitting a portfolio of the applicant's work. This program provides a workspace for a period of one to three weeks. In addition, 104–Paris offers a program, *Centquatre on the Road*, to disseminate in-house productions by supporting its associated artists in France and abroad in establishing collaborative agreements with theaters, museums, public spaces, companies, and schools. 104–Paris also presents an annual artistic program that includes performances, concerts, exhibitions, festivals, and installations both showcasing the works of artists-in-residence and the work of others. 104–Paris also allows access to some of its outdoor spaces on a first-come-first-serve basis and free-of-charge.

As a consequence, these shared spaces change physiognomy from courtyard or square to rehearsal hall or stage, and so on. They are available for anyone to practice art freely. This hybrid approach to using space at a personal and professional level generates an organic, creative, and ever-changing relationship with the structure and with the people who live in these spaces daily.

THE RELATIONSHIP WITH THE CITY — 104–Paris promotes various initiatives aimed at strengthening its relationship with the fabric of the city by developing specific projects to channel certain groups, such as students from local schools, toward its artistic programming. *Le Cinq*, a project intended for local associations and individual residents of the eighteenth and nineteenth arrondissements of Paris, operates along these lines. Each year *Le Cinq* welcomes more than

pp. → 46

20,000 people, offering the opportunity to take free classes, workshops, and training programs in its spaces, and engaging them in various activities that are part of its general program. Great attention is also given to the younger generations: children are accompanied through a series of visits and meetings to familiarize with art and specific projects. *La Maison des Petits*, where girls and boys up to five years old and their parents can spend time together, play, create, and meet other children, always under the supervision of a team of childcare workers. Finally, 104–Paris houses a brasserie, café, restaurant, pizzeria, and an organic market, as well as a number of businesses concerned with the issue of sustainable consumption, such as Emmaüs Défi, an affordable and fair-trade store for used clothing and objects, and L'Effet PAP', a boutique selling objects, gifts, decorations, and wellness products made by French eco-sustainable companies.

→ Centquatre–Paris, the Nef Curial.

OPENING THE GAZE

-

Just as the 104–Paris spaces are used for different activities and practices, the artistic programming conceived by Gonçalvès pursues a similar idea of heterogeneity and openness by putting together a series of activities including avant-garde contemporary creations, performances, and exhibitions aimed at drawing the attention of the general public while maintaining an open dialogue with the latest in pop languages familiar to the younger generations. Mixing genres, articulating the local and the international dimension, and interweaving a number of art forms—contemporary theater, visual arts, dance, circus, and magic shows—that highlight the vitality of art and its ability to dialogue with the environment are the mainstays of the director's artistic programming. All forms of "street art" are welcomed, the finest examples being showcased from time to time. For dance, Gonçalves has always given emphasis to hip-hop, perhaps the most iconic urban dance style ever. Furthermore, at 104–Paris street dance is practiced freely within its open spaces. The same approach shapes the music and visual art programming: quality, heterogeneity, participation, and a refreshing breath of "pop" are combined with an innovative artistic commitment to engage as diverse an audience as possible. Thus, the music program includes concerts, live and DJ sets, sound installations touching on a wide range of genres: electronic, classical, rock, jazz, pop, spoken word, etc. The art program embraces solo and group exhibitions, ranging from photography, painting, and sculpture to digital and street art.

Two episodes that speak well of 104–Paris's approach to conceiving its artistic mission are the Keith Haring retrospective in 2013 and the display of the BIC Collection in 2018. The first was the result of collaboration between 104–Paris and the Musée d'Art Moderne de Paris and celebrated the artist perhaps most present in the collective imagination, whose works originated on the very streets of the city. During the retrospective, three large sculptures were installed in the courtyard of 104–Paris, also visible from outside: a choice confirming the desire to create links with the public, to let art overflow into the city. The second was an exhibition including installations, sculptures, videos, designs, and fashion creations of a collection born in 1998 for an exhibition in Italy for which artists were asked to create works related to the company founded by Marcel Bich. In this exhibition, the BIC pen—perhaps one of the most widely used objects in our time—became a medium for artistic creation, inspiring more than 150 works by over 80 international artists.

The two exhibitions enabled 104–Paris to consolidate its standing both in the city and internationally. Thus, art leaves behind the narrow horizon of the museum or gallery to unleash its ability to speak to people in an inclusive environment, where artistic language manipulates and comments on communal feelings, in which it becomes possible to reconstruct a collective and shared horizon. ❡

MATADERO MADRID

MATADERODMADRID.ORG

— *An ever-changing cultural ecosystem*

↑
Centro de Creación Matadero Madrid.

Moving farther south in Europe, we have another remarkable example of urban redevelopment that follows the logic of cultural promotion and the relationship between architecture, urban development, and the performing arts explored in the previous example. We are again in a suburb but now in Madrid, in the southern part of the city, within an architectural complex that once housed Madrid's abattoir, one of many industrial buildings transformed during the twentieth century and designated for a cultural function.

Just as with 104–Paris, the story of Matadero Madrid also tells us about the dynamics of European cultural policies, but presents some differences from the French case. Firstly, the architecture of Matadero Madrid is a fine example of the Neomudéjar style, a late nineteenth-century architectural movement that became the "Spanish" variant of the Neo-Moorish architectural style, characterized by the use of ornaments, tiles, or bricks to form abstract patterns.

Matadero Madrid, as the website states, is "an international center of culture and artistic creation" that hosts a program of exhibitions, theater performances, festivals, live music, film and audiovisual projects, conferences, workshops, artistic residencies, educational programs, and family activities. All these are born from the specificities of the institutions that inhabit the center, interweaving their areas of activity and building international networks and collaborations. "Matadero encourages the meeting of languages in search of exchange and contamination between different modes of cultural production, thus facilitating interdisciplinary experiences. It is an ecosystem that accommodates a wide range of uses, initiatives, and agents in its buildings," the website reads.

If the 104–Paris defines itself an "organism" on its website, Matadero Madrid chooses the metaphor of the "ecosystem," emphasizing "the diversity of the institutions that form part of the center." Indeed, Matadero's management model envisages the coexistence of several collaborating entities, each offering their own activities and program lines—a transversal dynamic fostering a varied landscape to articulate the public function of this space. Heterogeneity and a hybrid nature characterize not only its cultural mission and end users but are intrinsic traits of its very structure and organization. This dimension also emerges in the use of another term: interdisciplinarity rather than multidisciplinarity, in the sense of a place that not only accommodates different languages and forms of expression, but also aims to bring them together and intersect, resulting in hybrid artistic practices and works.

→→
Eugenio Ampudia, *Every word is like an unnecessary stain on silence and nothingness*, Matadero Madrid, 2015.

FROM ABATTOIR TO PUBLIC SPACE

Located in the Arganzuela neighborhood, Matadero Madrid consists of forty-eight buildings covering over 165,000 square meters, which served as an abattoir and cattle market in twentieth-century Madrid. As in other urban centers, over the decades its facilities became obsolete, together with its function of supplying fresh meat to the city. From the 1980s onward, the various buildings were used for sociocultural purposes, the first steps in transforming the defunct past of this place into a present of life and art. Indeed, in the 1990s the old stables were converted to the headquarters of the National Ballet of Spain and the National Dance Company; in 1996, the remaining area of the abattoir was finally decommissioned and assigned to the 1997 general urban plan.

In the 2000s, the city administration issued a public tender to entrust these spaces to a private operator, but the initiative was unsuccessful, and in the meantime, several local associations requested to use these spaces for their activities. As we saw in Paris, then-mayor José María Álvarez del Manzano took matters into his hands, aiming to implement a project of urban transformation with an ecological slant to redevelop not only the site of the former abattoir but also the area adjacent to the Manzanares River.

In 2003, under a new municipal government, the overall strategy for the redevelopment of the Matadero changed to become part of a wider program to rehabilitate Madrid's historical heritage. The city administration decided to convert the space into a large laboratory for the creation and production of contemporary art, giving Madrid its own cultural center capable of addressing a wide range of audiences and disciplines, something which up till then it did not have.

At the time, there was no legal framework to manage this project, and so the decision was taken to create an institution that would support creative work and also link the various existing cultural centers in Madrid, which had previously operated as independent entities. This institution would act as a metropolitan contemporary cultural center while maintaining the specific character already operative in each individual building. Thus, a management model was created that brought public and private bodies together to act as a not-for-profit entity.

The new project, presented in 2006, was designed as a support program for creatives, collectives, and cultural workers in the Spanish capital. Its aim was to provide for the diverse needs in creating contemporary works by supporting alternative and independent realities, developing collaborative processes in the capital, fostering international mobility, and providing assistance in the production of new works and the circulation of existing ones.

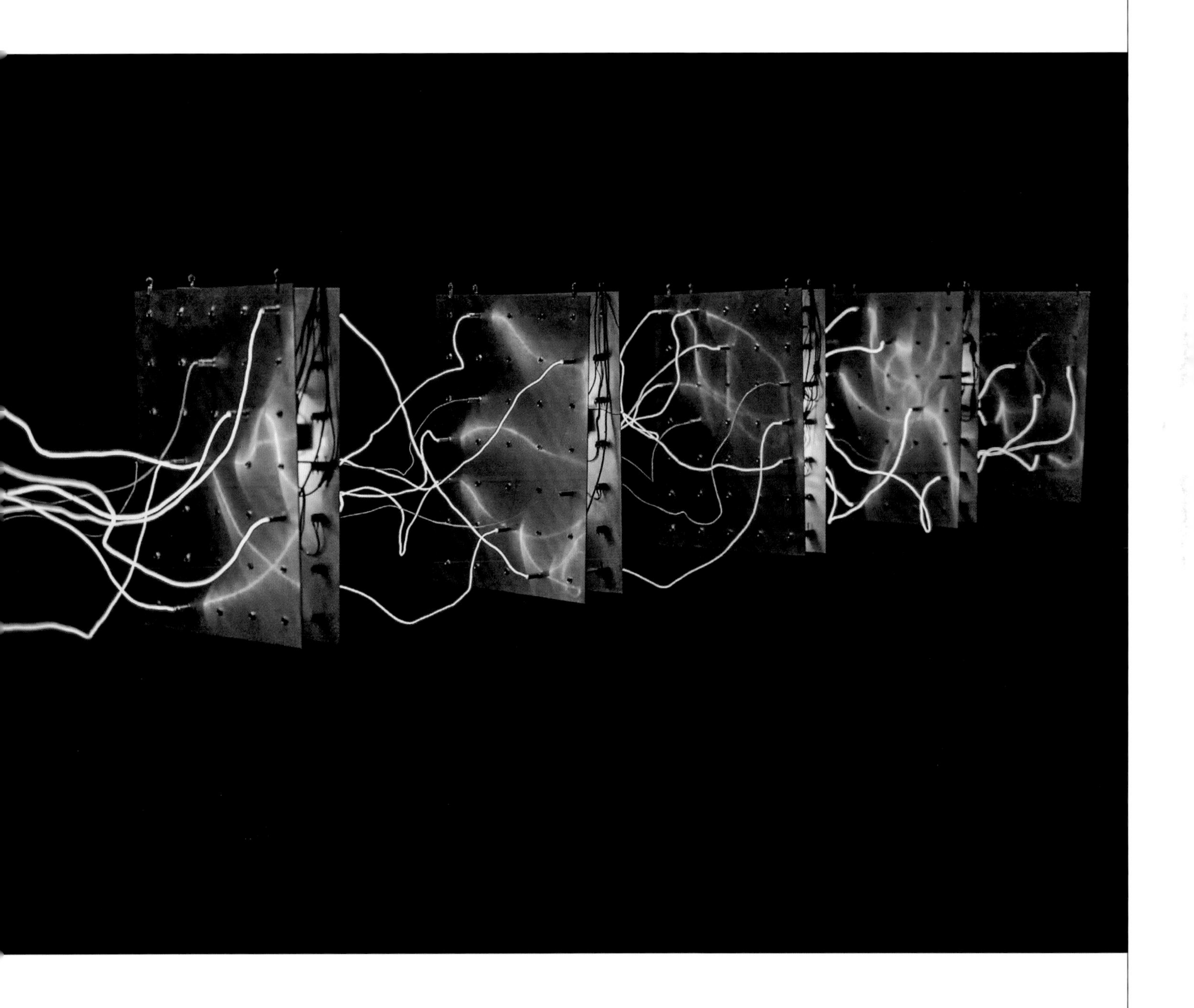

↑

L.E.V. festival,
Matadero Madrid, 2021.

Matadero Madrid opened in 2007, while parts of the center were still under construction. The management feared a negative public reaction to the "in progress" nature of the space, but only positive feedback was received. Indeed, Matadero was perceived as a "creativity workshop," a definition that still defines its identity today. From 2007 to the present, the Matadero facility has seen an increase in spaces available for activities, through the renovation and reactivation of further pavilions and the design of specific programs aimed to meet the growing requirements of the city and the artistic community.

The year 2008 was marked by the beginning of an international financial crisis that affected the entire planet; though, for the implementation of the Matadero project, it represented an opportunity, rather than a setback, thanks to substantial European funding and investment that the Spanish state activated to jump-start its economy. The Matadero became a top priority for the municipal government and its development advanced rapidly: most of the work was completed in seventeen months.

WHAT IS MATADERO MADRID TODAY? — Let's return to the Matadero website to try to find our way into its spacious pavilions, each being the result of a specific architectural design that combines the recovery of elements and materials from its industrial past with contemporary architectural requirements and styles.

To date, Matadero Madrid is a Center for Contemporary Creation sponsored by the Department of Culture, Tourism and Sports of the Madrid City Council. Under the artistic direction of Rosa Ferré through the Oficina de coordinación, in charge of managing transversal projects, its activities are organized as follows: the *Intermediae* program, the *Centro de residencias artísticas* and *Medialab en Matadero* (both public centers with independent artistic directions), *Cineteca Madrid*, and *Naves del Español en Matadero*, with a series of private partners whose initiatives contribute to the broad and multidisciplinary program, *Central de Diseño, Extensión AVAM,* and *Casa del Lector*. We will now examine these entities one by one.

The *Intermediae* program includes the design of projects targeted to the residents of the Matadero neighborhood. The objective is to involve local citizens in artistic and cultural activities and in hands-on work with the artistic and cultural fabric of the city, while fostering a strong international component. *Intermediae* was Matadero's debut program when it first opened to the public in 2007, and thus, for more

↑
La Hoja by FAHR 021.3, Matadero Madrid, January 2023.

→→
Cineteca Madrid, Matadero Madrid.

than a decade, it has been a landmark in the city's cultural life, as well as a solid example of community-oriented design and programming. The Intermediae Pavilion hosts exhibitions, book presentations, and other activities ranging from boxing or dance sessions in collaboration with local associations to meetings on permaculture, childhood, education, and participatory urban design groups.

The *Centro de residencias artísticas* offers residency programs and workspaces to artists, educators, curators, researchers, and other professionals through various programs designed for the benefit of individuals as well as groups or associations, thus providing Madrid's creative fabric with economic resources, tools, and institutional support in a framework of creativity and sharing.

Artists-in-residence are invited to share with the public their creative experiences developed within the Matadero spaces.

Medialab en Matadero is a meeting place for the production of open cultural projects. Under the premise that culture is a place for experimentation and sharing, *Medialab* provides a series of working groups (in which anyone can make proposals and everyone can take part) for participatory design, shared research, or the creation of learning communities. A wide range of topics are covered, from workshops on innovation and urban design to data processing, programming, and audiovisual experimentation. Special attention is paid to the use and development of open-source software and the documentation and prototyping of processes to render them replicable and modifiable.

Founded as a cinema specializing in documentaries, *Cineteca Madrid*'s current programming pays attention to new audiovisual forms, with a focus on independent, alternative, and nonfiction cinema. It also includes a number of spaces—the Archivo, Vestíbulo, Cantina, and Patio—hosting various activities, including workshops, seminars, and festivals. *Cineteca* produces its own projects but seeks to intersect with the city's independent artistic production, setting as its goal the development of critical thought in the audiovisual field.

Regarding the private partners, *Central de Diseño* is a platform for the promotion of design run by the Fundación Diseño de Madrid (DIMAD). Since 2007, this center has been entirely dedicated to design culture in all its forms—from graphic design to industrial and interior design—with the intention of making Madrid one of the international capitals of design. The *Central de Diseño* works on three different levels: exhibitions and display of international projects; training and outreach; hosting experimental laboratories that offer services to third parties. *Central* is equipped with a technological floor, a wide range of equipment, and more than 100 workstations, as well as rooms for exhibitions, pop-up stores, training activities, conferences, presentations, and showrooms.

AVAM – Artistas Visuales Asociados de Madrid is an association that gathers Madrid-based visual artists. Formed from the union of several groups and associations, its goal is to affirm the professional status of the "artist." It does this by operating as an interlocutor between the art community, institutions, and administrations, ensuring

↑
Casa del Lector, Matadero Madrid.

support for individual artists, working for the improvement of work conditions and the protection of the rights of art workers. The space managed by AVAM within Matadero (*Extensión AVAM*) is reserved for members, who can organize their own exhibitions and/or events here lasting for a maximum of fifteen days, taking advantage of the visibility generated by both the association and Matadero itself.

Casa del Lector is an international center for research, development, and innovation in the fields of reading and literature. Opened in 2012 and managed by the Fundación Germán Sánchez-Ruipérez, the center is devoted to readers and reading. These spaces are home to literary culture in all its forms, which are promoted through exhibitions, lectures, training courses, workshops, and artistic events that focus on digital innovation and experimentation, and on professional training. *Casa del Lector* allows the public to touch, read, and cherish books, so that both reading and publishing remain central to contemporary society.

ARTISTIC PROGRAMMING — Matadero Madrid has its own general artistic direction that operates through a coordinating office and a number of programs that interlink the activities of the different structures and pavilions. Each pavilion or program has its own dedicated staff, with its specific artistic direction or curatorship managing the projects on offer, thus giving the public the opportunity to engage with a truly broad, topical, and in-depth cultural offering. In addition to performance, audiovisual, literature, and design, attention is also given to the interconnection of technologies as well as artistic and cultural activities in general. This is found in the range of Medialab activities mentioned earlier, and especially in the forthcoming *Centro de Exposiciones y Proyecciones Audiovisuales Inmersivas*, a new center devoted to digital arts and the application of new technologies to artistic creativity and enjoyment, through which Matadero aims to make its mark as an innovator in the cultural industry. This attention to technology is fostered by Matadero's "workshop" approach, which is also seen in the close relationship between its programming and the architecture of its spaces. In this regard, we must mention one of the most interesting programs offered by Matadero, namely *Abierto X Obras*, which is located in the former cold storage room. This is an artistic program dedicated to "site-specific" exhibitions and installations, commissioned in equal measure to established and young or emerging artists who are invited to create an artistic work in relation to this very particular space. Covering over 800 square meters, this hall still retains its original character, including traces of a fire that broke out in the 1990s. The intimate atmosphere of this space, which is characterized by its exposed structure highlighted by arches and columns, has been conserved through minimal interventions. ¶

SESC POMPÉIA

SESCSP.ORG.BR/UNIDADES/POMPEIA

— Architecture of democracy

↑
SESC Pompéia, São Paulo.

Let's now travel to the city of São Paulo, Brazil, and, more specifically, to the Vila Pompéia neighborhood in the Perdizes district, west of the city, an area that is in some ways similar to the neighborhoods explored previously in Paris and Madrid. It is indeed a former working-class neighborhood, an industrial district that came into being in the first decade of the twentieth century and was inhabited at that time mainly by Italian, Spanish, and Hungarian immigrants attracted by the job opportunities in the large industries located there. These include a metal drum factory that remained in operation until the 1970s, when it was then taken over by SESC – Serviço Social do Comércio, a private nonprofit corporation of the merchants' guild that provides social welfare services for its employees and their families, as well as for the community at large. SESC then decided to build a recreation center to offer cultural services and activities to the public, and so commissioned Lina Bo Bardi—Italian-born but naturalized Brazilian and one of the most important South American modernist architects—to build it.

Born Achillina Bo, she trained between Rome and Milan and soon started her collaboration with the studio of Gio Ponti, becoming part of the artistic and intellectual circles of Milan in the 1940s. Then she moved with her husband to Brazil, which would become her country of choice; indeed, she left an important mark on the country's cultural development. Because her work had a political and militant vein, her professional development grew hand in hand with social and civic engagement, whereby architecture was at the service of people's everyday lives, and the architect was a creative figure able to enter into deep dialogue with popular culture. Lina Bo Bardi's involvement proved to be decisive in guiding not only the restoration but the very function and vocation of SESC Pompéia.

At a time when the practice of rehabilitating old industrial sites was not yet so widespread, Bo Bardi proposed to establish the center directly within the former Pompéia factory, taking advantage of its extensive concrete structures and completely revolutionizing its style and function, ultimately transforming the appearance of the entire area. SESC Pompéia was inaugurated in 1986 and is still a multipurpose center of more than 16,000 square meters that houses public services—a reasonably priced cafeteria and dental center, a newspaper library, public swimming pools, spaces to host various types of classes—as well as a cultural program of exhibitions, installations, theatrical performances, and concerts.

pp. → 62 | 63

SESC Pompéia exemplifies the close relationship between architecture, culture, and society while presenting a decidedly specific model, different from the examples previously examined: cultural policy is understood here in a strictly social sense and is conducted by a private entity performing a public function. “Performing Culture” is practiced in a broad sense and within a welfare approach that, alongside the arts, encompasses sport, health, and mental and physical well-being.

"A RAY OF LIGHT IN A SAD CITY"

Located in a neighborhood known as "the Brazilian Liverpool," because of the coexistence of industrial architecture and musical culture (Arnaldo Baptista and Sérgio Dia of Os Mutantes, among the founding bands of the avant-garde music movement "Tropicália," hailed from here), SESC Pompéia came to life inside a former factory that had a specific architectural peculiarity from its inception. Built in 1938 by architect and engineer François Hennebique, it was already a state-of-the-art structure at that time, built with a precast concrete system organized in a regular grid to delineate large open volumes.

When the factory operations ended, as of 1973, SESC Pompéia began to informally use the building to organize leisure activities for its employees and their children: this use of space was what Lina Bo Bardi decided to prioritize when she was commissioned to build a recreation center. Indeed, her plan was to exploit the former workshops of the Pompéia factory for that very purpose.

The initial plan was to raze everything and construct new buildings on the factory site, but the cost of the operation would have been too high. Bo Bardi thus proposed to work directly on the structure by reconverting its spaces, imagining a regeneration that sought not to erase the site's past but to maintain its qualities while radically transforming its function. A major shift occurred in the very perception of the site—from a place of work and toil to a place evoking a sense of community, joy, and pleasure.

The center was built in several stages between 1977 and 1986. Defining her project as "a ray of light in a sad city," Lina Bo Bardi designed a structure with functional yet refined, extravagant, and imaginative architectural features. She succeeded in transforming major technical and structural difficulties into a series of new architectural opportunities for additional, imaginative spaces. For example, to overcome the complications deriving from the Águas Pretas stream flowing underneath the building, the main hall was divided in two by a concrete pool where its waters emerge.

← SESC Pompéia, São Paulo.

The interiors of SESC Pompéia affirm the desire to generate a public space at the service of people, a place of conviviality and leisure, creating a strong link between inside and outside, between public and private, between architectural innovation and respect for the identity of the place. As we have seen in 104–Paris and Matadero Madrid, here too, architectural insight and practice have devised different uses of spaces, while still leaving the possibility for visitors attending the place to appropriate and eventually rewrite them.

pp. → 64 | 65

SESC Pompéia's activities seem to be fueled by the wave of populism originating partly from the country's political history and partly from Bo Bardi's militant conception of architecture and culture. On the one hand, the SESC organization strives to respond to the need to improve the quality of life of the lower classes, thus making sports, leisure, and recreational activities accessible. On the other, the architect's theoretical and political training led her to develop a humanistic and civic approach to architecture, which is not the result of a creative impulse for its own sake but something designed with the specific objective to serve the community. According to Bo Bardi, culture should be interpreted as a part of everyday reality and not as something special, or a domain reserved for a highly educated elite, as these words of hers, published in issue 16 of *Harvard Design Magazine* (2002), tell us:

> I am unable to design a bank, a private mansion, or a hotel. Maybe I would have liked to have been called to design a hospital, a school, a community center, but it never happened. Basically, I see architecture as a collective service, and as poetry. Something that has nothing to do with art. A kind of alliance between duty and scientific practice.

The principle of integration and sustainable development is also reflected in the choice of materials used in the construction of the building, favoring local, simple materials and avoiding waste, always maintaining a respectful balance with the environment and the spirit of the place. This approach is fully expressed in the implementation of the ventilation system, which was designed to promote natural ventilation inspired by traditional Brazilian know-how. The first stage of redevelopment of the old factory was completed in 1982 and the facility was opened that same year, while the sports facilities, which remain in use to this day, were opened to the public in 1986.

WHAT IS SESC POMPÉIA TODAY? — The venue retains its multipurpose character, as desired by its creator and owner: a polyfunctional space in which dimensions of leisure and necessity can coexist through the understanding that culture is a commodity of primary necessity, a right to be enjoyed within a collective context.

Approximately 16,000 square meters are divided into different spaces: the large sheds of the former factory house an 800-seat theater, restaurant, brewery, library, and a large recreation and play area. The elements built from scratch are the prismatic-base

→ SESC Pompéia, São Paulo.

towers and a third cylindrical element taller and narrower than the former constructions. The towers house sports facilities: the larger one, with its five-story irregular openings, has gyms and a swimming pool; the other, of eleven stories with square openings, houses dance halls, gyms, bars, and locker rooms. The third element, a 17-meter-tall tower, contains the water tank for the entire complex.

Unlike the previous examples in Paris and Madrid, SESC Pompéia has no dedicated website but enjoys a special section within the São Paulo SESC's general website. If the specificity of this place lies in its architecture, Bo Bardi's design did nothing more than try to express through volumes, materials, and the distribution of spaces the very function that this place embodies: to deliver a wide variety of services not only to the community of which it is an expression (merchants, tourist agents, etc.) but to society in general, in a political context where poverty and necessity demand a plural and collective commitment.

The section on the Pompéia Recreation Center lists its programs and activities. To simplify, we have classified the activities and services into three major groups.

CULTURAL AND RECREATIONAL SERVICES — SESC Pompéia offers various spaces and activities that are intended for cultural or leisure purposes: the *Área de Convivência* is a large communal space that hosts free exhibitions, installations, and performances; the *Library* is used for reading and lending books while the *Reading Room* is a place to consult current newspapers, use free Wi-Fi, and play chess or checkers. There is also a *Playroom* reserved for children up to six years old and their parents for free playtime or staff-led activities. The 774-seat *Teatro*—for which Lina Bo Bardi even designed the furnishings—has an extremely varied program of music, theater, dance, and conferences; the *Espaço Cênico* is an 80-seat hall designed for multidisciplinary artistic practice, from circus to performance and music. Among the most unique services that Pompéia offers are the *Oficinas de Criatividade*, a series of equipped ateliers to carry out individual or collective practices such as ceramics, sewing, photography, carpentry, and other artistic disciplines. The aim is to trigger artistic awareness through shared or communal practice and theory to nurture and

→

Flávio Império, 1997, celebrating the 20th anniversary of SESC Pompéia, São Paulo.

CHOPERIA

encourage artistic processes. Furthermore, among the novelties specifically related to the pandemic is *Anexa*, SESC Pompéia's new digital space in which experimentation through artistic languages fosters dialogue between artists, curators, researchers, pedagogical experts, and the general public.

Finally, there is a café and restaurant where meals can be bought at affordable prices, and a shop where goods such as books and records produced or published by SESC can be purchased.

PHYSICAL ACTIVITY — This remains at the heart of SESC Pompéia's mission. The sports facilities consist of three gyms, five playgrounds, a hall hosting different kinds of classes such as yoga, pilates, aerobics, etc., and a swimming pool with a 600-person capacity. Some of the sports activities are reserved for people registered with SESC (i.e., workers in the trade, service, and tourism sectors and their families), while others are open to the public, with specific times and rules for access.

SOCIAL AND HEALTH SERVICES — SESC Pompéia plays an important social role by offering some health services and programs aimed specifically at youths and children, primarily intended for SESC members but also available to the general public with specific times and access criteria. These include a dental center and several programs for social inclusion and development, including *Programa Curumin*, an informal education program for children aged seven to twelve aimed at broadening their development through educational, cultural, and recreational activities. This initiative promotes values such as play, respect for the environment, and the exercise of citizenship, as well as the importance of establishing social relationships based on friendship, sharing, and respect for diversity. *Programa Juventudes Alta Voltagem* is a socio-educational program for teenagers aged thirteen to seventeen, envisioned as a space for coexistence and discussion, in which topical issues of adolescence are addressed through various activities—plastic arts, literature, sports, theater performances, cinema, etc.—that emphasize cooperation, responsibility, empathy, and pleasure in interpersonal relationships. Finally, *Relacionamento Empresa* is a consulting desk offering services for companies in the field of trade, services, or tourism. By creating dialogue between the programmed activities and elements of architectural design, SESC Pompéia still has a direct influence on many people's daily lives, where collective well-being is elected as a priority, in its effort to build a vibrant and egalitarian community whose members can enjoy the same opportunities and rights. The arts are understood here as a required component in the realization of this ideal community, on a par with health and social services, because art enables individual growth, disregards the sense of duty to make room for pleasure, the possible, and the imaginary, and provides a unique opportunity to gather around practices and objects in which one can recognize oneself as part of a community. Unlike the previous two centers, the artistic direction of SESC Pompéia appears to be less prominent, or at any rate less recognizable, as the authorial gesture of an art curator or organizer. It is, however, clear that artistic programming is one of the important activities offered by the center, based on a vision of culture and inclusiveness that sees art not only as an instrument to promote growth but as a necessary element for the realization of people's well-being, alongside sports and health. ¶

←
Flávio Império, 1997, celebrating the 20th anniversary of SESC Pompéia, São Paulo.

RADIALSYSTEM V

RADIALSYSTEM.DE

— *Dialogue between tradition and innovation*

↑

Radialsystem V, Berlin.

We are now back in Europe, in Berlin, the capital of Germany, where industrial archaeology and architectural regeneration penetrate the living heart of the city, defining a distinctly "industrial" urban landscape. The center we explore now is Radialsystem V, on the Spree River, and housed in a building that, until the 1990s, was one of twelve water-pumping stations for the city's wastewater system.

The site is located in the eastern part of the city, specifically in Friedrichshain, a former working-class neighborhood and now one of Berlin's best-known destinations for underground culture. Berghain —the mecca of international club culture—is housed inside a former industrial plant in the same neighborhood.

Radialsystem V became a cultural center in 2006, retaining its name and in a certain sense the same function, but refurbished in an artistic-cultural sense. If before it pumped water that circulated throughout the city, today it produces art that is distributed from this center to the most diverse and widespread audience possible. Thus, there are two traits that define the identity of this place: on the one hand, the concept of dialogue, of continuous exchange between subject and idea, of movement from within to without and vice versa; on the other, the meeting of old and new, of tradition and innovation. Within an exceptional location made of brick, glass, and steel overlooking the banks of the Spree, it connects artists, creators, and culture enthusiasts by developing new cultural formats and genres.

Radialsystem V is home to four major companies that are among the most recognized in the international dance and music scene: Akademie für Alte Musik Berlin, Sasha Waltz & Guests, Solistenensemble Kaleidoskop, and Vocalconsort Berlin. Here, the future of "cultured" music is constructed through a risky process of experimenting with avant-garde practices, while contemporary choreography re-elaborates traditional repertoires and produces an artistic plan that brings languages together, nurtures them through hybridization, and makes them accessible to everyone and free from any elitism.

Radialsystem V has a complex administrative model: the building is a protected heritage site, but the cultural center is owned by the two founders, Jochen Sandig and Folkert Uhde, who have been running it since 2006. Compared to 104–Paris, Matadero Madrid, and SESC Pompéia, Radialsystem V has an additional mechanism to manage its artistic mission, as it was

→→
Sasha Waltz & Guests performing *In C* at Radialsystem, Berlin, 2021.

born from the initiative of private entities with a business dynamic in which all profits are reinvested on programming.

Until 2018, Radialsystem V received no public funding but sustained its activities on income from other businesses and the rental of spaces. This model was feasible due to the specificity of the German system for financing artistic production, which focuses on local creativity: individual artists receive public grants to realize their projects and then contact venues directly to present or develop their works.

Thus, Radialsystem V represents an intersection of the private and public dimensions: the public sector finances artistic production through the support of individual artists; the private sector provides space and supplies equipment, personnel, communication, promotion, and know-how. With this model, we see how "profit" and economic interests substitute public sector support for arts by virtuously integrating into the funding system for cultural activities, which in turn encourages private initiative and total autonomy in terms of artistic choices.

HISTORICAL LEGACY AND MODERNITY

Built on Holzmarktstraße in 1881 and expanded in 1905, Radialsystem V was the largest water-pumping station in Berlin's wastewater management system. The large building is in the style typical of industrial architecture of this region, such as the Charlottenburg Power Station (1900) and the Oberbaumbrücke (1896). The architect, Richard Tettenborn (1857–1923), designed the pumping station using decorative elements of the "Märkische Backsteingotik," a Gothic brick-based architectural style typical of the Brandenburg region, incorporating large windows facing the street. Tettenborn followed the lead of James Hobrecht, the engineer responsible for the design and construction of Berlin's sewer system, who insisted on the need for cleanliness and elegance in architecture and industrial technology.

During World War II, one third of the Radialsystem V was destroyed. Part of the building was quickly repaired and put back into service, although signs of war damage can still be seen behind the foyer bar today. Radialsystem V continued to serve the districts of Mitte, Prenzlauer Berg, and Friedrichshain until 1999, when it was replaced by a new pumping station. Radialsystem V was declared a historical heritage site of the city that same year and conservative restoration of the structure began in 2004.

↑
Christos Papadopoulos & Dance On Ensemble performing *Mellowing* at Radialsystem, Berlin, January 2023.

Gerhard Spangenberg, the architect who took over the restoration, was tasked with maintaining the original facade, modernizing the two inner halls, and completely renovating the west wing, which suffered most from war damage. Thus, we owe to him the search for a specific style that preserves the historical legacy of the structure while combining modernity and innovation through the addition of new contemporary elements. Spangenberg also carried out numerous other similar projects, such as the reconstruction of the Staatsoper Unter den Linden (2001) and the design of Die Tageszeitung (1991) and the Allianz Treptowers in Berlin (1993–98), demonstrating a predilection for theaters and stages, among other typologies.

A glass structure was built on the west side, adding an element of modernity and seeking continuity with the building's original character by using raw materials —concrete, steel, and glass—to emphasize functionality through minimalist elegance. This new addition not only creates an aesthetic contrast enriching the original style with its multiple transparent and opaque facets, but also triples the available space within the building. The restoration and construction work took a year, and the building was reopened as Radialsystem V – New Space for Arts and Ideas in September 2006.

WHAT IS RADIALSYSTEM V TODAY? — It is a space animated by the idea of dialogue. This concept is metaphorically embodied in its architecture, with its interesting symbiosis of old and modern, and is also propagated through the artistic programming—classic artistic genres are unconventionally interwoven following an interdisciplinary approach—and in the activities that take place inside the center, where cultural undertakings complement commercial initiatives.

This dual vocation is reflected in the figures of its creators. Jochen Sandig is a playwright, cultural entrepreneur, and founder of four cultural institutions, including Kunsthaus Tacheles (one of Europe's most famous social centers, occupied in 1990 by artists and collectives, a key venue for independent underground culture internationally) and the dance company Sasha Waltz & Guests, founded in 1993 together with choreographer Sasha Waltz and now one of the resident artistic ensembles at Radialsystem V. Sandig's work has always been focused on the idea of the city as a public space for the arts. Folkert Uhde, on the other hand, is a music manager and communications expert. Since 2002 he has staged and organized several festivals, including the biennial Alter Musik Zeitfenster in cooperation with the Konzerthaus Berlin. From 1997 to 2008, he was conductor and dramaturg of the baroque orchestra Akademie für Alte Musik Berlin, and since 2015 he has taken over the management of Bach Festival Days in Köthen, which takes place every two years. A scholar and lover of classical music, his approach aims to devise innovative formats with which to disseminate and produce it in contemporary times. In 2009, he received an award for this as Berlin's best cultural manager.

To date, Radialsystem V consists of a 600-square-meter main hall (the *Halle*), the former engine room of the pumping station which retains its historic architecture, with its three large arched windows and an original crane bridge. Thanks to a movable grandstand, the *Halle* can accommodate up to 260 guests, increasing to 500 when removed. The smaller 400-square-meter *Saal* has also been conservatively restored and still features original elements of the former pumping station, reinforced with modern components, exposed concrete walls, and columns. Like the main hall, this too is an extremely flexible space that can be modulated according to needs. These two rooms, facing the bar facility, are accessed through the *Foyer* and are characterized by glass and exposed concrete walls with terraces overlooking the Spree. The *Cube* is a 50-square-meter space with fully windowed walls, ideal for workshops and conferences.

Located on the top two floors of the new south-facing wing, *Studios A, B, C* also have glass facades. The 400-square-meter Studio A occupies the entire fifth floor and is regularly used as a rehearsal room. Studios B and C on the fourth floor are both 200 square meters and are interconnected but can be used independently. On the second floor of the new wing are the smaller *Ateliers*, five rooms ranging from 13 to 42 square meters that host workshops and meetings or can be used as offices. Finally, the *Terrace on the Spree and Deck* is a 400-square-meter outdoor terrace overlooking the river and a 42-meter-long pier for parties, outdoor activities, or workshops.

RESIDENT COMPANIES — The Akademie für Alte Musik Berlin is one of the world's most famous chamber orchestras. In collaboration with the Sasha Waltz & Guests ensemble, the Akademie has produced *Medea* (2007), *Dido & Aeneas* (2005), and the choreographic concert *4 Elements - 4 Seasons* (2007), which consolidated its reputation as a creative and innovative ensemble internationally.

Sasha Waltz & Guests, one of the most important institutions for contemporary dance in Berlin, has worked continuously with Radialsystem V, producing several projects such as *Medea* (2007), *Jagden und Formen with Ensemble Modern* (2008), as well as the projects *Dialoge 09 - Neues Museum* for the opening of the Neues Museum in Berlin and *Dialoge 09 - MAXXI* for the opening of the new MAXXI in Rome (2009). With more than one hundred international and national performances every year, Sasha Waltz & Guests is one of the most active companies on the international arts scene.

Founded in 2006 and part of Radialsystem V since 2008, the young chamber orchestra Ensemble Kaleidoscope offers innovative and creative concert installations. The ensemble also collaborates with artists from other disciplines such as architecture, literature, dance, theater, and lighting design to establish forms of expression and performance beyond the traditional concert scene.

Founded in 2003, Vocalconsort Berlin specializes in baroque and early music as well as in modern interpretations, from romantic to contemporary music. The ensemble's flexible instrumental variety ranging from quartet to choral concerts favors both stage and opera performances. Vocalconsort Berlin has performed all over the world at numerous festivals and concert halls.

→ Sasha Waltz & Guests performing *Dialoges 09*, Neues Museum, Berlin, 2009.

ARTISTIC PROGRAMMING — Radialsystem V's spaces are particularly attractive for rental and are suited to a wide variety of activities. In addition to rental operations, Radialsystem V is one of the most lively and attractive venues from the point of view of artistic production and programming, offering a programming specifically related to dance and music, with the aim of bringing different generations together under the same roof and attracting a younger audience through various initiatives. An example is the now-famous *Nachtmusik*, night concerts performed by small ensembles and soloists, with the audience listening while lying on mats, rugs, and cushions, thus revolutionizing through a simple twist the appreciation of so-called "cultured music" by a more diverse audience. Another example is *Barock Lounge*, a format that brings to life the experimental dialogue between baroque and electronic music, providing an unexpected and interesting synthesis. The baroque ensemble Elbipolis performs its repertoire in a relaxed atmosphere, with electronic artists such as Tim Exile or Brezel Göring of Stereo Total transforming these pieces into electro sounds through their own devices, creating a hybrid of classical concert and club culture that combines their musical structures and enhances their specificities.

In addition to these formats, Radialsystem's program also includes lecture-concerts, concerts and performances that revisit classical musical works, festivals, dance and music performances by international artists or major concerts by leading musicians, musical theater projects with specific programming for children, and projects aimed at the community. While focusing mainly on the languages of dance and music and their interactions, this layered plan also offers formats and works capable of connecting with a range of ages and socially diverse audience. The interaction between culture, politics, economics, science, and media has been part of Radialsystem V's concept from the very beginning. Ensembles and performers such as RIAS Kammerchor, Rebecca Saunders, Ictus Ensemble, Arditti Quartet, Elbipolis Barockorchester Hamburg, Christine Schäfer, Barbara Sukowa, Wir sind Helden, and Kim Kashkashian have performed here.

Radialsystem's history is that of one of the most vital cultural centers in Europe, through which artistic production of the highest level has passed through over the years, providing a point of reference within a particularly fragmented and dispersive artistic system such as Berlin. In this case, economic sustainability becomes a prerequisite not only for the well-being of the single enterprise, but more importantly to play an indispensable role in supporting emerging creativity and the local cultural scene. ¶

BENESSE ART SITE NAOSHIMA / CHICHU ART MUSEUM

— Nature is architecture, architecture is art

↑
Aerial view of Chichu Art Museum, Naoshima.

Blue skies, crystal clear waters, and rolling green hills in which curious architectural forms can be seen, such as a large polka-dotted gourd on a pier overlooking the sea. We are in Naoshima Island, nestled in the Seto Inland Sea in the heart of Japan. The large yellow gourd we mentioned is a work of art created by the artist Yayoi Kusama, and what might look like a typical fishing island, ready to welcome vacationing tourists during the summer season, is instead a place almost entirely dedicated to contemporary art, housing a vast complex of works and architectural buildings brought together under the name Benesse Art Site Naoshima. Here, in the early 1990s, the Fukutake Foundation and the then-mayor of the island decided to initiate a unique experiment: create an area where unspoiled nature would welcome contemporary art, making the entire island—and beyond—an open-air temple for the celebration of beauty, nature, and the well-being that these dimensions generate in human beings. In true Japanese style, Naoshima is the perfect place to immerse oneself within a pure aesthetic experience of contemplation, where art, architecture, and natural landscapes come together like different facets of the same experiential prism. This art-lover's paradise, desired and brought to life by Benesse Holdings, Inc., is home to a series of installations by international artists and museum buildings that are mostly the work of architect Tadao Andō, highly renowned internationally and strongly rooted in traditional Japanese aesthetic imagery. What is special about Naoshima is that art has been used to open up the natural and historical beauty of the island, promoting the revitalization of the entire surrounding area by making what was once an island of simple fishing villages a unique destination for art tourism. The goal of relating contemporary art and architecture to the pristine nature of the Seto Inland Sea has been achieved by weaving an intense dialogue with local residents, giving rise to an operation that has now been going on for about two decades and has set in motion the economy not only of Naoshima but also of adjacent islands. We read on the Benesse Art website the concepts that clearly illustrate the vision underlying the project:

> Using the Setouchi Islands as a canvas. Art that conveys a message to modern society finds its home on the islands of the Seto Inland Sea, where the Japanese landscape is still pristine, thus transforming a region that was losing its vitality. With this goal, the world's first symbiosis between islands and art began in Naoshima. Our goal is to give people a way to see, and to do so not through a conventional exhibition that asks them, "Can you see the beauty of this thing?" Here, it is not art at the center. At the center is the island and the people who live there, and art is something that brings out the island's charm. It is not just about looking at art, but what can be seen through art.

→→
Walter De Maria, *Time/Timeless/No Time*, 2004.

Naoshima expresses the conception of an aesthetic experience translated into something spiritual and almost mystical, in which art is understood in its broadest and purest sense, as a relational technique and instrument between human beings and nature, the unity of which must therefore be recovered.

The Benesse Art Site Naoshima is a complex consisting of multiple buildings and artistic places of interest which have grown over the years, also expanding on the nearby islands of Teshima, Inujima, Shodoshima, and Megijima. Exploring the island, we can find several museums and galleries, some open-air art installations, and architectural structures that reinterpret the Japanese tradition in an authorial and contemporary way, including, for example: the *Art House Project* that involves one of the island's villages, in which artists take up residence inside vacant houses and transform their spaces into works of art, weaving together stories and memories of the time when the buildings were lived in and used; the *Naoshima Bath "I ♥ 湯,"* a structure created by artist Shinro Ohtake where visitors can take a typical Japanese bath; and the *Naoshima Plan "The Water,"* a traditional house renovated by architect Hiroshi Sambuichi.

REINVENTING WELL-BEING: THE BENESSE ART SITE NAOSHIMA

The history of this large complex dedicated to art, located in a beautiful natural place and capable of expressing the profound relationship between environment and culture, brings us back to what was already addressed in the previous pages in relation to the urban context. Naoshima and the nearby beautiful and remote islands were in fact the focus of the intense process of modernization that Japan pursued after World War II. A number of copper refineries were installed here, and the toxic emissions and industrial waste polluted the air and the water. In time, the area began to depopulate as younger residents left for the attractions of the city and the economy of the area became almost irremediably depressed. The founding of the Benesse Art Site Naoshima had the beneficial effect of regenerating and revitalizing the region by enhancing its strengths: the beauty of the landscape and the presence of a rural community whose traditional identity and culture remains intact to this day.

The birth of this large-scale art project was due to an understanding between two men and their shared vision: Tetsuhiko Fukutake, a Japanese entrepreneur and founder of the Fukutake Publishing company who dreamed of creating a place dedicated to recreation and bringing together young people

↑ Chichu Art Museum, Naoshima.

from around the world, and Chikatsugu Miyake, then-mayor of Naoshima, who aimed to revitalize the south of the island by developing a cultural and touristic project. The meeting between the two took place in 1985, but unfortunately the following year Fukutake passed away, before the project could even come to life. His legacy was taken up by his son Soichiro Fukutake, who continued to develop the idea and carried out his father's dream by commissioning Tadao Andō to bring the center to life. This was initially conceived as a place where people could immerse themselves in nature and the outdoors, so much so that there were no permanent buildings but only Mongolian yurts. Thus, in 1989, *Naoshima International Camp* was opened, the first step toward what would become the Benesse Art Site Naoshima. The same year, *Frog and Cat* by artist Karel Appel was the first artwork installed on the site. In 1992, the center began to take on a semblance of what it is today. The *Benesse House Museum*, designed by Tadao Andō and embodying the spirit of the Benesse Art Site, was built and opened that same year: both a hotel and a contemporary art museum, it was conceived based on the concept of the "coexistence of nature, art, and architecture." Inside, artworks do not occupy special rooms but are scattered among the spaces of the hotel, while large windows opening to the outside let the nature outside enter the building. The artistic life of the site began with the installation of exhibitions, the creation of site-specific artworks, and the display of Soichiro Fukutake's personal collection. It was a decade later, however, that Fukutake came up with the idea for the Chichu Art Museum, specifically after seeing, in Boston, an exhibition on Monet and purchasing the *Water Lilies* series. Tadao Andō was again involved in the design of this structure, which was to be devoted entirely to art.

↓
Yayoi Kusama,
Pumpkin, 2022.

LETTING ONESELF BE IMMERSED INTO THE WORKS — Not the first, but certainly the most remarkable of all the constructions on Naoshima, the Chichu Art Museum is located in the south of the island, its name already revealing something of its structure: "Chichu" means "in the ground," and indeed the museum literally penetrates deep underground to avoid as much as possible human intervention in the natural landscape and to embody in a literal and natural way the ideal fusion of architecture, art, and nature. The ultimate goal is to evoke or create a total experience for those who pass through it. Built underground, the dominant element of its structure is geometry and when seen from above, it appears as a large triangle and a buried rectangle connected by a rectangular walkway that is also sunk into the ground.

Tadao Andō's design for the interiors appears minimal and rigorous in the use of materials such as concrete—one of his favorite, along with glass and steel—as well as in the alternation of solids and voids. The clear volumes of the rooms are determined by light, which penetrates into the space through an elegant interplay of angles and contours, scanning the space with natural luminosity and shadow.

This structure makes the Chichu Art Museum not only an anti-monument, despite the brilliance of its design, but also a non-museum, as its exhibition halls are not neutral containers that adapt to the works on display, but actual structural elements that define the very conditions of enjoyment. In this sense, Tadao Andō succeeded in a decidedly ambitious dual intent: on the one hand, he disrupted the "white cube" approach, highlighting how space always influences what happens within it; and on the other, he placed architecture on the same plane as the artworks. His idea was that interaction with the structure contributes to its development and in part complements its artistic and anthropological significance. In this sense, we may consider the Chichu Art Museum almost an art installation in its own right, rather than just a museum space exhibiting works for viewing. As we will see in the next section, this aspect also relates to the performative nature of the path that viewers are requested to follow inside, which involves a series of prescribed actions and specific modalities to undertake the visit. In addition to the exhibition halls, the museum itinerary is marked by three open spaces: a concrete corridor and two inner courtyards. The first is a triangular courtyard, its floor covered with roughly hewn stone; the second is square and covered with horsetail; and the third is a beautiful garden that mimics, in a small way, that of Giverny, Monet's inspiration for his celebrated *Water Lilies*. The Chichu has another special feature: the museum exhibits the works of three artists only, each in their own room. This is an exhibition concept that is closer to site-specificity and total immersiveness rather than mere presentation.

The museum hosts five canvases from Monet's *Water Lilies* series, *Time/Timeless/No Time* by Walter De Maria, and the installation *Open Sky* by James Turrell. Despite being underground, the atmosphere of the spaces is dictated by the natural light and airiness, which are the true protagonists and the ultimate goal of the museum structure. Tadao Andō's brilliant design, between functionalism and traditional Japanese style, concurs with the works to create a very special aura that changes as the hours of the day and the seasons go by, enveloping viewers in an environment in which form and content, aesthetic experience and contemplation, echo and enhance each other. Therefore, the performing culture pervades all planes in the Chichu Art Museum, embodied in what one might describe as a true museum dramaturgy, springing from the very idea that gave it life, continually re-actualized by the visitors and the works, which literally come alive through the specific conformation of the space and light, and the enjoyment of visitors, accompanied by the museum staff along a trajectory that requires specific timing, actions, and bearing.

→
Lee Ufan, *Porte vers l'infini*, 2019.
Lee Ufan Museum.

MUSEUM DRAMATURGIES: VISITING THE CHICHU ART MUSEUM — Since its opening on July 18, 2004, the museum has welcomed some 200,000 visitors a year, who were allowed to enjoy an experience that seems to be more akin to a ceremony than a simple museum visit. Indeed, the visit is the very keystone of the whole Chichu Art Museum raison d'être. In addition to allowing people to enjoy the works on display, the real peculiarity of this museum lies in the fact that its structure was devised imagining the type of fruition required to admire the works—two of the three created specifically for the spaces that house them—in order to produce a precise effect on the visitors called on to participate with their bodies in an experience meticulously prepared by architect Tadao Andō and his accomplices, the artists. This element takes us back to our main theme, which is the exploration of the performativity of culture, which should be understood not only as the content of works but also as the aesthetic and

phenomenological status that shapes all levels involved in contemporary cultural production. Similar to a play or performance, the museum visit is imagined as a kind of dramaturgy. Space, light, color, and materials provide the setting in which each performance/visit is staged, animated by the museum staff accompanying visitors and instructing them about how to use the space, and by the visitors themselves, who are at the same time protagonists and recipients of this highly transformative experience.

As in the true tradition of Japanese ritual, a visit to the Chichu involves a series of practices and contrivances that are essential to safeguard the effectiveness of the journey and, consequently, to experience its deeper meaning. The route to be followed is immersed in silence and rarefaction: a limited number of visitors enter the rooms to contemplate the works to the fullest by participating in an intimate dialogue with them and with the space. The introduction sheet handed out at

the entrance asks visitors not to touch the works, film, photograph, or reproduce them, use ink pens, smoke, use cell phones, carry bags, drink, or eat outside the areas provided for that purpose. Rather odd to the eyes of the typical Western museum-goer is the requirement to remove shoes and wear slippers to enter the room dedicated to Monet: a seemingly simple request—as well as one that is particularly common in Asia when entering private enclosed spaces—that nevertheless radically changes the emotional perception of the space, introducing a sense of intimacy and care for our surroundings.

The museum staff contributes to this immersive experience from a practical, aesthetic, and "scenic" point of view. Unisex, streamlined uniforms, whispered directions, intangible limits on access to the works: the staff accompanying visitors not only have the task of informing and respectfully warning to maximize the enjoyment of the museum, but themselves embody the code of behavior the space requires. Their uniforms are also true pieces of art, conceived by the renowned Japanese designer Taishi Nobukuni, who wanted to transcend gender, time, and place in the same way as the Chichu Art Museum was designed to last at least 1,000 years.

Let's now explore the works a little more in detail.

CLAUDE MONET SPACE — The room dedicated to Claude Monet houses five paintings from the *Water Lilies* series, the pictorial cycle that engaged the master of Impressionism in the last years of his life. By 1883, Monet had moved to Giverny, a lovely, small village near Paris, where he began to set up a luxuriant garden with a host of plants and flowers such as daylilies, various types of irises, Agapanthus, flowering annuals, and willows. The garden also included a pond surrounded by flowers and ornamental plants, including roses, irises, tulips, bluebells, gladioli, wisteria, and weeping willows, and was literally covered with water lilies. Moreover, the pond was crossed by a Japanese-style wooden bridge. The creation of this garden proved crucial to the last phase of the painter's work: in this enchanting personal paradise, Monet could immerse himself daily in the play of light, the iridescent reflections on the water, the detail of shapes and the variation of colors in the changing light, which he tried to capture in ever more detail through painting, in a daily exercise of abstraction and idealization of form. This almost repetitive practice led him to create a series of as many as 250 paintings. Interestingly, there is a very strong correlation between Monet's lived experience and the atmosphere that envelops the visitors of the room dedicated to him in the Chichu Museum, and more generally, the inspiration behind the entire Benesse Art Site Naoshima operation. Indeed, the ability of light to sculpt space and transform objects, the aesthetic contemplation of the landscape, and art as a tool for inquiry and the material connection between humankind and nature are also embodied in Tadao Andō's conception of space in the Chichu Art Museum. The goal is to engage visitors in an immersive experience that can lead them back to an original dimension of harmony with the environment and matter, a phase preceding language, meaning, and cultural implications.

←
Claude Monet, *Water-Lily Pond*, diptych, c. 1915–26, oil on canvas, 200 x 300 cm each.

The five paintings from Monet's series are all housed in a large, square, all-white room. Great attention is paid to the size of the room, the materials used, carefully selected to determine a precise color and texture. The space is lit only by indirect ceiling light, and the five *Water Lilies* are arranged symmetrically on the sandblasted white plaster walls. The floor is covered with a mosaic of white Carrara marble tiles and the works are protected from the salty air by large transparent panels. This dazzling and almost mystical feeling is immediately offset by the boldness of the five works, imposing in size, their materiality and vividness emphasized and amplified by the essential starkness of the space. The room acts as a mise en abyme of the paintings and as a metonymy of the museum itself: just as Monet absolutized his gaze of the floating water lilies in Giverny, increasingly disengaging himself from form and representation to seek a deeper, more primal sensation unleashed by the sight of that everyday spectacle of nature, so the space invites viewers to immerse themselves deep into the ritual of aesthetic (and ecstatic) contemplation of nature, as reimagined and reproduced by the artist. In parallel, the natural environment surrounding the Chichu Art Museum engages the visitors in its own incessant dialogue.

This continuous exchange between reality and representation, between natural and artificial, is perpetuated by the Chichu Garden, occupying an area of about 400 square meters and containing more than 200 species of plants and trees, including some of the same water lilies of the famous pictorial series.

WALTER DE MARIA — The room reserved for Walter De Maria contains the work *Time/ Timeless/No Time*, produced in 2004 especially for the Chichu Art Museum at the invitation of Fukutake, after the American artist in 2000 had created the works *Seen/Unseen Known/ Unknown* on the island. This is the largest of the three exhibition spaces. Its interior is occupied by a large staircase divided into two levels hosting the installation: a dark, reflective sphere 2.2 meters in diameter placed in the center, and twenty-seven elongated, geometrically shaped prismatic gilded wooden sculptures arranged on as many altars along the walls. Only direct natural light is used, which changes throughout the day, allowing for a different experience depending on the time of the visit.

Minimalism, monumentality, and a relationship with time and space are defining features of the work of Walter De Maria, one of the leading exponents of Land Art, who passed away in 2013. Here too we can detect many points of contact between the artist's poetics and the general layout of the museum through an approach that aims to blur the distinction between artwork and architecture, and between architecture and the landscape. Indeed, the uniqueness of this hall and of the one hosting James Turrell's *Open Sky* installation lies precisely in the fact that they were created jointly by architect Tadao Andō and the two artists in a kind of site-specific collaboration: the museum is built and exists in function of those very works, commissioned to those very artists and created specifically for this location. As in the space dedicated to Monet, De Maria's installation here is catalyzed by the architectural space, which amplifies its effect on the visitors, who are also prepared and readied by Andō's gallery giving access to the hall. Attention to detail, simplicity, rarefaction, and compositional virtuosity suggesting order and clarity unite the space and the work, setting up a perceptual and physical experience for the viewer who, as if at the end of a spiritual journey, finds himself contemplating the very essence of things. The objectivity and concision that confront the visitors do not imply emptiness or absence of significance, but constitute a condition for the vibration of matter to manifest itself and resonate in the living body of those in its presence.

JAMES TURRELL — The third and final room presents three works by James Turrell, the world-renowned American artist whose activity focuses on the perception of light and space. *Afrum, Pale Blue* (1968), *Open Field* (2000), and *Open Sky* (2004), the latter devised and made especially for the Chichu Art Museum, represent Turrell's long career, allowing visitors to admire his creative evolution through time in a kind of concise retrospective journey.

If in De Maria's work it is form and matter that are emphasized, here light is the absolute protagonist; as is typical in Turrell's work, it makes itself an art form. The manipulation of natural light through encumbrances, openings, and closures, and the creation of luminous and chromatic environments, act directly on the bodily sphere of the observer, activating perceptual, cognitive, psychological and, above all, emotional chain reactions. The Night Program is available regularly only on Fridays and Saturdays.

The visit—or rather, the journey—into the museum is concluded. The building, however, also includes a garden and a café, where a large window offers the visitor a panoramic view overlooking the Seto Inland Sea. This wide horizon offsets the museum's subterranean pathway and yet dialogues with the visitor's experience inside the museum through wooden tables and chairs, also designed by architect Tadao Andō, that invite relaxation and meditation. Similar to Lina Bo Bardi's SESC Pompéia, again it is the architect who acts as a true director, skillfully guiding the gestures and emotions of visitors to the museum, from the moment they step inside until they leave.

Over the years, the Benesse Art Site Naoshima has continued to expand, witnessing the production of numerous art projects nurturing relationships and exchange with the local community, including installations and site-specific works throughout the island, so much so that it has become one of the largest and most renowned open-air museums in the world. Today, the Naoshima island is a multifaceted center dedicated to contemporary arts and its influence extends to the other islands of the archipelago as well, in a kind of contagion or encroachment that over the years has managed to revitalize the image and economy of an entire geographical area. An example to illustrate this is the nearby island of Teshima, where in 2010 the award-winning artist Christian Boltanski initiated his "utopian" project *Les Archives du Cœur*, which aims to bring together in one place the sound recordings of the heartbeat of humankind. ¶

INSTITUTO INHOTIM

INHOTIM.ORG.BR

— *The garden of art*

↑
Aerial view of *Invenção da cor, Penetravel Magic Square #5, De luxe* by Hélio Oiticica.

We now travel to the Brazilian state of Minas Gerais and its capital, Belo Horizonte. This inner region of the country is considered the "world's mine" because of the richness of its soil. More precisely, we are in the city of Brumadinho (40,000 inhabitants), which became infamous in 2019 for being the site of an environmental disaster, the collapse of an iron mine tailings pond in which 300 people lost their lives. We enter what might appear at first glance to be a large botanical garden, rich in tropical plant species, refreshed by pools of water, and traversed by stone walkways. Instead, we are in the Instituto Inhotim, an open-air museum covering 140 hectares. Now directed by Antonio Grassi, Inhotim welcomes about 350,000 visitors each year with a focus on the local community, to which educational programs and social initiatives are directed.

As in the case of Naoshima, here the starting point is the connection between art, architecture, and the natural environment, which is once again approached from the perspective of protecting the biodiversity of the area and the relationship with the local community, as well as the ability to generate an experience that is out of the ordinary: a sort of total performance. As Naoshima and SESC Pompéia, Inhotim too is a space of extraordinary cultural and social value that owes its existence to the will and economic resources of a private investor whose vision and audacity have been directed toward the community. Indeed, this initiative offers the public not only the chance to connect with the works of some of the most important contemporary artists, but also to experience the natural heritage of an area that is home to about 70 percent of the world's plant biodiversity, contributing to the preservation of a region now severely tested by deforestation and agribusiness interests.

Inhotim was created thanks to a substantial investment by Bernardo Paz, a wealthy Brazilian iron magnate who created a lush botanical park and an unprecedented collection of contemporary works that form this vast garden-museum, which has grown to become the largest contemporary art museum in South America. With all its contradictions or gray areas—first and foremost, the megalomania of its founder, in addition to the various accusations of money laundering, exploitation of child labor, and environmental damage that have been raised against him—this enterprise has unquestionably had the merit of revitalizing the economy of one of the least viable areas of Brazil, subjected to the continuous and intensive exploitation of its geological resources. Indeed, over the years Inhotim has received awards as well as international and institutional recognition.

→→
Kaleidoscope at Instituto Inhotim, Brumadinho.

Established in the early 2000s, initially as a private garden and then opened to the public in 2006, Instituto Inhotim is now a private nonprofit organization receiving donations as well as private and public funding. It is recognized as an OSCIP (Organização da Sociedade Civil de Interesse Público) and as a Jardim Botânico by the Comissão Nacional de Jardins Botânicos.

If we were to give a schematic summary of the cultural reality of Instituto Inhotim, it would read as follows: the art-nature performance, the enhancement of artistic and botanical biodiversity, an interactive activity of fruition, and the relationship between the local and global dimensions.

HISTORY OF A UTOPIA

The Instituto Inhotim was founded on the initiative of Bernardo Paz, a mineral magnate and art collector, who in the 1980s took over an old fazenda (the typical Brazilian farm or homestead) to house his vast collection. The fazenda belonged to a wealthy Englishman named Timothy, known in the surrounding area as "Mr. Tim," or "Inhô Tim" in the local dialect—hence the name it has kept to this day. This choice refers to one of the axes around which this cultural reality takes shape, namely the close link with the local context, with the identity of the location, and with traditional culture by inscribing these within precise Brazilian artistic and architectural trends. As with the Benesse Art Site, Inhotim's form and goals were born by bringing together different figures, each capable of making their own ideational and imaginative contribution toward the realization of the project. Similar to Naoshima, where the relationship between Fukutake, the architect Tadao Andō, and a number of artists was crucial in defining the vocation and aesthetics of the site, here the dialogue between Bernardo Paz, the landscape architect Roberto Burle Marx, and artists Tunga and Cildo Meireles marked some of the fundamental steps in the current physiognomy of Inhotim. Initially, Paz's idea was not to create a site dedicated to art, but rather a botanical garden, a place where intellectuals, artists, critics, and businessmen could meet while immersed in the peace and beauty of the landscape.

Apparently, this idea came to Paz as a result of a health problem. He began working with his friend Roberto Burle Marx—a key figure in the development of modern Brazilian architecture and public building—by defining an idea of public space embodying a dialogue between landscape and architecture. Marx's contribution was an element of connection with the tradition of the great private museums that sprang up in Brazil around the 1940s. These include the Museo de Arte de São Paulo (MASP), the Museu de Arte Moderna do Rio de Janeiro (MAM), and the Museo de Arte Moderna de São Paulo (MAM-SP), where wealthy entrepreneurs and Brazil's most distinguished architects—including Lina Bo Bardi—collaborated in the creation of major public works dedicated to the arts and culture. If, however, underlying the foundation of these other centers was the relationship between architecture and urban life, Inhotim reflects the rural dimension that is still present in Brazilian culture. Mary was the first figure to promote the creation of the garden at Inhotim, introducing various plants and helping to define the design of its landscape, which would take ten years to see the light of day. In its early stages, Inhotim was a vast natural area housing Paz's private collection of primarily modern artworks, but then it came to represent the dialogue between two leading figures in the Brazilian contemporary art scene that would mark the course of the garden's development: Tunga and Cildo Meireles. The creative artistic practice of Tunga—who passed away in 2016 and is considered one of Brazil's most influential and eclectic artists—included highly diverse artistic languages, from drawing to sculpture, installation, photography, performance, film and video, and writing. Meireles is a conceptual artist and sculptor, best known for his installations dealing with political themes to spur the interaction of the viewer. Both close to Paz in the years of Inhotim's foundation, it is to them that we owe the "deviation" from the intended lush garden for a few selected people to one of the most important open-air art centers dedicated to contemporary languages. Building on what was already taking place inside Inhotim, where critics, intellectuals, artists, and entrepreneurs would be invited to visit Paz's private collection, Tunga and Cildo convinced him to open that experience to the general public and not just a lucky few. The second key step in defining the Inhotim project as we know it today, promoted primarily by Tunga, was that the collection should not only contain modern art but also contemporary works. The garden was seen not only as an exceptional container of artworks, but as a place of inspiration and creation where leading international artists could create new works in close relationship with the context.

This was a double operation that brought about the aesthetic repositioning of the collection, which was opened to the public. In line with the populist utopian wave that we saw animate the creation of the SESC Pompéia, now the public has access to a place of immeasurable value, dotted with the most innovative works from around the world, offering to everyone knowledge, beauty, wealth, and well-being. A "post-contemporary Disney World," as Paz himself defined it, where all members of society in general and regardless of social class, can enjoy art and take advantage of socially inclusive educational programs, projects, and employment opportunities aimed toward the revitalization of the general economy and tourism of the area. In 2006, what was intended to be an exclusive venue became the most important contemporary art museum in South America and one of the largest botanical gardens in the world, accessible to everyone and becoming a popular tourist destination, while still a fundamental element in the education, growth, and emancipation of the region's rural community. It is a place entirely dedicated to the preservation of the precious, unique, and necessary resources of both nature and art, continually animated and activated by educational programs, inclusive projects, and social initiatives but also performances, concerts, temporary exhibitions, seminars, and festivals and located in a region of Brazil which is still rural and rather off the main tourist routes. With about 700 works displayed since its founding, today Inhotim houses creations of about 60 international artists from 40 different countries, approximately 550 outdoor pieces and installations distributed over the museum spaces, and 23 galleries and 52 pavilions dedicated to individual works. The botanical collection consists of around 5,000 species from all continents (1,300 of which are various palm species), with at least eight thematic gardens.

IGNITING BIODIVERSITY — "A living collection, with art and nature in constant dialogue. At Inhotim, every visit is a new experience." This is how the section illustrating the Instituto Inhotim collection on the facility website reads, referring to both the collection of artworks and botanical species, thus placing these two categories on the same level of importance. These words highlight two key points characterizing Inhotim and demonstrate a certain similarity with the earlier example of the Benesse Art Site Naoshima. On the one hand, the relationship between art and nature, different but intertwined, which together offer human beings a special kind of spiritual nourishment within a fragile but powerful biodiversity that needs protection and support. On the other hand, the centrality of the visitor's experience; visitors are called upon not only to wander through the exhibition spaces and enjoy the collection—which is both artistic and botanical—but to actually interact with these spaces, to explore the various paths, thus living a synesthetic experience that is intended to be a truly transformative moment. To explore in detail an artistic/natural project as wide and complex as Inhotim is not possible here; however, we can trace some of the directions that have influenced its development and focus on some works that are perhaps among the most significant in the garden.

↑
Chris Burden, *Beam Drop Inhotim*, 2008.

At the center of Inhotim's curatorial project is definitely the collection, which is enhanced through research, visual and editorial documentation, bibliographic material, as well as exhibitions and online activities. These initiatives bring out the specificities of the works and delve deeper into the themes and concepts conveyed by the artists' works and personalities. To schematize, we could say that the entire design of the garden-museum revolves around a fundamental principle, which is expressed in various directions: the idea that Inhotim is constantly evolving, such that it demands an active involvement of all those who inhabit it, be they artists, curators, or spectators, thus implicitly promoting a form of transformation. Dealing with Inhotim entails an interaction that will inevitably lead us to give—and perhaps leave—something of ourselves. This principle is manifest in the very nature of the curatorial project of the museum-garden: from commissioning site-specific works to the continuous dynamics between the permanent exhibition, the creation of new works, and the reactivation of collected pieces through events, projects, and visits. This is complemented by strong bonds with the artists, who are not mere guests of the garden-museum but veritable aesthetic-thematic mainstays who contribute significantly to shaping the space that hosts their work. They activate an interactive relationship with the public, both through the implicit experiential fruition that the garden-museum activates, and through the individual works, many of which are installations requiring some form of viewer participation; together with other curated activities, they aim to bring the collection to life through the visitors' involvement.

From the very moment Inhotim opened to the public, it was conceived as a dynamic museum, a place of both vision and creation and, more generally, a place for the unleashing of expressive possibilities and the unfolding of knowledge. This was made possible thanks to the creation of a special commission with the task of animating the curatorial project and facilitating an active relationship between artists, curators, and space by taking into consideration various physical, cultural, and imaginative perspectives. The site-specific mode is the most favored approach at Inhotim: artists are invited to create works specifically for the garden, thus establishing an intimate connection with the natural and

non-conventional museum environment. Similar to Naoshima, the garden-museum itself is considered an artwork in its own right, springing from the continuous interaction between its space and the installations and the development of a significant relationship between curators and artists, as well as the brilliant spatial dramaturgy that creates connections between the works on display.

↓ The True Rouge Gallery on the Lago Ornamental.

Together with site-specific installations, the Instituto Inhotim collection also includes sculptures, photographs, videos, performances, drawings, and paintings dated from the 1960s to the present day. Of the 23 on-site gallery spaces, four are dedicated to temporary exhibitions that are constantly updated through the development of new projects. There are four storage rooms where other works from the collection, such as sculptures, paintings, photographs, and videos, are kept.

The 19 galleries housing the permanent collection feature works by Tunga, Cildo Meireles, Miguel Rio Branco, Hélio Oiticica & Neville d'Almeida, Adriana Varejão, Doris Salcedo, Victor Grippo, Matthew Barney, Rivane Neuenschwander, Valeska Soares, Doug Aitken, Marilá Dardot, Lygia Pape, Carlos Garaicoa, Carroll Dunham, Cristina Iglesias, William Kentridge, and Claudia Andujar. Let's now focus on one of the most significant works in the garden-museum.

TRUE ROUGE, TUNGA, 1997 — Recognized as one of Brazil's leading artists of the 1970s, Tunga uses a wide variety of materials to create installations that are activated through the language of performance. Conceiving the installation as something closely related to action, the performers' bodies, gestures, and movements are used to instill life to the most disparate materials, thus aligning the artists' poetics with the spirit animating the Inhotim garden-museum. Art appears here as a multidisciplinary language where philosophy, natural sciences, and literature overlap with visual creativity, acting on a plane somewhere between reality and fiction, between concreteness and imagination. Tunga's *True Rouge* was purchased in 1994 by Bernardo Paz for his private collection. After being displayed in New York, Paris, and the Mercosur Biennial, in 1997 it reached Inhotim, where it was eventually installed in the True Rouge Gallery, the first-ever museum-garden gallery built specifically to display the work of a single artist on a permanent basis. Nets, wood, blown glass, glass beads, red paint, sea sponges, billiard balls, bottle cleaning brushes, felt, and crystal balls are all found in *True Rouge*. Several containers are suspended in irregular positions thanks to a system of supporting red wires and ropes. From time to time, these can be set into motion by a group of performers who interact with the pieces, animating an imagery that mimics biological processes, life cycles, and the workings of the human body on the one hand and alchemy on the other.

As mentioned, Tunga was central to the birth and development of the Instituto Inhotim, so much so that he was attributed a second gallery in 2012, the Tunga Psychoactive Gallery. He is the only artist in the museum-garden to have two pavilions dedicated to his work.

→
Edgar de Souza, untitled sculptures, 2000, 2002, and 2005.

THE BOTANICAL COLLECTION — The vibrancy and diversity seen in Inhotim's art collection connects with the natural vitality of the garden, thus offering the public not only a museum of contemporary artworks but also an exhibition and living gallery of plant species: Arecaceae (23%), Araceae (11%), Orchidaceae (10%), Bromeliaceae (4%), as well as Cactaceae and Acanthaceae.

Inhotim is located in a naturalistically interesting location, a remnant of the Atlantic forest and the Cerrado tropical savanna, two of the most threatened biomes on the planet and among the most valued and rich in biodiversity. This makes it a key place for scientific research, conservation, and environmental education. In 2021, Inhotim Institute was certified by the BGCI Global Botanic Garden Fund, an international award for the support of environmental conservation projects.

At the forefront of research and preservation of plant biodiversity, Inhotim has implemented several initiatives, including the *Viveiro Educador*, an educational seedbed in which to train knowledge and environmental awareness, as well as scientific outreach projects; a *Laboratório de Botânica*, dedicated to the conservation of biodiversity and the propagation of rare plant species, where they also practice *in vitro* cultivation of endangered species, such as *Cattleya walkeriana Gardner*, a species of orchid native to the Cerrado; the *Seed Bank*, which contains more than 220,000 seeds of thirty-four species, all native to the Atlantic Forest and the tropical savanna of the Cerrado. The laboratory also conducts research on native and endangered species of Brazilian flora, as well as studying specimens typical of the Brumadinho region, developing protocols and galvanizing action for their conservation.

THE WORLD IN A GARDEN: THE RELATIONSHIP WITH THE REGION BETWEEN LOCAL AND GLOBAL — One of the priorities characterizing the work

of Instituto Inhotim is the relationship with the region, understood both from a geographical and human community perspective. This entails training, development, and improvement of general living conditions through the activation of projects, social actions, and educational programs aimed at schools. One of the special features of Inhotim, as noted by scholar Maurício Barros de Castro, is that this utopian and visionary project, albeit not devoid of contradictions or disputable facets, has been built in a rural area little visited by international tourism and even less by Brazil's artistic and cultural milieu. What has now become a prestigious world hub for art and environmental research, a potential of enormous cultural, scientific, and economic interest, is located several hours by air from the main world capitals. The presence of Inhotim in such a faraway land has resulted not only in a significant economic boost to the region, it has also elevated a specific, rural-based segment of Brazilian society to a global scale, helping to project its traditions in a contemporary scenario by renewing its image and meaning through the language of art.

Not only are conservation and collection activities continuous, but both plants and artworks constantly evolve through artistic creative processes and botanical regeneration. So, local and global perspectives intersect in this garden-museum, creating a unique example of a proactive center of culture and knowledge. Inhotim's founder, Bernardo Paz, is fully aware of the importance of being able to serve a community with such a unique collection (which only extraordinary levels of financing such as his could create in a single place), even if this is in the middle of nowhere. A possibility and responsibility that is expressed through a series of actions ranging from educational programs curated by Inhotim's education department to other services for the region, such as the *Território Específico* initiative.

EDUCATIONAL PROGRAMS — The Inhotim department dedicated to didactic and educational projects works with a multidisciplinary approach to accompany children, students, and local residents in the discovery of the museum-garden collection. They offer a series of experiences aimed at spurring dialogue and reflection around the themes addressed by the artworks, as well as broadening awareness and sensitivity toward art in general and environmental issues.

These activities include guided tours—in-person or digital—that follow different itineraries to target specific audiences (teachers, primary or high school students), aimed at eliciting interaction between the participants and the works or plant species examined. There are also a number of special educational programs for children and young people, such as *Espaço Ciência Inhotim*, which includes meetings and play activities focused on the popularization of science; and two continuing programs for teenagers in Brumadinho: *Jovens Agentes Ambientais*, inviting young people to develop environmental actions from the Institute's artistic and botanical collections, and *Laboratório Inhotim*, in which young people can experiment with artistic languages after visiting the museum-garden collections.

Educational programs also include a music school that, unlike the other educational activities, is supported by public funding and caters to the Brumadinho community with an Escola de Cordas, which provides free music classes for 80 participants, the Orquestra de Câmara Inhotim, composed of 25 musicians from the Escola de Cordas, and a choir, the Canto Coral, a choir for young people and adults.

SOCIAL PROGRAMS — In addition to the educational programs offered by Inhotim's education department, the Instituto has introduced a number of actions to involve local inhabitants in social and political processes, creating a platform for Brumadinho residents to come together, network, and share with the Institute's researchers, personnel, and social or cultural workers a series of services to facilitate the less affluent segments of the population. These include *Nosso Inhotim*, a program created for the local residents who can access at a reduced fee all events organized by the institute; the *Inhotim Library*, specializing in visual arts, botany, environment, heritage conservation, etc.; and the *Rede Educativa Inhotim*, a virtual platform that fosters the meeting of actors involved in research and education on issues of culture and biodiversity.

Finally, it's worth mentioning the *Território Específico*, an object of research and programmatic direction that shaped the development of Inhotim's program in 2021–22. Modeled on the work of Brazilian geographer Milton Santos, *Território Específico* is a field of research in which the notion of "territory" is approached from the point of view of the forms of life and community that inhabit it, providing the conceptual framework around which the Institute questions its relationship to the social and geographic context it inhabits, opening up reflection to the outside world as well. Artists, researchers, scientists, and the general public were invited to investigate the role of institutions and art in the relationship with the local environment, as well as the potential of the museum-garden itself, in the face of the most pressing issues of contemporary society. ¶

←
Yayoi Kusama,
Narcissus Garden, 2009.

CHINA
USA
MEXICO
IRAN
FRANCE
UNITED KINGDOM
ITALY
LITHUANIA

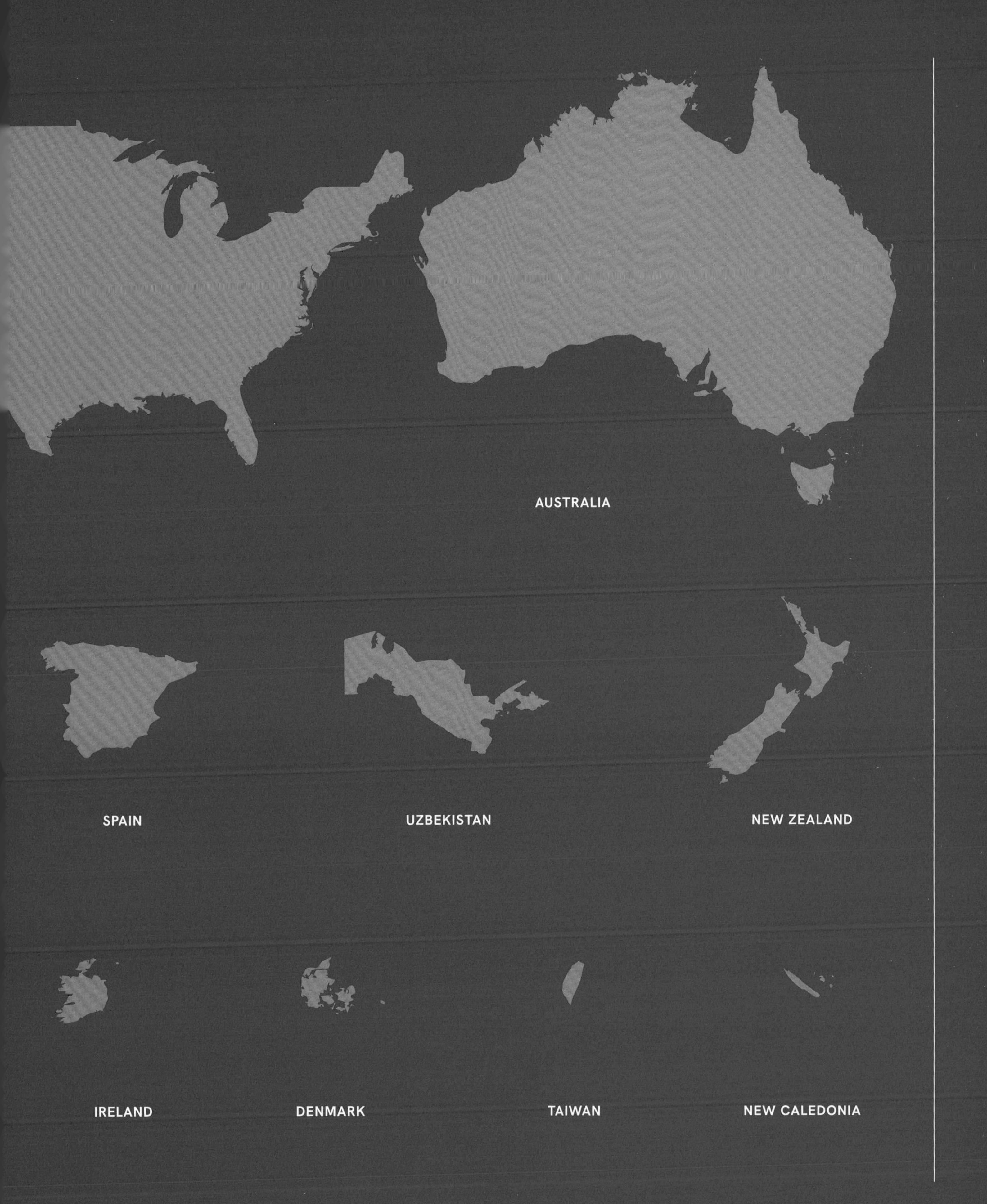
AUSTRALIA
SPAIN
UZBEKISTAN
NEW ZEALAND
IRELAND
DENMARK
TAIWAN
NEW CALEDONIA

-42° 48′ 73′′ N 147° 15′ 30′′ E

MUSEUM OF OLD AND NEW ART (MONA)

HOBART / AUSTRALIA

↓ Museum of Old and New Art (MONA), Hobart.

MONA is a museum displaying ancient, modern, and contemporary art located in Hobart, Tasmania. Opened in 2011, its exhibition spaces house the collection of the eclectic billionaire and philanthropist, David Walsh. The creative idea behind it is more than the mere display of a collection. Through the museum structure, MONA has redefined the landscape that hosts it. Indeed, this project is part of a process to re-evaluate the Tasmanian territory, known for having been the largest penal colony in the southern hemisphere.

39° 48′ 77″ N 64° 26′ 48″ E

SITORAI MOKHI-KHOSA

BUKHARA / UZBEKISTAN

←
→
Sitorai Mokhi-Khosa, the Summer Palace of the Emirs, Bukhara.

Built between 1912 and 1918, the Palace of Stars and Moon was originally the home of the Emirs of the city of Bukhara. In 1927, the museum opened its doors thanks to Moussadjan Saïdjanov, the first Uzbek curator in history participating in the organization. Its rooms, once a demonstration of the Emirs' opulence, today house the city's Museum of Decorative and Applied Arts. The Sitorai Mokhi-Khosa hosts many examples of Uzbek wood and metal workmanship, with a special focus on *suzani*, the traditional art of embroidery typical of Tajikistan, Uzbekistan, and Kazakhstan.

43° 38′ 10′′ N 5° 25′ 39′′ E

CHÂTEAU LA COSTE

LE PUY-SAINTE-RÉPARADE / FRANCE

↓
Louise Bourgeois,
Crouching Spider, 2007.

In the heart of Provence, between Aix-en-Provence and the Luberon National Park (source of much inspiration for Paul Cézanne), we find Château La Coste, an estate of more than 200 hectares that brings together art, architecture, food, and wine. Created in 2010 by the collector and businessman Patrick McKillen, Château La Coste is an ongoing project that welcomes new works and programming each year. Leading international artists and architects have contributed to the fusion of art and nature in what is a true open-air museum. The site includes works by Renzo Piano, Tadao Andō, Frank O. Gehry, Paul Matisse, Guggi, Kengo Kuma, and many others.

22° 56′ 18″ N 120° 13′ 44″ E

TEN DRUM CULTURE VILLAGE

TAINAN / TAIWAN

↓

The old sugar refinery at Ten Drum Culture Village, Tainan.

Ten Drum Village is an arts and cultural village founded by the performance collective Ten Drum Band and housed in a former Japanese colonial sugar factory converted in 2005. The innovative Taiwanese collective transformed the premises of the Tainan factory into a theater for their performances, while conserving strong links with the historical matrix of the host spaces.

39° 58′ 59″ N 116° 29′ 26″ E

798 ART ZONE

BEIJING / CHINA

In 2002, a former factory that produced electronic components in the Dashanzi area of northeast Beijing was re-evaluated and recontextualized: an example of industrial archaeology transformed into an art district. Artists and cultural organizations have divided, rented, and rebuilt factory spaces that have gradually started to accommodate galleries, art centers, artist studios, designers, restaurants, and bars.

→ An exhibition of contemporary art with sculptures displayed on old machinery, 798 Art Zone, Beijing.

↓ 798 Art Zone, Beijing.

Tomoyo

-22° 15′ 22″ N 166° 28′ 54″ E

CENTRE CULTUREL JEAN-MARIE TJIBAOU

NOUMÉA / NEW CALEDONIA

↓
Centre Culturel Jean-Marie Tjibaou, designed by Renzo Piano, Nouméa.

Named after pro-independence politician Jean-Marie Tjibaou, and designed by Renzo Piano in the 1990s, this cultural center is dedicated to New Caledonia's Kanak culture. Founded as a symbol of pacification between the people of New Caledonia and France, it houses a museum complex dedicated to the language, culture, arts, and traditions of the Indigenous people.

45° 26′ 39″ N 9° 12′ 19″ E

FONDAZIONE PRADA

MILAN / ITALY

↑ Fondazione Prada, Milan.

Opened to the public in 2015, the Milan headquarters of the Fondazione Prada were designed by the architectural collective OMA, headed by Rem Koolhaas. The project involved the renovation of a former gin distillery, though it has transformed into an architectural work that hybridizes preexisting spaces with new construction. Now a reference venue for contemporary art in Italy, Fondazione Prada brings life to its projects through research characterized by multidisciplinarity, with the aim of forging a powerful link between all the visual arts.

PROMOCIONDELARTE.COM/TABACALERA

40° 24′ 38″ N -3° 42′ 17″ E

LA TABACALERA

MADRID / SPAIN

→→ Fighter Adam Chase (right) from The Level team makes a flying kick over Pimp Ross (left) from Project Rangers team during a wrestling show at La Tabacalera, Madrid, February 2016.

Located in Madrid's Lavapiés neighborhood, the city's historic tobacco factory, decommissioned in 2000, has been redeveloped and is now a self-managed social and cultural center, La Tabacalera. Fully administered by the local community, the center hosts exhibitions and workshops, as well as offering free-of-charge spaces to be used by artists of all disciplines. Its operations and activities are conducted under the principles of horizontality, transparency, inclusion, and sustainability.

↑ Young people relax in the yard of La Tabacalera, Madrid.

56° 5′ 19″ N 10° 13′ 25″ E

MOESGAARD MUSEUM (MOMU)

HØJBJERG / DENMARK

MOMU, a museum dedicated to anthropology, archaeology, and ethnography, was inaugurated in 2014 in a suburb of Aarhus, Denmark. Designed by Henning Larsen Studio, the structure harmoniously blends with the setting, offering unconventional opportunities for its visitors to enjoy the surrounding landscape by extending the museum spaces outdoors. The exhibition spaces house an extensive collection of Danish archaeological artifacts and more than 50,000 objects from around the world.

← Moesgaard Museum (MOMU), designed by Henning Larsen, 2015.

→ Replica of *Stone Age Man* and visitors of Moesgaard Museum.

-36° 31′ 12″ N 174° 26′ 56″ E

GIBBS FARM

MAKARAU / NEW ZEALAND

↑ Anish Kapoor, *Dismemberment*, 2009.

In the Kaipara district near Auckland, the New Zealand collector and entrepreneur Alan Gibbs created Gibbs Farm, an open-air sculpture museum set in 400 acres of parkland. The works featured, all commissioned to world-renowned artists, dialogue harmoniously with the surrounding natural environment.

55° 54′ 15″ N -3° 25′ 17″ E

JUPITER ARTLAND

EDINBURGH / SCOTLAND

↓
Jupiter Artland, Edinburgh.

→→
Christian Boltanski, *Animitas*, Edinburgh, April 2016.

In Edinburgh, in the heart of Scotland, the husband-and-wife team Robert and Nicky Wilson created one of the world's most recognized contemporary sculpture and Land Art gardens in 2009. Nominated ArtFund's Museum of the Year in 2016, the Jupiter Artland includes numerous sculptures by Anish Kapoor, Christian Boltanski, Phyllida Barlow, and others, as well as several indoor galleries. Over time, the institution has also strived to encompass a focus on art awareness and education.

19° 35′ 33″ N -101° 59′ 55″ E

FÁBRICA DE SAN PEDRO

↓

Mauricio Rocha, *Taller*.

URUAPAN / MEXICO

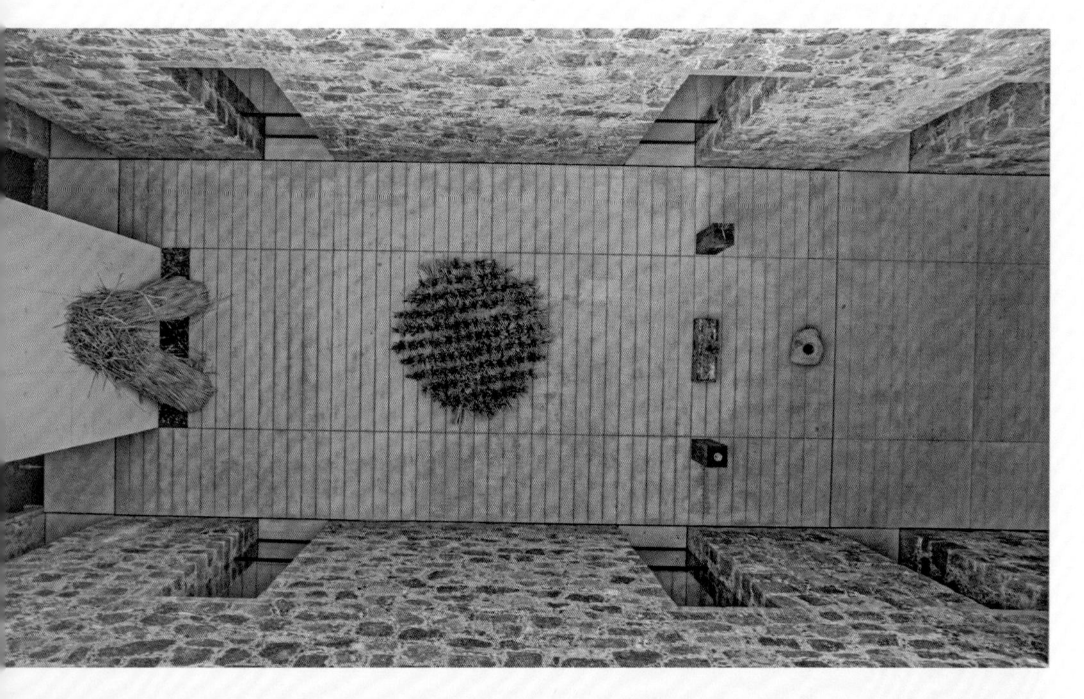

In 2017, the Fundación Javier Marín created the Fábrica de San Pedro inside a former textile factory: a cultural center dedicated to art, design, and gastronomy. In addition to its exhibition function, it is also a research hub focusing on the textile art of the Uruapan area. Its main objective is to encourage the convergence of contemporary culture and tradition through a series of workshops.

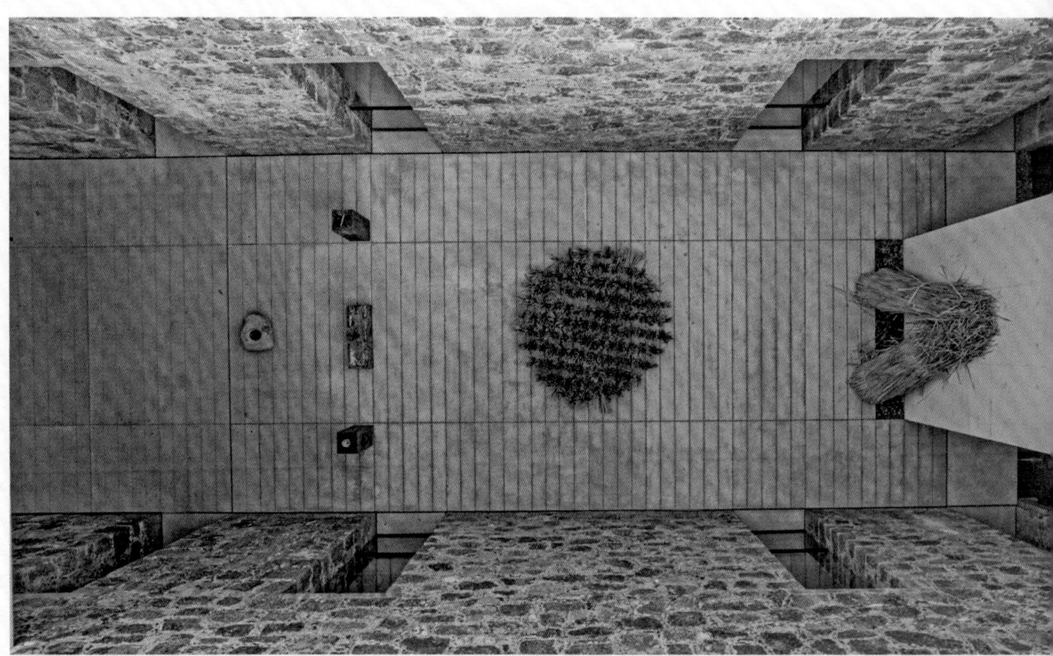

53° 13′ 23″ N -7° 43′ 39″ E

LOUGH BOORA SCULPTURE PARK

BOORA / IRELAND

↑

Lough Boora Park, the Black Forest in evening light with the remains of 5,000-year-old black oak trees, County Offaly, Ireland.

Inspired by the wilderness and industrial heritage of the area, sculptor Kevin O'Dwyer created the Lough Boora Sculpture Park in 2002 in the wetlands of Lough Boora. Each year artists who live in the area are invited to dialogue with the surrounding landscape by producing site-specific works that interact and harmonize with the specificity of the landscape.

54° 41′ 30″ N 25° 16′ E

LUKIŠKĖS PRISON

VILNIUS / LITHUANIA

↓
Lukiškės Prison, Vilnius.

→→
Young people at Lukiškės Prison, Vilnius.

After its definitive shutdown, Lukiškės Prison in central Vilnius—a tangible sign of the oppression of various occupying regimes—was transformed into a cultural center. After the band Solo Ansamblis inaugurated its re-opening, the project *Lukiškės Prison 2.0* was born to reevaluate prison sites with the aim of implementing creative spaces to be used by the Lithuanian people.

Jack&Jones
DAVAI
AUKELĘ
GOOD VIBES

Thank You!
THE LION KING

34° 4′ 37″ N -118° 28′ 32″ E

GETTY VILLA

LOS ANGELES / USA

Opened by oil magnate J. Paul Getty in 1954 to expand his own museum, the Getty Villa was inspired by the design of the Villa of the Papyri in Herculaneum and incorporated several elements from other ancient sites. The villa also includes a garden with Mediterranean vegetation and an ancient Roman theater. The collection consists of about 44,000 pieces devoted primarily to Greek, Roman, and Etruscan art.

35° 41′ 58″ N 51° 25′ 18″ E

ARGO FACTORY

TEHRAN / IRAN

↑
Argo Factory in Tehran's business district.

←
Courtyard of the Getty Villa in Los Angeles.

Argo Factory is a contemporary art museum and cultural center located in a former brewery in Tehran, which was completely restored by the Iranian architect Ahmadreza Schricker (ASA North) and is today one of the headquarters of the Pejman Foundation. The Argo Factory is the first post-revolution contemporary art museum in Iran and aims to give space and voice to Iranian artists of the past and present.

45° 25′ 59″ N 12° 19′ 8″ E

PUNTA DELLA DOGANA

VENICE / ITALY

A historic building in Venice (once the Dogana da Mar of the Republic of Venice), Punta della Dogana is one of two sites, along with Palazzo Grassi, that houses the collection of François Pinault. Restored in 2017 by architect Tadao Andō, it is a landmark venue in Italy for research and the dissemination of contemporary art.

↓

Installation view of *IV Luogo e Segni 5*: Félix González-Torres, *"Untitled" (Blood)*, 1992, Punta della Dogana, Venice, 2019.

55° 58′ 9″ N 12° 32′ 32″ E

LOUISIANA MUSEUM OF MODERN ART

HUMLEBÆK / DENMARK

→ Alexander Calder, *Little Janey-Waney (Stabile Mobile)*, 1964–76, Louisiana Museum of Modern Art, Humlebæk.

Considered one of the milestones of Danish modern architecture, the Louisiana Museum was created in 1954 by Knud W. Jensen with the objective of disseminating contemporary art in Denmark. Its architecture—a synergistic meeting of art and landscape—is complemented by the outdoor sculpture garden. A landmark of contemporary art in Europe, the museum has an extensive permanent collection featuring works from World War II to the present day.

41° 52′ 31″ N 12° 28′ 22″ E

MATTATOIO

ROME / ITALY

Starting as an idea of the Zoneattive collective, a former abattoir from the late nineteenth century in Rome's Testaccio neighborhood was restored and reopened to the public in 2010. Since 2018, the Mattatoio has become part of a redevelopment plan to create a hub for contemporary artistic research and production. Its pavilions are dedicated to visual research in all its forms, always in relation to the host place and city

↓ Olivier Saillard and Tilda Swinton, *Embodying Pasolini*, 2021.

THEATERS: MATRIX SPACES

THEATERS: MATRIX SPACES

Leaving behind the highly varied horizon of cultural centers, in the second chapter we will explore the seemingly more uniform horizon of theaters, focusing mainly on the European context (itself a varied and complex microcosm), and attempt to describe different realities, each defined by its own specificities in terms of artistic programming, cultural function, managerial structure, and funding system. Each of the realities we will examine articulates its own *modus operandi* based on the choices of artistic direction, the available spaces, and the art scene with which it dialogues, but above all, on the political, economic, and administrative framework that each country presents.

What is surprising when one analyzes these structures is the high degree of heterogeneity and multiformity contained within a single definition. Prose theater, opera theater, Italian-style theater, dance theater, puppet theater, documentary theater, narrative theater, figure theater, physical theater, and so forth. Theater is a place but also a genre, an artistic language containing numerous other subgenres, categories, and typologies, making its definition extremely elusive. Similarly, the theater space can take on different characteristics: it can have a raised stage or none at all, circular or frontal stall seating, boxes or seats, armchairs or cushions distributed around the stage. Performers may need only a few props or perhaps a set built by architects, powerful lighting rigs, and complex technological systems. Actors can wear professionally made, elaborate costumes or they can appear to the audience completely naked. Sometimes on stage there are animals, natural elements such as water, sand, soil; sometimes the bodies disappear and only voices remain. It is said that the show begins when the curtain rises, but in many theaters, there is no curtain! The theater itself can host performances with only one person on stage or large ensembles of actors, musicians, and dancers. Theater artists may use the body and movement as their main expressive element, or voice, words, music, or even wooden puppets, shadows, or silence. We have theaters in which the director's authorship is the driving force behind the work, or other cases in which the actors and actresses contribute to the composition of the dramaturgy in the same capacity as the director. The play can be based on a dramaturgical text—new, old, adapted, executed word-for-word—or constructed from actions, improvisations, musical sequences, etc. This long list is still partial and certainly not meant to negate any need for classification within the theater scene, but is instead to indicate how this is done within the conceptual framework of performing culture, and therefore, it is a fundamental process. In parallel to performance art, it is precisely the theatrical space that, especially in the twentieth century, enables the growth of an aesthetic and philosophical awareness of the nature of live performance by exploring the concept of "performativity" as an ideally opposed dimension to "representation." This distinction takes us back to John Austin's definition of the "performative act," but we must be aware that in the moment in which it is created, it cannot be practiced. Although distinguishable from each other, these two polarities are always intertwined and articulated in a configuration in which one will at best prevail over the other. It is not only languages or expressive "instruments" that multiply and characterize styles and genres, but also genealogies, generations, and the relationship with traditions and the past. Indeed, the tendency to conserve classical genres and repertoires—opera, ballet, tragic and comic works, prose theater—coexists in performance culture alongside a trend for more contemporary research and creation such as performance, contemporary choreography, video dance, digital theater, installation, and new dramaturgies that can, but not necessarily, choose to dialogue with tradition. Again, these definitions should not be seen as opposites or mutually exclusive, but more as rhetorical elements useful in describing the present state of performance culture in the theater scenario, or as the shifting reflection of the same image that takes on a meaning and function in the development of its own culture through its relations with others.

The dynamic that exists between public and private—closely related to the architectural space and the social context in each of these places—embodies an idea of community defined by tastes, needs, and internal dynamics. This constellates the performative landscape with many possibilities of being together and thus, regenerates the bonds that bind society together through one of the most ancestral forms by which human beings organize, re-elaborate, and make sense of their experience.

TEATRO REAL DE MADRID

TEATROREAL.ES

— The pulsating heart of history

Now we take a plunge into the velvety universe of European theaters starting in Madrid, with the Teatro Real, one of the many examples of nineteenth-century opera houses built to host grandiose opera, ballet, and symphonic music performances. Located in the Austrias district—a monumental area in the historic heart of Madrid overlooking the Plaza de Oriente, shared with the Royal Palace—this theater with a troubled history has hosted some of the most important artistic figures of the past, from Giuseppe Verdi to Nijinsky, Stravinsky, and Salvador Dalí. "El Real," as it is called by Madrileños, boasts one of the most impressive stage spaces in Europe, where the modern structures added during the twentieth-century restoration guarantee exceptional acoustics. El Real's artistic offering encompasses opera, dance, and music, bringing together major international productions, with concerts and music festivals, flamenco shows, and a substantial program for children.

A THEATER WITH MANY LIVES

The history of El Real is anything but linear, characterized since its inception by interruptions, slowdowns, and changes in its intended use, all of which have marked its development, including the very architecture of the building. The first construction works date back to 1818, during the reign of Ferdinand VII, as part of a general remodeling of Plaza de Oriente, as desired by the king. The new theater was built on the rubble of the old Real Teatro de los Caños del Peral demolished the previous year; it was intended to give Madrid a stage for opera that could compete with the major European theaters.

← Malin Byström in *Capriccio* by Richard Strauss, directed by Ahser Fisch, Teatro Real, Madrid, June 2019.

The project was entrusted to architect Antonio López Aguado, but the works suffered long interruptions, first due to lack of funds, then to the death of the architect and his replacement by Custodio Teodoro Moreno. The construction would not be completed until 1850, during the reign of Isabella II, when it was finally inaugurated. For the following 75 years, it would be one of the leading theaters in Europe, as well as the home of the Real Conservatorio Superior de Música de Madrid.

In 1925, the theater had to shut down due to structural problems; renovations were started and they continued for another 41 years. Between damage due to the Civil War and the country's subsequent post-war plight, the theater was closed until the second half of the 1960s. In 1966, it was decided to reopen it to the public as an auditorium, and it became home to the Royal Conservatory of Music and School

of Dramatic Arts. The city of Madrid still lacked a dedicated opera stage worthy of the great theaters of Europe. To this end, new restoration work on the building was undertaken on January 2, 1991, which lasted for nearly seven years. On October 11, 1997, King Juan Carlos and Queen Sophia officially reopened the Teatro Real, after the renovation works started by José Manuel González Valcárcel and, after his death, carried on by Francisco Rodríguez de Partearroyo, were completed.

Since its reopening in 1997, El Real has presented more than ten world premieres: *Divinas Palabras* by Antón García Abril (1997), *Don Quijote* by Cristóbal Halffter (2000), *La señorita Cristina* by Luis de Pablo (2001), *Dulcinea* by Mauricio Sotelo (2006), *El viaje a Simorgh* by José María Sánchez Verdú (2007), *Faust-Bal* by Leonardo Balada (2009), *La página en blanco* by Pilar Jurado (2011), *Poppea e Nerone* by Monteverdi-Boesmans (2012), *The Perfect American* by Philip Glass (2013), *Brokeback Mountain* by Charles Wuorinen (2014), and *El Público* by Mauricio Sotelo (2015).

↑
Prologue of *Peter Grimes* by Benjamin Britten, coproduction Teatro Real, Madrid, Royal Opera House, London, Opéra national de Paris, and Teatro dell'Opera di Roma, Teatro Real, Madrid, April 2019.

THE STRUCTURE OF EL REAL — It was the 1990s restoration that altered the Teatro Real's structure the most. Although it still retains its nineteenth-century architectural style and decor, it is now equipped with complex stage machinery and additional audience space was created by taking full advantage of the available height. Above the fourth and final tier of boxes, 15 new rows were added as new kinds of audience stalls, which are known by the unsurprising name of "paradise." With an additional 28 boxes on different levels, eight prosceniums, and a double-height royal box, the theater now has a capacity of about 1,800 seats.

The 1,472-square-meter stage is the theater's true jewel, consisting of nine platforms for moving sets on two levels and allowing for numerous combinations both on stage and in the orchestra pit. The building has many different halls and spaces, the main ones being the *Sala Principal*, with its exceptional acoustics and a state-of-the-art stage machine, making the stage suitable for the most complex productions; the *Sala de Orquesta* for orchestra rehearsals, with its distinctive wood-paneled and rounded ceiling designed to ensure the finest acoustics; the *Café de Palacio*, an elegant and modern bar with Lebanese cedar wood, stucco, and marble furnishings, housing a collection of paintings owned by the Centro de Arte Reina Sofía and with a wonderful view of the Plaza de Oriente from the sixth floor; the *Sala Gayarre*, with 190 seats, suitable for both performances and corporate events; a *Foyer*; and seven large, lavishly decorated halls, including the ancient *Salón de Baile*, completed in 1835, intended for masquerade parties and balls (and occasionally hosting meetings of the Spanish Parliament), with its unique "starry" ceiling in which 630 fiber-optic lamps reproduce the Madrid sky.

With the exception of the main hall used primarily for theater performances, all other spaces can be rented for private events, conferences, receptions, and institutional gatherings.

To date, the legal format of the theater is that of a public foundation chaired by the King and Queen of Spain, with the Ministry of Culture and Sports and the Madrid Municipality as founding partners, and with significant civil participation in its governance and funding. Indeed, the major supporters of Teatro Real include large multinational corporations, such as Telefónica S.A.

←
General rehearsal of *Rusalka* by Antonin Dvořák, choreography by Klevis Elmazaj, Teatro Real, Madrid, 2021.

(a Spanish telecommunications company operating primarily in Spain and Latin America, and the fourth largest in the world) and Endesa, the largest Spanish energy supplier, as well as many other partner companies and foundations that support the theater's activities. However, El Real also has another circuit of "patrons," the Amigos del Real, in which individuals can support the theater or become members at various tiers of support and can access a series of discounts, special events, meetings, and so on.

OPERA FOR EVERYONE — What is striking when taking an overall view of the activities of the Teatro Real in Madrid is certainly the attention toward inclusiveness and the dissemination of its excellent artistic mission. Not only opera and ballet, but a rich musical program ranging from a classical repertoire to contemporary genres, as well as a series of events dedicated to flamenco, the Spanish traditional dance and music style, which is still extremely popular.

Also included are programs specifically geared to children, as well as a "social" section featuring projects to foster participation and inclusion through music. Let us take a closer look at the lines on which El Real's artistic project is articulated.

PROGRAM — The vocation of the Teatro Real is to be an international reference venue for opera, which hosts major works coproduced with leading international theaters, while at the same time creating dialogue with the city's cultural institutions and playing a central role in the relationship with the area and its various audiences. To this aim, alongside programming of a traditional repertoire or more established operatic forms, it also looks to contemporary and experimental music productions, seeking to intercept the best of the moment.

The focus on diverse musical genres, which is expressed in the varied artistic programming—with prestigious opera productions as well as other genres, such as contemporary music or flamenco—is enhanced by the implementation of different activities to attract a wider audience to traditional genres, such as opera or ballet.

In addition, social initiatives are also organized where music becomes the object around which to build collective opportunities for exchange and entertainment. Alongside opera and dance, the cultural program includes concerts ranging from symphonic music, performances by small ensembles or soloists, and piano recitals, but also more popular genres such as fado. *Flamenco Real* is a program devoted entirely to evenings of music and dance, offering performances by both new talent as well as masters of the Flamenco genre. *El Real Junior are* events for children and families, including film screenings, meetings, performances, and "educational concerts," whereby younger audiences are introduced to classical music.

INNOVATIVE FORMATS — The *Universal Music Festival* has brightened up Madrid's summer cultural calendar for five years by bringing together pop and rock giants such as Sting, Steven Tyler, Elton John, Tom Jones, Iggy Pop, and Pet Shop Boys as well as Spanish and Latin American pop artists: Pablo Alborán, Miguel Ríos, David Bisbal, Niña Pastori, Rosario, Raphael, Manuel Carrasco, Luis Fonsi, and José Luis Perales, among others.

SPECIAL PROJECTS AND SOCIAL ACTIVITIES — In addition to the different sections of the cultural seasons, Teatro Real also organizes other activities with music—classical and otherwise—as their focus but with an explicitly social impact, thus harnessing the communal and imaginative potential of musical practice to galvanize the transformation and development of individuals.

These include the *Agrupación Musical Inclusiva del Teatro Real* foundation, an inclusion program for neurodiversity held in a place of musical excellence to encourage the participation of individuals with different forms of disabilities in musical collectives. In addition, the Teatro Real is the first opera house in Spain and one of the first in the world to be equipped with hearing accessibility technology within a protected historic building. The installation of a magnetic induction system allows people with hearing aids to enhance the sound reception of live music.

The previous illustrates the strategy of Teatro Real translated into action: to bring new life to tradition and make it part of contemporary society, and prevent traditional art forms that are unable to keep abreast with changing trends from disappearing or becoming increasingly elitist. El Real aims to make these more accessible and appealing by creating awareness that these art forms represent a common heritage of imagery and knowledge that is of fundamental importance today and has to be rediscovered and regenerated through practice. ¶

→

Marion Cotillard playing Joan of Arc in Arthur Honegger's *Jeanne d'Arc au Bûcher*, Teatro Real, Madrid, 2022.

→→

Irene Theorin in *Turandot* by Giacomo Puccini, stage direction and set and light design by Robert Wilson, music director Nicola Luisotti, Teatro Real, Madrid, 2018.

KAAITHEATER

KAAITHEATER.BE

— *A home for artistic vibrancy*

↑

Buren collective,
Spare Time Work, Kaaistudio,
Brussels, June 2022.

In the case of the Teatro Real in Madrid, it is history and artistic tradition that seek to penetrate contemporary society by devising new formats and contexts to attract audiences across the city. But Kaaitheater in Brussels works in a metaphorically opposite direction, inviting society to enter its structure with contemporary energies and imagery by offering a stable home to the lively and ephemeral flow of emerging creativity and artistic research. We are in Belgium, in a city that for different reasons has been one of the hubs of the international contemporary art scene in recent years, ousting or, at any rate, keeping pace with other more artistically vibrant capitals, such as Berlin and London. An enviable educational system, a network of welfare and public support for artists, and a proliferation of cutting-edge cultural venues have made Brussels one of the centers of the international art community, constantly seeking opportunities for exchange and networking, as well as concrete possibilities for production.

This is the context for Kaaitheater and the many other art centers operating in the city. Kaaitheater is housed in a building of considerable architectural standing, featuring a distinctive blend of Art Deco and modernism, which originally housed the Lunatheater. In addition to this main venue, Kaaitheater has a smaller secondary venue, Kaaistudio, a short distance from the first, which hosts about 75 shows per season every year, with a focus on ecological and social themes. The cultural activity offers a wide range of contemporary genres, languages, and formats: performance, theater, dance, meetings, music, workshops, lectures, installations, film screenings, readings, exhibitions, as well as publishing and audiovisual projects. In the 1980s, Kaaitheater was the launching pad for some of the most influential personalities in the international dance and performing arts scene, such as Anne Teresa De Keersmaeker and Jan Fabre.

Kaaitheater's history speaks of a strong political and social tension, of a fine balance between institutionalization and experimentation, of the search for radical organicity and adherence to common values that shape an entity and that, although experiencing several successive artistic generations and directions, has always held firm to its vocation of promoting the languages of art as imaginative tools for intervention on and transformation of reality.

→→
Angélica Liddell / NTGent in *Liebestod. Histoires(s) du Théâtre III*, Kaaistudio, Brussels, January 2023.

A HISTORY OF COMMUNITY

The story of Kaaitheater is an exemplary account of a cultural and artistic temperament that marked the development of European performing arts starting from an intersection of theater, choreography, and performance. Examining its various stages of life, we see the close relationship between the community dimension of the art scene and the cultural evolution of a given context. Kaaitheater's first manifestation was the socially extroverted festival format, which later shifted toward a sort of "nomadic" arts center and eventually became a stable, solid, and recognized cultural institution on the national and international creative scene.

Kaaitheater was founded in 1977 by the cultural manager and former theater director Hugo De Greef to connect the nascent Belgian art scene with international avant-garde productions. The aim was to echo other European festivals such as the Avignon Festival or the Edinburgh Fringe, which we will deal with later. Conceived by De Greef as something temporary, as a necessary propaedeutic element for the local artistic community to grow, Kaaitheater was to continue only "until a fresh and progressive theater movement is unleashed in the country." By 1985, after just five editions of the festival, the goal had been achieved: the so-called "Flemish Wave," which in 1977 showed the first signs of its emergence, was now mature and established. Jan Decorte, Anne Teresa De Keersmaeker, Jan Fabre, and Jan Lauwers could fearlessly hold their own against the greatest international artists. From the dimension of exceptional temporality typical of the festival, Kaaitheater was now in search of continuity and regularity, shifting from a function of promoting and presenting works to one of producing and accompanying local artists who were now becoming established. At that time, Hugo De Greef was also the organizer of Schaamte, an association of Flemish artists and companies born in that same period, and which provided the first nucleus for Kaaitheater's new mission; eventually, the two entities merged. In 1983, Kaaitheater obtained its first permanent home: the former Étoile brewery, which became, and still is, Kaaistudio. The goal of the new association —which kept the name Kaaitheater—was threefold: produce, present, and distribute produced work.

From 1987 to 1993, Kaaitheater was in charge of organizing performances in the main Brussels venues, as a sort of touring company in its own city; however, this left the artists and their work exposed to excessive uncertainty. This was contrary to Kaaitheater's goal, which was to provide continuity to an experimental artistic reality, detached from any commercial mechanisms, thus creating a strong link between artists and the public and taking on the difficult role of protecting the fragility inherent

↑ Troubleyn / Jan Fabre, *Mount Olympus*, Kaaistudio, Brussels, August 2016.

in artistic research processes. It was soon apparent that a fixed location was needed to consolidate its structure so as to initiate a closer and more stable relationship with the city of Brussels and its theatrical history. The 1992–93 season was thus the last "itinerant" one for Kaaitheater, which then settled into the Lunatheater premises. Operating from two different spaces made the challenge of sustainability even more complex. To cope with the new situation, Kaaitheater's core activity had to change again: from a group of artists to an art center, from production to programming and establishing relations with a wider public. Following cuts in municipal funding, the director Hugo De Greef left Kaaitheater and Johan Reyniers was appointed in 1998 to replace him. Reyniers's strategy was twofold: on the one hand, to ensure the continuity of the Kaaitheater project, and on the other to set in motion those changes necessary to guarantee the operation of a dual-location art center. The most important intervention in this regard was undoubtedly the expansion of the roster of artists, creating more space for newer generations while reducing that of the original and now established companies, which had also become more expensive. By differentiating its artistic mission, Kaaitheater chose to revive its now traditional function of

supporting emerging creativity, rather than continuing to promote a certain genre of artistic language or aesthetic. In 2008, the artistic direction was entrusted to Guy Gypens and Katleen Van Langendonck, who opened a new chapter in the life of the theater, questioning the political role of a cultural institution like Kaaitheater. Gypens and Van Langendonck felt the need to make the house more accommodating and intensify ties with local and international partners. Thus, in the following years, contents and activities conducted outside Kaaitheater venues would increase, as would interaction with new audiences through initiatives and festivals dedicated to individual themes—such as *Burning Ice*, on the socio-ecological crisis, or *WoWmen*, on gender issues—and collaborations with other cultural entities in the city.

Today Kaaitheater is "a stage for dance, theater, performance, music, and debate, rooted in Brussels and with its gaze directed toward the world . . . Convinced of the importance of art for the well-being of humankind, Kaaitheater explicitly sets out to research society. Located in the Brussels Canal Zone, where many of contemporary society's problems are exemplified, the artists narrate and shape the city of the future."

TWO PLACES FOR ONE PROJECT — As anticipated, Kaaitheater has two venues about a fifteen-minute walk apart and located on the Brussels Canal, the banks of which form a natural pathway connecting the two venues. Kaaitheater's two centers represent the two poles of its cultural activity and testify to the different phases that Kaaitheater has gone through during its lifetime. The Art Deco-style Lunatheater, built in 1932, once housed an auditorium, café, and some apartments, but over time the structure went through some problematic phases, including the risk of being demolished. Saved by the City of Brussels, after careful restoration in 2001 it became the main venue of Kaaitheater, which secured its destiny for the foreseeable future. The Kaaitheater hall is the pivotal venue for artistic programming, where most of the season's events are held as well as the presentation of important and innovative productions ranging in formats and disciplines, as we will see in the next section. The Kaaitheater structure houses the foyer, the Kaaicafe, and the large theater hall with its modern steel structure.

← Vania Vaneau in *Nebula*, Kaaistudio, Brussels, February 2023.

Kaaistudio is the minor hall, although this is where Kaaitheater began its activities as a production center. It functions primarily as a rehearsal room, workplace, and studio where smaller or less technically complex productions are also occasionally held. The space consists of three rooms: a foyer, a music studio with movable walls and panels to optimize the acoustics, and a theater studio with red-brick walls reminiscent of the building's industrial past, parquet flooring, and a tiered seating area. Both the Kaaistudio and halls of Kaaitheater can be rented for a variety of cultural activities and live performances.

THE MANAGERIAL SETUP — From a management point of view, Kaaitheater is organized around a shared management structure, whereby the two general and artistic directors—at the time of publication, Agnes Quackels and Barbara Van Lindt—are part of an artistic committee together with other figures in charge of programming, coordination of production, participatory projects, and audience development, as well as administrative coordination. Kaaitheater is headed by a board of directors that includes some government representatives and a general assembly, thus giving it the profile of a private association but with an organizational structure that incorporates the participation of political representatives of the Flemish community. Another characterizing element is the attention paid to interpersonal relations and human resource management, which reflects the intimately political vision animating Kaaitheater's cultural work.

Thus, importance is given to communicating the principles that underpin the association's physical workspace, conceived as "a healthy, welcoming, and respectful environment for everyone involved" (both employees and guest artists) in which racism, sexism, violence, and abuse of power are structurally rejected in favor of awareness of the responsibility required by a cultural institution actively engaged in topical social issues. Kaaitheater seeks to translate this responsibility into practices and reflections that are also capable of questioning its own automatisms.

Kaaitheater has partnerships with some of the city's leading art centers, including Moussem Nomadisch Kunstencentrum, Globe Aroma, Workspacebrussels, and Het TheaterFestival. It receives grants from the City of Brussels and various public bodies in the Flemish community.

NOURISHING THE CONTEMPORARY SECTOR — Beyond the spaces and operating model, what makes Kaaitheater stand out is undoubtedly its artistic programming and the intimate connection it established with its own history and the cultural history of Brussels and of Europe in general. We can say that Kaaitheater's identity, although rather recent when compared to other theaters examined here, is defined by its specific function and approach to the art scene rather than by a precise aesthetic choice of creative language or format. In this sense, any change in its artistic direction does not necessarily alter the nature of the project but updates it, fine-tuning it to the changes in contemporary reality. Contact with certain practices, or rather, with certain ways of conceiving artistic practice, and the close relationship with artists have been central to Kaaitheater's programming since its founding. Its status has changed over time, and, consequently, the status of the artists involved has also changed, due to the recognition and positioning achieved on the international art scene. Now we will explore how Kaaitheater's artistic mission is articulated.

RESIDENT ARTISTS — Following in the footsteps of the early days of its "settled" phase, Kaaitheater selects a number of artists defined as "resident," meaning that they are present in the theater's programming for a long period of time. The last residency, which started in 2017 and ended in 2021, involved six artists. The names selected for this five-year term differ in genres and disciplines and present experimental and highly diverse artistic and research practices: Benjamin Vandewalle, performer and choreographer; Christophe Meierhans, who trained as a composer but now works on stage schemes that question the theatrical format; Kate McIntosh, an experimentalist working in performance, theater, video, and installation; Michiel Vandevelde, choreographer, curator, and writer; Radouan Mriziga, dancer and choreographer; and Vera Tussing, also a choreographer and dancer. Despite evident differences, these six artists are indeed united by a profound and attentive gaze toward the world and the active involvement of the viewer in both theatrical contexts and public space, which is a continuation of Kaaitheater's same trajectory.

BILLBOARD — In addition to staging works by resident artists, Kaaitheater's artistic programming embraces the best of contemporary European production, presenting to its audience both local and international artists to of-

→
Johan Leysen performing a Beckett monologue in *ACT* by Kris Verdonck / A Two Dogs Company, Kaaistudio, Brussels, February 2020.

→→
Angélica Liddell / NTGent in *Liebestod. Histoires(s) du Théatre III*, Kaaistudio, Brussels, January 2023.

fer a broad overview of the current formats and scenic devices. The audience's experience of going to the theater can therefore turn out to be something very different, depending on the type of work they are confronted with. Here too variety is the rule and performances range from the theater and contemporary drama of Tg Stan (one of the main theater collectives of the past decade) to children's theater or costume operetta; then we have performances by Lotte Van Der Berg, Mette Edvardsen, and Markus Öhrn, all names perhaps little-known in general but of great prominence in contemporary performing arts, who offer the audience uncustomary formats to be enjoyed; and the dance of Christodoulos Panayiotou, a key figure in contemporary choreography, or the sound performances of Jonathan Burrows and Matteo Fargion.

The program often presents companies previously formed at Kaaitheater that are now

established and renowned, who return to the same stage where they started. These include the ensemble Rosas with its founder Anne Teresa De Keersmaeker—one of the very first artists produced by Kaaitheater—whose influence has marked the development of contemporary dance worldwide, or Jan Fabre, who is regarded as one of the most innovative and versatile personalities on the international scene but recently also at the center of a major scandal over abuse reported by some of his company's dancers.

In addition to performances, Kaaitheater's programming features a series of events, meetings, debates, and talks covering very specific yet diverse topics, from ecological issues to contemporary philosophy, feminist thought, new media, and artistic languages. Interestingly, this area of activity is not considered separate from the artistic one, highlighting an increasingly widespread curatorial approach that considers artistic practice and theory closely linked to critical thinking, theoretical reflection, and specialized knowledge from the natural and social sciences.

FESTIVALS — An important space in Kaaitheater's programming is given to the festival format. Some events are produced directly by Kaaitheater, whereas others are produced in collaboration with different cultural venues in Brussels that, from time to time, can be distributed throughout the city or focused in the Kaaitheater venues. The curatorial line of these festivals was, and still is, primarily thematic, with the aim of articulating a precise discourse in a specific field of knowledge or of the arts. The aim is to attract a target of enthusiasts, thus creating an audience that does not usually attend the theater.

The exception to this "thematic rule" is *Performatik*, a festival dedicated to performing arts and, more specifically, the relationship between performing and visual arts. Over the years, this event has become a true urban festival thanks to the curatorial collaboration of several city partners such as Wiels, Argos, Bozar, De Centrale, Museumcultuur Strombeek, QO2, and Beursschouwburg.

SIDE ACTIVITIES — Kaaitheater's cultural and artistic mission appears particularly varied and layered—indeed, it is somewhat similar to the examples of multipurpose cultural centers seen in the previous chapter, but differing from them in terms of organicity and curatorial vision. In this sense, what we define as side activities should not be considered as such, as they also play an important part in the overall design, thus contributing in shaping the artistic programming of a cutting-edge venue like Kaaitheater. If the talks, meetings, and theoretical focus groups are an integral part of its activities, similarly all the other events are to be considered as central. These are the workshops for adults or young people, conducted by artists participating in the cultural season; the festivals hosted at Kaaitheater; installations; exhibitions; book presentations; the *lecture performances* with film and documentary screenings; parties; and, finally, even some activities related to meditation, spirituality, and ritual.

Well before the pandemic, Kaaitheater was already engaged in the production of multimedia content: interviews, video documentation of meetings, audio recordings, and theoretical texts, which are accessible on the theater's website and online platforms. ¶

ERT – EMILIA ROMAGNA TEATRO

EMILIAROMAGNATEATRO.COM

— Disseminating creativity

We now move to Italy, to the region of Emilia-Romagna that has historically been a theatrical hotbed, especially during the second half of the twentieth century, a period of economic development, political drive, and active citizenship. Emilia-Romagna has a long history of excellence for its public and private initiatives in theater, and in the arts and cultural sectors in general. The region is home to a dense network of cultural centers and facilities that are financed by public funding, private initiatives, and bank foundations. This is a networked and layered landscape, in which large public theaters, small but proactive provincial halls, schools and training venues, residency and production centers, private rehearsal halls, festivals, and distribution circuits, are all potential platforms for emerging artists; in this scenario, cultural awards flourish. Emilia-Romagna has seen the birth of some of the most innovative artistic experiences in Italy and Europe, such as Socìetas Raffaello Sanzio by Romeo Castellucci, Chiara Guidi, and Claudia Castellucci, today among the most prominent names in the international theater scene; the Santarcangelo Festival, once Santarcangelo International Festival of Theater in the Square, with over fifty annual events; the experience of Teatro delle Albe by Marco Martinelli, Ermanna Montanari, Luigi Dadina, and Marcella Nonni; and Teatro della Valdoca, founded by Cesare Ronconi and Mariangela Gualtieri, both true masters of Italian research theater.

Emilia-Romagna is home to the Premio Ubu, considered by those in the industry to be the Oscar of Italian theater, the Vetrina della Giovane Danza d'Autore, as well as some of the most important opera houses in Europe, such as the Comunale di Bologna. Peter Brook and the Living Theater, two giants of twentieth-century research theater, have passed through here; furthermore, Bologna was home to the first experiment in Italian university degree programs dedicated to the arts, music, and live performance, the now mythical DAMS. This is the vibrant setting for our next case study, the ERT – Emilia Romagna Teatro Fondazione, one of the seven National Theaters formally recognized by the Italian Ministry of Culture. ERT is one of Italy's leading centers of theater production, which manages the cultural programs of seven theaters distributed over five cities and towns in the region: Modena, Vignola, Castelfranco Emilia, Bologna, Cesena. In particular, ERT is an example of a successful model of cultural policy that prioritizes networking and establishing close links between institutions of different

←
Arena del Sole, Bologna.

→→
Pippo Delbono in *Amore*, directed by Pippo Delbono, November 2022.

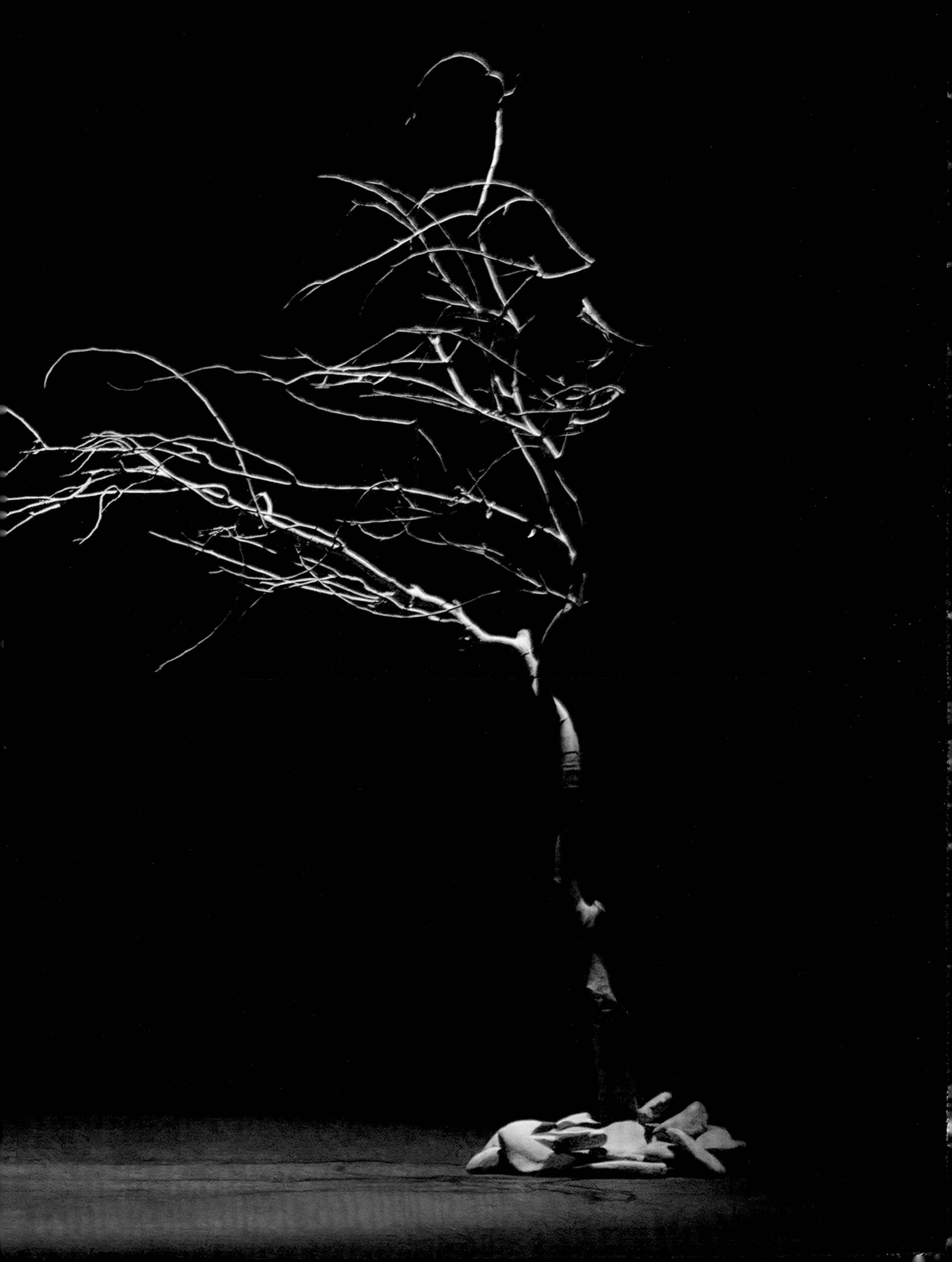

natures, such as public theaters and universities. Cultural action is seen in this context as a widespread public service, in which major urban centers participate as much as provincial towns, all connected with an effective transportation network. As proof of this, ERT's headquarters is not, as one might easily think, Bologna, but the smaller city of Modena.

↓
Antonio Latella, *Santa Estasi*, first performed in 2016 at Teatro delle Passioni, Modena.

BIRTH OF A THEATRICAL INSTITUTION

Some explanation is needed when analyzing ERT's history. As in the case of Kaaitheater, again we are dealing with a reality that was not born in a specific place but only later became established in a series of theatrical spaces. In this sense, ERT's history does not coincide entirely with the history of the theaters it now manages, with their own lives and histories that have only recently intersected with that of the Foundation. We will try to give an account for both levels, still paying more attention to the activities of ERT, which is the real topic of this section.

ERT's history actually has several points of contact with that of Kaaitheater, one of which is their shared date of birth, 1977. In addition, as in Brussels, the beginning of the Emilia-based foundation has a history of associationism, which then consolidated into an institutional structure that was publicly and formally recognized as a National Theater. Consequently, its status was transformed from a private to a public entity.

ERT first appeared as an identifiable body in 1977, when the ATER – Emilia-Romagna Theater Association shareholders' meeting established its own drama department. We can, however, go back to an even earlier date; in 1964 several city administrations in Emilia-Romagna formed an association that formalized a networking effort that had been informally ongoing for years. The aim was to "offer support for opera productions with collective agreements and support the management of theaters" in the region. Over the years, however, the association began to feel the need to devote a specific part of its activities to the production of prose works, leading to the establishment of an internal body dedicated entirely to that function. In 1977—the same year of its founding—ATER-ERT was recognized as a public theater, but it was not until 1991 that ERT gained autonomy from ATER, and in 2001 was transformed into a Foundation. It is worth mentioning that ATER gave birth not only to ERT but also to two other important entities in the Emilia-Romagna and Italian theater circuit: the OSER, the regional symphony orchestra, based in Parma, now the Toscanini Foundation, and the dance company Aterballetto, based in Reggio Emilia, now the *National Dance Foundation*. Both became autonomous entities in 1991.

In 2015, ERT joined the ranks of *Italian National Theaters*, receiving three-year funding from the Ministry of Culture to carry out its theatrical production, training, and programming activities, aimed specifically at prose but with some space dedicated to dance as well.

PERMANENT BUT OFF-CENTER — ERT thus has the distinction of being a "repertory of permanent theater," a solid and institutionally recognized structure with its own unique and autonomous artistic direction—at the moment under the guidance of its director Valter Malosti—branching out into its various venues.

To date, the founding members of the Foundation are the Emilia-Romagna Region, the Municipality of Modena, the Municipality of Cesena, and the Municipality of Bologna, together with other ordinary members, mostly from Emilian municipalities and foundations: the Emilia-based Bank BPER, Legacoop, and other groups and associations grouped together in the "Albo Speciale" or special register of supporters.

Therefore, ERT operates not only at a city level but at regional level, thus functioning as a true circuit in which the individual centers keep their own autonomy as concerns territorial relations and specific projects, but at the same time enjoy the support of a larger and more solid structure. Among the various theaters managed by ERT—seven in five cities—the most well-known are obviously those of Bologna, the regional capital, and Modena, home to the Foundation since its inception. The other three, however, offer many opportunities to articulate plans in which international programming and theater production converge in a local context. In addition to the theatrical activity, ERT also produces the *VIE Festival*, which is held in the Foundation's various venues and is primarily aimed at contemporary creativity and international performing arts, which will be discussed in the next section. Now we will examine more specifically the different venues managed by ERT.

Modena is the city where ERT has historically been headquartered and where it operates two different theaters. The first, Teatro Storchi, is a historic theater from the late nineteenth century that has gone through multiple architectural (dis-)adventures. It owes its name to the Modena merchant Gaetano Storchi, who founded it at his own expense, later associating it to a charity to raise proceeds for charitable purposes. The theater was opened in 1889, but over the years it was restored several times to make up for the many structural problems caused by the lack of investment during its construction. It remained under the control of the Opera Pia Storchi until the late 1960s and was then acquired

→ Sergio Blanco, *El Bramido de Düsseldorf*, Teatro Storchi, Modena, 2019.

by the City of Modena in 1989. In 1990, its management was passed on to Emilia Romagna Teatro. The Teatro Storchi is a typical nineteenth-century theater, with horseshoe-shaped stalls and three tiers of galleries, suitable for hosting classical works, dance, and ballet as well as new prose productions.

It is quite another story for the second Modena-based theater managed by ERT, the Teatro delle Passioni. Located just a few kilometers from the Storchi, it occupies a former industrial building converted in the late 1990s as part of a redevelopment project for an area of the city that is scheduled to become Modena's arts hub in the coming years. The Teatro delle Passioni complex is similar to the European cultural centers mentioned earlier, as it offers not only a theater hall for about 140 seats, but also a cozy foyer and a bar/restaurant, making this a meeting place outside ordinary theater programming. Its architecture makes it naturally oriented toward artistic research, contemporary creativity, and more experimental formats; not coincidentally, the Teatro delle Passioni is one of the main venues of the *VIE Festival*.

With these two theaters, ERT in Modena is able to articulate a multifaceted artistic plan—a more traditional or "mainstream" program in the choice of performances and audience numbers, and a more experimental and contemporary one—by aligning the programming to the specificity of each venue. In addition to the main programming, ERT in Modena has special activities for children, including performances, workshops, and events in the city's schools.

ERT's activities in Bologna follow the Modena model; since 2014, it has managed two different venues, each with its own vocation—the larger and more institutional Arena del Sole, with two halls, located on one of the main streets of the city, and Teatro delle Moline, a small atelier in the Bologna university area. The Arena del Sole is a historic building, opened in 1810 as a "place dedicated to daytime performances," as stated by the engraving that stands out on the Neoclassical facade. Originally, the Arena was actually an open-air structure built in the area of the

Dominican convent of St. Mary Magdalene to host summer performances, starting at Easter and ending in October. It was not until 1916 that a removable roof was added, making the structure accessible both in summer and winter, and not only as a theater but also as a movie house. Indeed, the appeal of movies was so strong that in 1946 theater programming was discontinued and the Arena del Sole became a movie house only. In 1984, the building was acquired by the City of Bologna, which took steps to restore it to its original function as a theater, following major renovations. Two new halls were built—one larger, the Leo De Berardinis Hall (in honor of the director who renewed the theater scene) with about 884 seats, and a smaller one, the Thierry Salmon Hall (dedicated to the late Belgian actor and theater director), with 160 seats—as well as the Cloister, which can be used for outdoor events and performances, four foyers, and three rooms that can be used for lectures, meetings, and conferences. The "new" Arena del Sole reopened to the public in 1995 and was entrusted to the Nuova Scena cooperative, founded by Dario Fo, Vittorio Franceschi, and Franca Rame, which managed the spaces until 2014.

← La Veronal, *Opening Night*, Teatro Bonci, Cesena, 2022.

The Teatro delle Moline is located inside Palazzo Bentivoglio, a prestigious building from the second half of the sixteenth century. It was founded in 1973 by Luigi Gozzi, a playwright, director, and university lecturer from Bologna, who made the space the headquarters of his company Teatro Nuova Edizione. The theater has a small hall of about 60 seats used for rehearsals, a space open to the public for artistic residencies and workshops and sometimes used to host productions by young emerging companies.

The interconnection between these two venues precedes the period of ERT's management, once again testifying to the tendency toward a networking model often adopted by organizations and entities based in Emilia-Romagna. The two theaters, headed by some of the most prominent Italian directors on the national and especially the Bologna scene—Franca Rame, Vittorio Franceschi, Luigi Gozzi, and Marinella Manicardi—had already "shared the same cultural trajectory . . . promotional activities and collaboration" for some time, as stated by the then-director of the Arena del Sole Paolo Cacchioli. In the light of this collaboration and the increasing bureaucratic complexity of working as separate theatrical companies, the two merged in 2006, thus bringing the smaller but very active Teatro delle Moline under the umbrella of the Arena del Sole. Since 2014, the two spaces have been managed by ERT, which also takes care of their cultural programming and other activities in an integrated manner; thus both venues maintain their specific function in the cultural landscape of the city of Bologna.

The Teatro Alessandro Bonci in Cesena is one of ERT's most important theaters, both historically and architecturally. Accounts of fifteenth-century Cesena contain records of theatrical performances and events held in the stately palaces and squares of the city; during the eighteenth century, Palazzo Spada became the main venue for theatrical activity, accessible to all the city's inhabitants; this is why the aristocratic families of Cesena decided to build the first wooden theater in that very site. The theater was then leased by the City Hall, which rebuilt it and made it the Municipal Theater, later dedicated to the Cesena-born tenor Alessandro Bonci. The construction of the new theater was entrusted to Vincenzo Ghinelli, an architect specializing in theatrical buildings, the Cesena theater representing his most notable work. The new Teatro Bonci opened to the public in 1846. Built in the Neoclassical style, it features a balanced distribution of space, harmonious organization of volumes, and elegant decorative elements. From a scenic point of view, the excellent technical and acoustic qualities of this theater made it one of the most important opera houses in Europe for over a century. The history of the Teatro Bonci confirms its prominent role in opera and other traditional genres, hosting major premieres and leading artistic figures of the past. Albeit this role was partly undermined in the postwar period by the gradual decline in popularity of opera, it then recovered by the 1970s, when the Bonci again became widely frequented by audiences interested in prose and new drama. Since 2001, it has been under the management of ERT, which still organizes its multidisciplinary program of plays, concerts, and dance, as well as important programs for schools, including the *Festival Nazionale del Teatro Scolastico Elisabetta Turroni*, one of the most important events dedicated to school theater and now in its twenty-second year.

ERT's last two venues are located in two very small towns in the Modena hinterland: Castelfranco Emilia, with its fine Teatro Dadà, and Vignola, home to the modern Teatro Ermanno Fabbri. The former is located inside an Art Nouveau building, which was once the Zucchini-Solimei kindergarten, where the original eighteenth- century municipal theater moved in 1913. Following a series of renovations, shutdowns, and re-openings, it was finally taken under ERT management in 1995. The latter is a recently built theater dating from 2010 and owes its existence to the far-sightedness of a local entrepreneur, who invested in the construction of a new theater hall where the old Ariston Cinema once stood. Indeed, still today the theater houses a small museum dedicated to cinema.

ERT'S TERRITORIAL INITIATIVES — ERT is in charge of the management and programming of seven theaters distributed throughout the Emilia-Romagna region, each differing in size, characteristics, and vocation but all articulating a common and coherent artistic mission, while maintaining a close relationship with the region. It is beyond the scope of this publication to review the programming of each theater from the perspective of their relevant artistic choices, but we will try to highlight the main points and functions that unite them within a single overall design, identifying each theater as a single node in a much wider network of territorial cultural initiatives.

PRODUCTION AND PROGRAMMING — Since its origins, ERT has operated primarily in the field of artistic production. In some texts and press releases it is referred to as a "company," reflecting the fact that it is a "proposing" entity in the theatrical scenario, this function being considered a prerequisite by the Italian legal system for the recognition of a "national theater." In Italy, a theater is not so much a venue that merely hosts a performance but a center that creates the conditions for the public presentation of a performance. Specifically, it is formally in charge of all operations from start to finish, involving contact with the artists, management of all administrative details, staging, and distribution in the theatrical circuit. Hence, the great responsibility of National Theaters toward the national artistic community.

We cite ERT's website in this regard: "With the creation of more than 200 shows under its belt, ERT develops its theater policies along two basic trajectories: collaboration with artists on the one hand and, on the other, the search for alternative performance and spatial typologies for a large audience, under the banner of a diverse and more complex meeting with the public."

Scrolling through ERT's archive we can understand how its production activities are

↑

Kornél Mundruczó, *Imitation of Life*, Arena del Sole, Bologna, 2019.

aimed not necessarily at a precise aesthetic or artistic language but leave space to highly diverse projects, while giving precedence to what is defined as spoken word or prose theater. ERT has produced and co-produced original works by leading contemporary Italian directors such as Antonio Latella, Pippo Del Bono, Roberto Latini, and Elio De Capitani, to name just a few. These include new dramaturgical writings or re-adaptations of classic texts as well as more experimental works, including digital languages, readings, participatory performances, and so on. Another important element to note in ERT's archive are the numerous international coproductions involving theaters in France, Spain, Greece, Switzerland, Croatia, Japan, and many other countries with which ERT coproduces or cofinances works destined for international audiences and presented through extended multi-country tours.

Another goal of a National Theater like ERT is to be an "accessible and receptive space to host productions from other theaters or to accommodate artistic residencies," to again quote its website. To this end, ERT allows national and international works to circulate primarily between the different venues managed by the Foundation and inserted into a program specifically designed for each. In the program of ERT's seven theaters—in addition to its own productions or prose performances—both contemporary dance and ballet are included, as well as music, symphonic and otherwise.

This multidisciplinary approach is also seen in the *VIE Festival*, which in 2005 replaced *Le Vie dei Festival*; from 1994 to 2004, the latter brought some of the most interesting examples of national and international summer festivals to Modena. The *VIE Festival* adopts a more concentrated timeframe, following the customary model of European performing arts festivals. It is distributed over all of the Foundation's theater venues and organically complements ERT's programming by offering a glimpse into contemporary performing arts. The focus, however, is on experimental and vibrant creative languages and formats, intercepting both international and new national works, thus introducing new formats for audiences to enjoy. Alongside performances, the *VIE Festival* offers side activities, including meetings with artists and theorists, workshops, and special projects, which contribute to the renewal and expansion of the reference communities of the various theaters in the area.

Finally, all ERT-managed theaters pay special attention to families and younger audiences and dedicate part of the program to children's theater, as well as curating numerous projects in schools of all levels in Emilia-Romagna. This widespread activity helps create awareness and forms a rich groundwork on which theatrical arts can flourish—something that is always woven into the social fabric of the region.

TRAINING, RELATIONSHIP WITH THE REGION, AND OTHER PROJECTS — Historically, the region of Emilia-Romagna boasts a very intense relationship with the theater scene and is home to important venues, festivals, and production centers that regularly host the work of artists and companies that have made international theater history. This virtuous cycle is possible first and foremost thanks to economic resources and active policies that have guaranteed continuity to the cultural realities in the

→
Valter Malosti,
Se questo è un uomo, first performed in 2019 at Teatro Carignano, Turin.

area over decades, as well as to the tendency to create networks that enhance the merits of each individual entity, thus creating a common heritage of experiences and good practice. This virtuous process is also assisted by the regional educational authorities and a renowned public institution, the University of Bologna Alma Mater Studiorum, among the first in Italy to offer degrees in theater. They consider education, pedagogy, and training as indispensable components in the languages of art; therefore, they nurture close links with the artistic reality of the territory.

A healthy theater system is one that invests in the training of future artists and operates toward making the arts a mainstay of a region's cultural offer, incorporating theater and arts-related projects into the school curriculum, amplifying opportunities for contact with the performing arts in a simple and direct way, and creating opportunities for professional training, which is a prerequisite for the arts of the future. This role is taken on and implemented by ERT in different ways. An example is the initiative aimed at professional training delivered by Scuola di Teatro Iolanda Gazzerro, directed by Valter Malosti and envisioned as a "permanent workshop for actors," capable of providing aspiring professionals with "full insertion and qualified permanence in the theatrical labor market, with knowledge and skills capable of affecting the processes of innovation and qualification of the current production system."

ERT also offers numerous specialized courses for the theatrical professions in areas such as theatrical writing and dramaturgy, actor training, performance staging, and in various other areas. These are organized in collaboration with the city's cultural institutions, including the University of Bologna and the Fondazione Cineteca di Bologna, and with the support of the Emilia Romagna region.

In addition to these initiatives, children's theater performances are also programmed in collaboration with local schools, as well as participatory projects aimed at the general public. Some of the latter projects are supported by the European Union, as in the case of *Atlas of Transitions*, a European project concluded in 2020 that involved the implementation in seven EU countries of a series of meetings, productions, and workshops that involved citizens, migrants, and asylum seekers in the creation of participative contexts and sharing through artistic practices.

Finally, and again to promote theatrical languages in all their nuances and making them more accessible, since 2018, in partnership with the Sossella publishing house, ERT has produced the editorial series *Linea*, an anthology of new dramaturgical texts related to ERT productions; in 2019, *LineaExtra* was added, dedicated to foreign dramaturgy and writings of individual authors in line with ERT's goal of fostering greater internationalization.

Thanks to its decentralized yet very solid model, ERT is now an "industrious laboratory of confrontation between spectators and creators, stubbornly faithful to its role as an institution of public relevance," conceived as "a great open theater" whose powerful arms are capable of embracing a vast territory. This is why ERT stands as a valuable ally for all national and international entities that wish to undertake any production or promotion activity for the theatrical arts. ¶

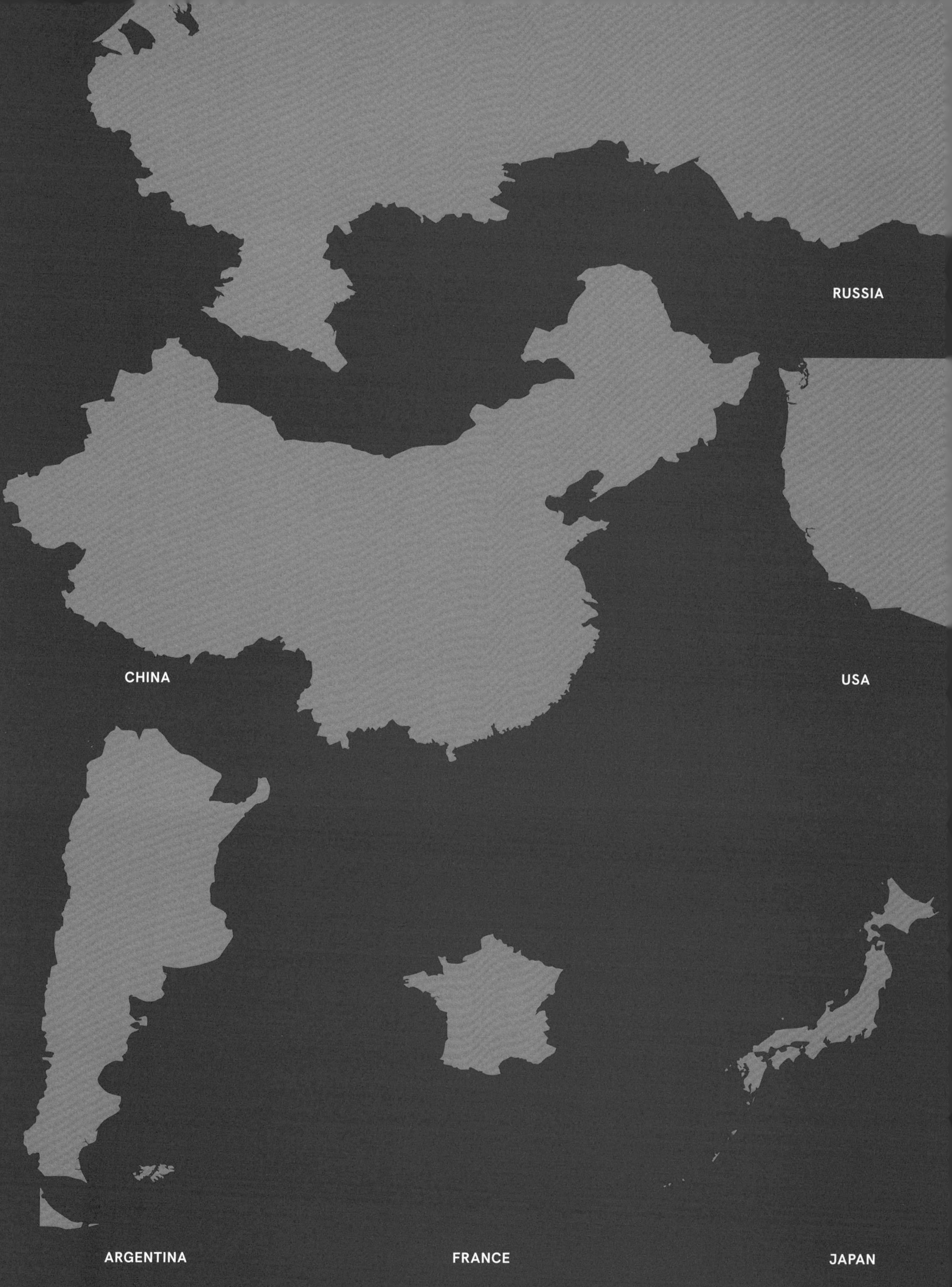

RUSSIA

CHINA

USA

ARGENTINA

FRANCE

JAPAN

AUSTRALIA
UNITED KINGDOM
ITALY
UNITED ARAB EMIRATES
DENMARK
TAIWAN
ISRAEL

55° 45′ 36″ N 37° 37′ 7″ E

BOLSHOI THEATER

MOSCOW / RUSSIA

Opened in 1826, the Bolshoi or Grand Theater is Moscow's primary historic venue and one of the world's shrines of classical ballet. This is also the home of the Bolshoi Ballet, the world's largest ballet company with about 200 dancers. The Bolshoi has also been the site of many historical premieres, hosting works by Tchaikovsky and Rachmaninov on its stage.

↑ The Bolshoi Theater Ballet Company, backstage.

45° 28′ 3″ N 9° 11′ 21″ E

TEATRO ALLA SCALA

MILAN / ITALY

↓
Maria Callas performing in *Medea* by Luigi Cherubini, Teatro alla Scala, Milan, 1953.

→→
Roberto Bolle at Teatro alla Scala, Milan.

The brainchild of neoclassical architect Giuseppe Piermarini, the Teatro alla Scala was built in 1776 and opened two years later at the behest of Empress Maria Theresa of Austria. The greatest composers, singers, conductors, and opera performers, such as Verdi, Rossini, Toscanini, De Sabata, Callas, Abbado, and Muti, have debuted and performed on its stage. Following a complete overhaul, today La Scala pursues an idea of theater that straddles the so-called *season* and *repertoire* programming.

35° 40′ 57″ N 139° 41′ 10″ E

NEW NATIONAL THEATER (NNTT)

TOKYO / JAPAN

Since opening in 1997, the NNTT has been the hub of contemporary performing arts in Japan. Designed by architect Takahiko Yanagisawa, the theater, along with the adjacent Tokyo Opera City Tower, soars over the Shinjuku area of central Tokyo. In addition to theater production, the complex hosts training programs for young artists, an extensive library dedicated to the performing arts and a museum space; performances for children and young students are also staged.

↓
Hamlet by William Shakespeare, directed by Antonio Latella, 2020–21.

45° 28′ 0″ N 9° 11′ 5″ E

PICCOLO TEATRO

MILAN / ITALY

↑ *Asters*, music by Akira Nishimura, February 2019.

Founded in 1947 by Giorgio Strehler, Paolo Grassi, and Nina Vinchi Grassi, the Piccolo Teatro in Milan is Italy's first permanent theater. The Piccolo is known for its strong and international-oriented mission, with a specific focus on multidisciplinarity, contemporary dramaturgy, and plurality of artistic expression.

51° 30′ 47″ N -0° 7′ 27″ E

COVENT GARDEN

LONDON / UK

←

Orchestra rehearsal for Michael Tippett's *The Midsummer Marriage*, directed by Bernard Haitink, Covent Garden, London.

A neighborhood much-loved by street performers and merchants since the 1500s, Covent Garden is home to several historic theater institutions. The Royal Opera House, the city's main opera house; the Theatre Royal Drury Lane, built in 1663 and now dedicated to musicals; and the St. Paul Church, better known as Actors' Church because of its association with theater, are all found in the nearby streets.

↑
The British Royal Family attend the reopening of the Royal Opera House at the end of World War II, February 1946.

→→
La Bayadère by Léon Minkus performed by the Kirov Ballet Company at the Royal Opera House, Covent Garden, London, 2001.

Built in 1732 within the Covent Garden district by architect Edward Middleton Barry, it is now home to two very important companies, the Royal Opera and the Royal Ballet. Considered one of the most renowned opera houses in the world, it has hosted numerous debuts, such as that of Friedrich Händel. Today it is renowned for its collaboration with well-known contemporary composers.

-34° 36′ 2.7684 N -58° 23′ 0″ E

TEATRO COLÓN

BUENOS AIRES / ARGENTINA

Opened in 1908 with a performance of *Aida* directed by Luigi Mancinelli, Teatro Colón is the largest and most renowned opera house in South America. Famous for its exceptional acoustics and impressive architecture, Teatro Colón houses the Colón Fábrica, a veritable forge of imagination and workmanship where everything needed for theatrical productions, such as scenery, costumes, wigs, and special effects, are produced.

←
President of Argentina Juan Perón and his wife Eva Perón at Teatro Colón, Buenos Aires, 1950.

40° 50′ 15″ N 14° 14′ 59″ E

TEATRO DI SAN CARLO

↓

Teatro di San Carlo, Naples.

NAPLES / ITALY

Built in 1737 at the behest of the Bourbon King Charles III, the Real Teatro di San Carlo is the oldest opera house in the world still in operation. Since 1812, it has been home to Italy's oldest ballet school—the renowned dancers Fanny Cerrito, Fanny Elssler, and Maria Taglioni trained within its walls. In addition to its classic opera production, the theater is engaged in the reconstruction of the history of Italian opera through the MEMUS museum.

-33° 51′ 26″ N 151° 12′ 54″ E

SYDNEY OPERA HOUSE

SYDNEY / AUSTRALIA

↓

Sydney Opera House on Sydney Harbor.

A UNESCO World Heritage Site since 2007, the Sydney Opera House is one of the finest examples of twentieth-century architecture, with its trademark sailboat-like structure that naturally blends in with the surrounding bay. Designed by Danish architect Jørn Utzon and opened in 1973, the Sydney Opera House contributed to revolutionize the traditional concept of a theater by being a multipurpose center, also dedicated to other cultural and leisure activities.

25° 11′ 4″2 N 55° 16′ 19″ E

DUBAI OPERA

DUBAI / UAE

↑ Aerial view of downtown Dubai and its opera theater.

In 2016, the Dubai Opera opened in the heart of the city. It is a state-of-the-art 2,000-seat facility that hosts a wide variety of events, ranging from opera to ballet and symphonic concerts. Inaugurated with a performance by Placido Domingo, the complex towers over Dubai's Opera District, a cultural neighborhood housing high-end hotels, galleries, museums, and design studios.

32° 3′ 39″ N 34° 45′ 51″ E

SUZANNE DELLAL CENTER FOR DANCE AND THEATER

TEL AVIV / ISRAEL

The Suzanne Dellal Center aims to support and promote the art of contemporary dance in Israel. Founded in 1989 by the Dellal family in honor of their daughter Suzanne, the center is the result of the renovation of a nineteenth-century building in Tel Aviv's historic Neve Tzedek neighborhood. Focused primarily on educational activities and the promotion of Israeli and international choreographers and dancers, the Suzanne Dellal Center is a focal point for the local and national dance culture.

↓ *Living Room* performance by Inbal Pinto, original production by Suzanne Dellal Center, Tel Aviv.

25° 2′ 13″ N 121° 31′ 9″ E

NATIONAL THEATER AND CONCERT HALL (NTCH)

TAIPEI / TAIWAN

↓ Chiang Kai-shek Memorial, Taipei. To the left, the National Concert Hall; to the right, the National Theater.

Completed in 1987, the NTCH is a twin structure built in Taipei's Liberty Square, the city's main public piazza. Designed by the Chinese architect Yang Cho-cheng, these buildings, which contain elements of traditional Chinese palaces, are landmarks for modern performing arts in Asia. A hybrid between a cultural center and performance space, over the years the four halls have featured performances by leading international artists such as Philip Glass, Rudolf Nureyev, Placido Domingo, Luciano Pavarotti, Yo-Yo Ma, John Walker, Pina Bausch, and many others.

pp. → 206 | 207

48° 52′ 19″ N 2° 19′ 54″ E

OPÉRA NATIONAL DE PARIS

PARIS / FRANCE

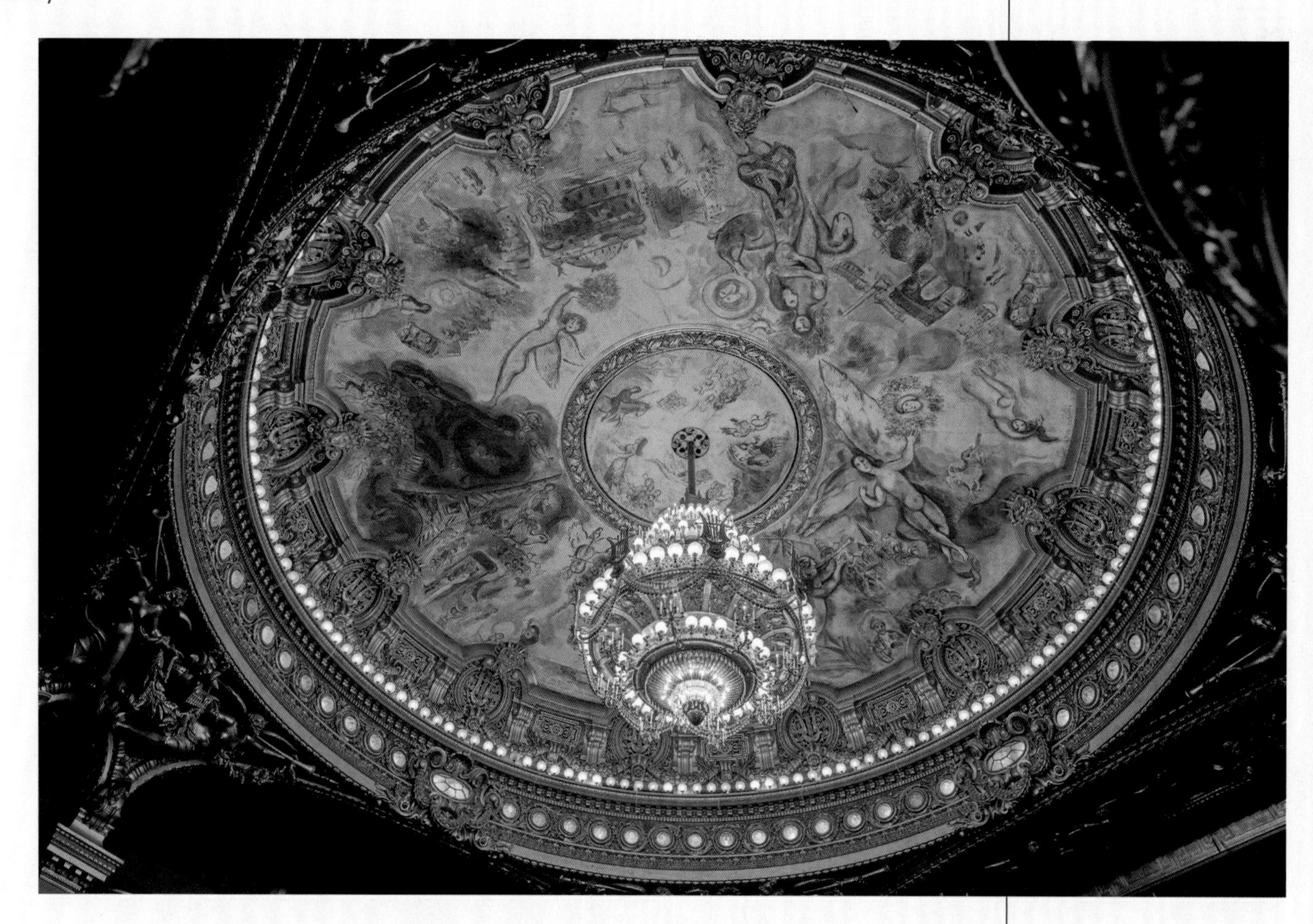

↑
Detail of the Opéra Garnier ceiling, painted by Marc Chagall, Paris.

Founded in 1669 by Louis XIV as the Académie d'Opéra, the Opéra de Paris is one of the best-known opera houses in the world. Today, its production is distributed between two different venues, the historic Palais Garnier, commissioned by Napoleon III in 1887, and the more recent Opéra Bastille, opened in 1989 and dedicated primarily to baroque opera and dance. The Opéra de Paris has seen great composers and choreographers, such as Gioacchino Rossini, Richard Wagner, Charles Gounod, Francis Poulenc, George Balanchine, Rudolf Nureyev, Roland Petit, Maurice Béjart, and Pina Bausch, among many others, debut and perform on its stages.

LINCOLNCENTER.ORG

40° 46′ 21″ N -73° 59′ 3″ E

LINCOLN CENTER

NEW YORK / USA

Built in 1962 following the initiative of John D. Rockefeller III, Lincoln Center is a complex dedicated to the performing arts, located in the heart of Manhattan, New York City. Several resident arts organizations are part of Lincoln Center: the Chamber Music Society, the Film Society, Jazz at Lincoln Center, the Juilliard School, the Lincoln Center Theater, the Metropolitan Opera, the School of American Ballet, the New York City Ballet, the New York Public Library for the Performing Arts, and the New York Philharmonic.

↓ Lincoln Center, New York.

31° 19′ 20″ N 120° 42′ 6″ E

SUZHOU BAY GRAND THEATER

SUZHOU / CHINA

↓

Suzhou Bay
Grand Theater.

The Suzhou Bay Grand Theater is part of a cultural center designed by French architect and urban planner Christian de Portzamparc and opened in 2020. The double-ellipse structure divides the center into two different but closely interconnected spaces, one housing the Grand Theater and a music school, the other hosting a museum and exhibition spaces. The design of the center blends in perfectly with its surroundings by connecting the new physical space with the sky above and the sea flowing through it.

4° 3′ 8" N 118° 14′ 37" W

WALT DISNEY CONCERT HALL

LOS ANGELES / USA

Designed between 1999 and 2003 by architect Frank Gehry, the Walt Disney Concert Hall is one of the four halls of the Los Angeles Music Center, home to the Los Angeles Philharmonic and the Los Angeles Master Chorale, and is now the city's cultural hub. Commissioned by Walt Disney's wife Lillian, the hall is characterized not only by its distinctive exterior but also by its spectacular acoustics, designed by Gehry in collaboration with Minoru Nagata.

↓ The Walt Disney Concert Hall, Los Angeles.

55° 40′ 55″ N 12° 36′ 3″ E

COPENHAGEN OPERA HOUSE

COPENHAGEN / DENMARK

←
Jakob Oftebro and Sicilia Gadborg Høegh in *Doll's House* by Henrik Ibsen, directed by Anna Balslev, Copenhagen Opera House, 2022.

The brainchild of Danish architect Henning Larsen, the Copenhagen Opera House was inaugurated in 2005. Located on Holmen Island opposite the Royal Palace, the theater is a state-of-the-art facility that blends naturally with the harbor and the surrounding port landscape. The complex also includes an adjacent small theater, the Takealot, which is dedicated to experimental productions.

23° 5′ 35″ N 113° 19′ 19″ E

GUANGZHOU OPERA HOUSE

GUANGZHOU / CHINA

↓ The Guangzhou Opera House.

Designed by Zaha Hadid and opened in 2011, the Guangzhou Opera House stands on the banks of the Pearl River in the heart of the city. The outer structure, composed of "twin boulders," reflects its surroundings and its symbiotic relationship with the nearby river. Inside, a steel skeleton runs through the entire complex and performance halls, creating a hyper-technological dimension for the enjoyment of the most striking performances.

MULTIDISCIPLINARY FESTIVALS

MULTIDISCIPLINARY FESTIVALS

If the artistic work is a "content" that, once produced, is distributed in different "containers" such as theaters or cultural centers, festivals are also containers of artistic events that provide, in a well-defined time span, the opportunity to participate in a series of events linked by specific artistic characteristics. This description, however, is inadequate to convey the permeability and effervescence that a festival season can generate. It is this vitality that creates the specific identity of a festival (albeit nuanced, and each with a life of its own), which is capable of generating real dialogue both between the projects hosted in the artistic program and the single disciplines from the surrounding art scene. Aside from their historical role on the world stage, and whether they involve theater, dance, music, or circus, festivals usually spring from the need to showcase a specific artistic vision or discourse through the construction of a program of events involving artists and audiences.

Radicalism, singularity, stratification, flexibility, and community are the key words to describe the experience of any festival, even the most institutional ones. If we consider the art projects as notes, and cultural venues as the score that dictates their spatial organization, then organizing a festival is like composing a musical phrase that brings together notes and lines to assemble something more complex than the simple sequence of events: a single entity that brings together and transforms the individual inputs. What is special about festivals is that by taking place over a limited and concentrated period, they manage to condense great energy and intensity and unite a community otherwise scattered in the fragmented space of our urban settings. This establishes a strong and intimate relationship with the audience and generates a special form of loyalty. Festivals are a perfect context for the showcase of the live arts, enabling one to venture into areas where more customary artistic programs may be absent and to explore innovative, experimental, hybrid, and radical dimensions to help reformulate tastes and trends. The surprising heterogeneity of festivals embodies the main transformation of the performing arts scene, namely the multiplication and hybridization of disciplines. The festival is now one of the most widespread forms by which the arts—or more generally, cultural phenomena—present themselves to the public, producing a far-reaching impact not only from an artistic standpoint but also in economic and communication terms. For this reason, instead of being mere containers for content, festivals themselves become content.

Defining what a festival is can cause heated debates. A broad definition might be "an event limited in time and space that develops a specific artistic project and takes place at regular intervals." As we will see later, the recent growth in the number of festivals has led to a major transformation within the events industry, so each of the terms of the previous definition is now debatable. The international comparative study *Music Festivals: A Changing World*, edited by Emmanuel Négrier at al., summarizes the criticisms that may arise from this classic definition (p. 242):

> The temporal limit of festivals has become relative when we consider that festivals offer activities outside of their season dates. The spatial limit also tends to lose some of its meaning when we observe the development of strategies of decentralization of spectacles, and certain festivals may take place on several sites, travel from site to site, or even be duplicated in other regions or countries. Likewise, the concept of the artistic project is also being modified by contemporary practices. The artistic niche in which a festival is born can later become merely one reference point among many present within the event, as festivals try to renew themselves by bringing together different aesthetic registers within hybrid programs. Thus, there is an artistic project, but it is not always tied to a specific style. As for the periodicity of a festival, besides the death rate affecting certain sectors or countries during a period of recession, we note that it can vary from one to two years.

Festivals are certainly not a recent phenomenon—in fact, they are an integral part of the history of performing arts. Many were created centuries ago and still continue today, such as the Bayreuth Festival in Germany, which was founded by composer Richard Wagner to disseminate his work. Indeed, the legacy of the festival concept can be traced back to Ancient Greece. Established in the sixth century BC, the Pythian Games were held every four years and featured musical and athletic competitions in honor of Apollo. The element of competition has endured over the centuries: the Green Man Festival, held annually in mid-August in Wales, traces its lineage back to a twelfth-century competition. Today competition is not between artists but between festivals, as they try to offer the most attractive lineups in their effort to gain greater advantage in a saturated market.

None of the festivals we will investigate offer an exclusively theatrical program but consider their artistic proposal in a broadly multidisciplinary sense by adding other activities and formats, which can be related to other disciplines such as literature, theory, film, and so on, to accompany and intersect with the main program.

This allows festivals to nurture the main artistic discourse and attract a specific audience that sometimes feels excluded from the fruition of artistic languages considered the preserve of experts and enthusiasts. Tapping into a sense of community and sharing the exceptional experience that the festival can generate, which is somewhat detached from space and time, is the ideal dimension to disseminate, rework, experiment with, and innovate the most contemporary artistic languages.

Despite the many forms of economic support, which often include a mix of public contributions and private sponsoring, all festivals share a number of features: a strong relationship with local and national political entities on which funding, agreements for venues, and various other forms of support depend; and the ability to create networks and operate within a complex system of relationships, partnerships, and conventions with local authorities, cultural institutions and associations, and international realities such as other festivals and production centers, cultural institutes, embassies, and distribution organizations. International action, however, almost always goes hand-in-hand with a specific venue, one that may trigger a renewed relationship with the city's architecture and spaces, which are occupied in unconventional ways by art projects and urban communities.

A festival, however, does not necessarily need to involve innovative and emerging art forms; it can also focus on somewhat neglected disciplines in an effort to keep old traditions alive, sometimes with a strong connection to the area of origin. An example of these more conventional forms of performing arts are the numerous initiatives taken to enhance and disseminate the tradition of Sicilian puppet theater. This art is the result of a joint effort bringing together the various crafts and skills of blacksmiths, carpenters, and tailors—a small, regional treasure that is celebrated everywhere in Sicily. At the Morgana Festival, which has taken place over 40 times, puppets are featured. They are presented alongside performances from similar creative disciplines such as street theater and, more generally, international contemporary theater. Therefore festivals, as well as other events, can respond to the growing supply and demand—either for artistic or commercial purposes (or both)—or they can influence it by focusing exclusively on disciplines that are dying out or have exited the mainstream art scene.

↑
Parsifal by Richard Wagner, directed by Uwe Eric Laufenberg, Bayreuth, July 2016.

FESTIVAL D'AVIGNON

FESTIVAL-AVIGNON.COM

— The cathedral of performing arts

↑

The Black Monk by Anton Chekhov, directed by Kirill Serebrennikov, Avignon, July 2022.

Now we move to the Provence-Alpes-Côte d'Azur region of southern France, where the city of Avignon sits on the banks of the Rhône, just before it flows into the Mediterranean Sea. Today Avignon has a population of nearly 100,000, rich in history and culture, and most remembered for being the papal seat in the fourteenth century during the so-called "Avignon Papacy." The city's architecture has conserved its medieval past with several remarkable buildings, such as the famous Palace of the Popes, a UNESCO World Heritage Site. The Festival d'Avignon, one of the world's first and longest-running festivals dedicated to contemporary theater and performing arts, has been held in the streets and squares of this iconic town since 1947. It was founded "by accident" by Jean Vilar, a director, actor, and artist, among the best-known of his time, and from the very first festival has presented a new perspective on how to make and enjoy theater. Experimentation and contemporary languages are inextricably accompanied by a political emphasis on the social and collective dimensions. In an attempt to mend an apparent fracture between high and popular culture, between traditional French theater —whose repertoire was becoming stale and unpopular—and artistic innovation, the Festival proposed something radical, thus creating opportunities for transformation and new forms of collective interaction.

The vitality and expressive freedom of contemporary experimental theater became an opportunity to remodulate the relationship between art and society. Vilar's intuition was to take the most innovative artistic production to a province far from Paris, yet maintaining a continuous exchange with it. He chose to stage theatrical performances outdoors, taking advantage of Avignon's evocative medieval architecture. Almost violating the sacredness of the stage, he placed the theatrical act into direct contact with the city, its spaces, and its inhabitants—just like in the Middle Ages, when theater was a disruptive form of expression within the reach of everyone, especially the common people. This choice renewed the relationship among language, architecture, and community, and revitalized the very forms of scenery and staging. This redefinition of the relationship between center and periphery, between experimentation and the civic dimension of art creation rapidly became a paradigm, giving rise to a festival model that would soon be imitated in many other European countries. Initially in the month of September, then in July, every year Avignon has been transformed into a citadel of the arts for more than 70 years, drawing together a large community of enthusiasts, professionals, and aficionados around an artistic program that has constantly grown. Over the years, many choices

→→
François Chaignaud and Geoffroy Jourdain, *Tumulus*, Avignon, July 2022.

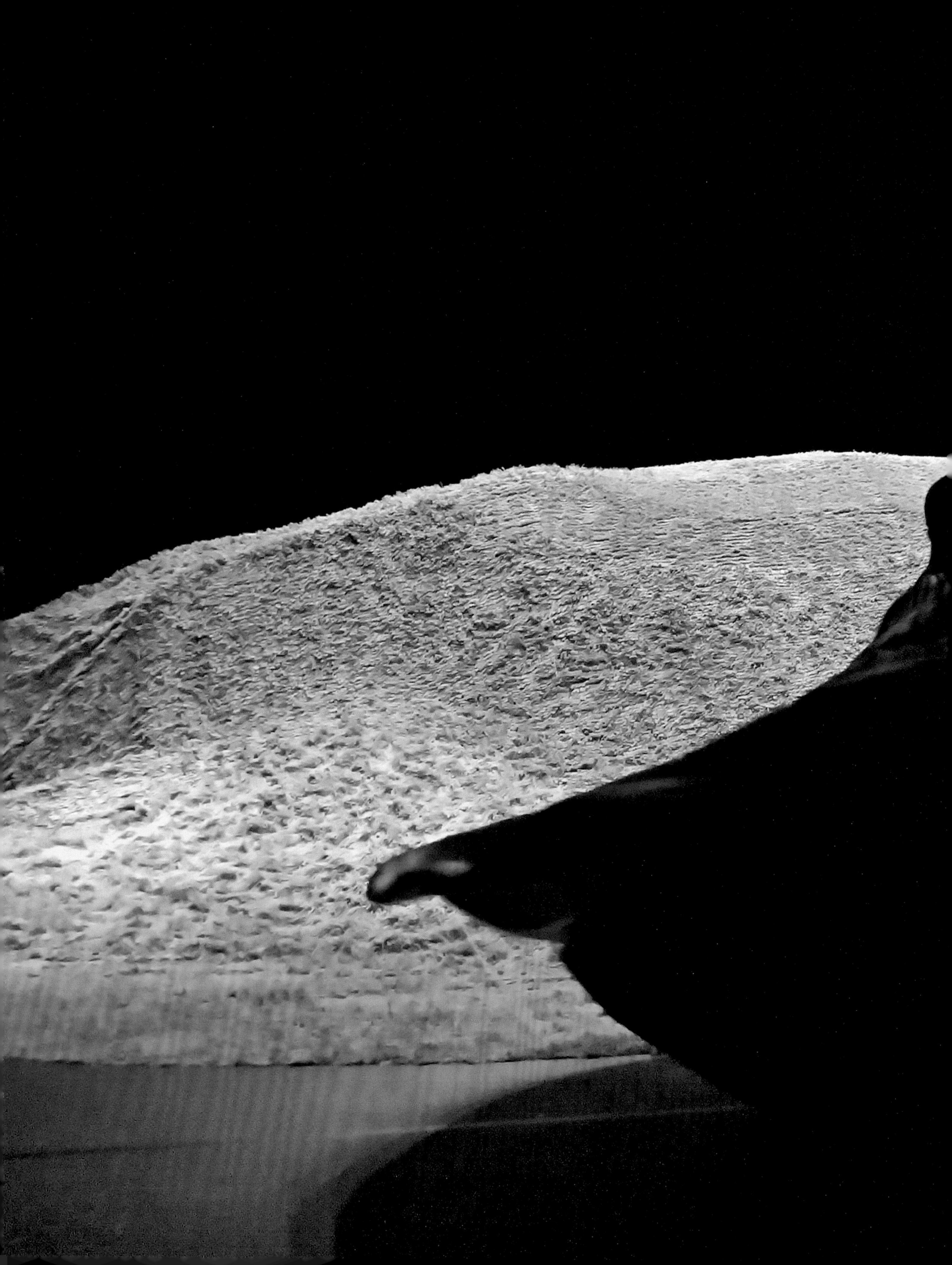

made by its forward-looking directors and managers have been considered benchmarks. Thanks to its openness and multidisciplinary approach, the continual dismantling of boundaries between disciplines, the layered programming able to appeal to and bring together different audiences, a focus on the involvement of local communities and the social impact of its activities, as well as its support to artists in the development of their careers, the Festival d'Avignon still sets the standard for other performing arts festivals that have sprung up since. Directed for almost a decade, until 2022, by the director, actor, and author Olivier Py, and recognized by the French state and various public institutions that provide much of its financial support, it is now a quintessential theater festival that continues to create and renew its community. Currently directed by Tiago Rodrigues, it plays a vital role in the production and circulation of contemporary works of the highest level —a guarantee of quality for its productions and an achievement for those who are part of the roster. In Avignon, the level of care, constant search for quality, and attention to the public role of the festival create the ideal conditions for a unique experience for the spectator. Here the artistic plan becomes an in-depth cultural project, but at the same time layered, broad, and capable of involving ever-changing audiences.

MILITANCY AND EXPERIMENTATION

In 1947, Avignon hosted an exhibition of modern art curated by the surrealist poet René Char and the art critic Christian Zervos. They suggested that the actor, theater and artistic director Jean Vilar present his latest work, T. S. Eliot's play *Murder in the Cathedral*, at the Cour d'Honneur of the Papal Palace in Avignon.

Accustomed to smaller stages, Vilar declined the invitation, considering the Cour d'Honneur too large and "formless." In addition, his rights to represent T. S. Eliot's works had expired. He thus made a counterproposal to Char and Zervos, offering to present three works during an "art week" (*une semaine d'art*, which was to become the name of the first festival) in September 1947. The nature of the three works marked the outline of what would become the artistic identity of the nascent festival: these were Shakespeare's *Richard III*, which was little-known in France at that time, *La Terrasse de Midi* by Maurice Clavel, an unknown work by an unknown author, and *L'Histoire de Tobie et de Sara* by Paul Claudel, which was staged for the first time on that very occasion. The festival was created as a showcase for unknown works from the universal repertoire, as well as modern writings. Jean Vilar's intent was "to renew theater and collective art forms by providing a more open space . . . to give a breath of fresh air to an art form that is suffocating in waiting rooms, basements, and halls; to reconcile architecture with dramatic poetry." This vision was a perfect fit with the plan of the Avignon Municipality to revive the city through reconstruction and culture after the April 1944 bombing; they supported the festival financially from the very beginning. Thus, in agreement with the Municipality, the Cour d'Honneur du Palais des Papes was converted to house Jean Vilar's new design, which was extended to another two venues in the city, the Municipal Theater and the Verger d'Urbain V. For that first festival, 4,800 spectators, with 2,900 paying, attended seven performances of the three works mentioned. Thus, the Festival d'Avignon had been born. In 1951, Jean Vilar took over the directorship of the Palais de Chaillot in Paris, renamed the Théâtre National Populaire (TNP). Actors such as Jeanne Moreau, Michel Bouquet, Daniel Sorano, and Maria Casares, who performed at the TNP during the season, also performed in Avignon that summer. The TNP and the festival had the same director and pursued a common cultural project that had inherited the activist spirit of the postwar period, in an effort to engage new audiences and reactivate the theater experience. This resulted in a decentralization of French cultural policy, creating a direct link between France's main cultural pole and a small peripheral center where the tradition of French theater was being rewritten every summer.

Avignon became a pivotal place for theatrical and artistic experimentation in those years. Up until 1963, the imprint of the festival was entirely due to the efforts of Vilar and his company; when Vilar left the directorship of the TNP to devote himself entirely to the Festival d'Avignon, a series of initiatives for renewal and certain questions regarding the festival were aired.

From that period on, more directors were invited to collaborate and new stages were inaugurated, but, most importantly, the festival programming began to accommodate other artistic disciplines. In addition to theater, dance made its first appearance on the festival stage in 1966, with Maurice Béjart and Le Ballet du XXe siècle; in 1967 cinema was added, with the screening of *La Chinoise* by Jean-Luc Godard in the Cour d'Honneur; and, finally, musical theater, with *Orden* by Jorge Lavelli. The audience continued to grow from one festival to the next and the city was crowded with thousands of people each summer, with younger generations and associations for the needy especially welcome. Schools were opened and campsites set up to accommodate the many spectators drawn to the festival, which by then had become a veritable cultural landmark, a place of meeting, exchange, and discussion for the international arts community.

pp. → 226

The festival management was becoming increasingly complex. In 1968—the year of the student uprisings and waves of strikes throughout France—protests were also felt at the festival: despite his attempt to engage with the protesters, Jean Vilar was challenged and suffered to the point of hospitalization. He died in 1971. Paul Puaux took over as director of the festival, carrying forward its approach of experimentation and decentralization of culture.

In the 1970s, the Avignon stages hosted primarily TPN companies that the festival had inherited when it was under Vilar's direction. But the celebrity and front-page ranking achieved by the festival was a magnet for many artists to perform, even though not part of the official program. Similar to the Edinburgh Festival Fringe, the concept of an alternative and independent "OFF Festival" began to take hold. Enlivened by local artistic companies and later by other young companies from all over France, Avignon became the right place to attract audiences, directors, actors, and practitioners, even without being on the official festival bill. Soon, the two sides of the festival started to dialogue and intermingle: actors from the "IN" would perform in the "OFF" and vice versa. In 2017, the OFF Festival hosted more than 1,400 performances.

The year 1980 was a watershed in the history of the festival, which by that time had reached its peak but needed to be modernized and rendered more professional

↓ Angélique Kidjo in *Femme noire* by Léopold Sédar Senghor, Avignon, July 2017.

to attract new generations of artists. The directorship passed from Paul Puaux to Bernard Faivre d'Arcier and, most importantly, the French state was now on the board, allowing the festival to be completely independent from an economic perspective. Facilities at the various locations were improved and a dedicated team was formed to launch the new trajectory: the festival was now one of the world's largest live-performance productions. A visible sign of this change is that the design of the posters for each year's festival was entrusted to a different visual artist every year.

In 1985, Alain Crombecque, former artistic director of the Festival d'Automne, took over as director of Avignon, continuing in the role for eight years. While maintaining the traditional festival layout, he stamped his mark on the artistic program: readings of contemporary poetry, meetings with leading actors, and contemporary music performances were now included in the program. Artistic traditions of non-European countries started to make an appearance, such as music from India, Africa, Pakistan, Iran, and other countries: Avignon's scope expanded to encompass other cultures, while remaining a fulcrum of French theatrical experimentation.

The Festival d'Avignon became a leading festival in Europe and a unique venue for the production of extremely large shows that were difficult to present elsewhere. Thanks to an increased budget, the guest capacity increased to accommodate 100,000 visitors and 40 productions, for a total of 300 performances in 20 different venues.

From 2004 to 2013, the direction was entrusted to Hortense Archambault and Vincent Baudriller. Their project aimed to strengthen the encounter between artistic creation and the general public, as well as the relationship with the local community. The festival organization moved from Paris to Avignon to optimize the planning phase with artists and strengthen ties with the region and partners. Initiatives were developed throughout the year for local audiences, aimed especially at younger participants. The festival also started to accompany and support the work of the theatrical companies more closely, following the technical and economic aspects of the productions, as well as their French and international tours.

Another important innovation is attributed to Archambault and Baudriller, namely appointing associate artists to work alongside the director in the conception of the annual festival, thus bringing a new sensibility and a different approach to the planning and programming processes. A new center, La FabricA, was inaugurated in 2013. This venue consists of a stage the same size as that of the Cour d'Honneur, 18 residences, and two adjacent technical spaces. This theater "factory" is the realization of one of Jean Vilar's dreams, designed to host residencies for creative collectives engaged in preparing productions for the Festival d'Avignon. La FabricA, which is open to the public all year round, changes its function during the summer and becomes one of the main sites for festival performances.

From 2013, the festival was directed for almost a decade by Olivier Py, director, author, and the first actor to direct the festival since Jean Vilar. His work was a perfect fit with the festival's new focus on appealing to younger audiences, an openness to international and Mediterranean cultures, decentralization through itinerant performances, and investing in poetry, contemporary literature, digital technologies, and performing arts, which are all considered as vectors for social and cultural integration.

The festival has become a platform for discussion and for theoretical and political dialogue, increasingly connected to topical contemporary issues such as gender equality, sexual identity, and other similar subjects. This was achieved through several successful and innovative formats, including *Les Ateliers de la pensée*, founded in 2015, in which some 12,000 visitors took part in debates and exchange with artists, thinkers, journalists, and politicians.

This approach embodies the political positioning, militant vocation, and the pivotal role as a transformative cultural agent that the Festival d'Avignon has built up over its more than 70-year history, as expressed by Olivier Py in his editorial on the 2018 festival:

> We hope for a change of political agenda that no longer assigns our future to economic necessity and the dark gods of finance. We are learning to want something else, so that future generations can keep the euphoric flame of the possible alive.

GREATER THAN A CITY — Today, the Festival d'Avignon is one of the most important cultural institutions in Europe in the realm of performing arts, a well-established and historicized reality yet capable of reinventing its forms and function, thus keeping in touch with the development of successive generations. In order to maintain an effective and tangible cultural and economic impact, the festival undertakes the vital task of monitoring, analyzing, and interpreting its data. Examining the following numbers can help give an idea of the entity of the festival.

AVIGNON IN NUMBERS — A snapshot of the festival shows each year about 50 performances scheduled, from France and the rest of the world, and nearly 250 performances in all, plus a vast program of meetings with artists, readings, film screenings, and exhibitions. Two-thirds of the performances are produced especially for the festival or performed for the first time in France. The festival involves more than 20 venues, most of them historic, offering a wide range of stage spaces both in terms of architecture and size, accommodating from 50 to 2,000 people. Each year, the festival sells about 120,000 paid tickets, with approximately 30,000 spectators attending free-of-charge events.

The Festival d'Avignon is not only a point of reference for performing arts audiences, but also for the trade press and practitioners, artistic directors, and people working in the sector. More than 500 journalists are accredited and about 3,500 entertainment professionals from all over the world participate annually.

In terms of communication, the festival has several instruments for its various audiences: a guide for operators, programs, and catalogs for the public, as well as a program guide for children, a website, social channels, and even an app for mobile devices.

More than half of the festival budget comes from public grants—state, municipal, regional, and others—while the remaining portion is covered by its own income: sales of tickets and in-house productions, sponsors, and commercial and non-commercial partnerships. Indeed, the festival is supported by leading international cultural institutions and bodies, but it also has long-standing relationships with sponsors, first and foremost the Fondation Crédit Coopératif, as well as the 15 or so small- and medium-sized enterprises of the "Cercles des Entreprises Mécènes" and the individual investors of the "Cercle des Mécènes," specific bodies created by the festival to bring together its supporters. The festival generates from 23 to 25 million euros in economic benefits for the city. Finally, at the same time as the "IN" Festival, the "OFF" Festival invites more than 1,000 artistic companies to perform and showcase their own productions in about 100 different venues on a self-financing basis.

SUSTAINABILITY POLICIES — The Festival d'Avignon devotes part of its activity to the new frontiers of the international cultural organization, namely those of environmental sustainability, inclusiveness, and accessibility for specific audiences such as people with disabilities; people who are racially and socially discriminated against; and those who are marginalized. There is an ethics policy for all relations with its workers and employees. In addition to being a member of

the Collectif des Festivals Éco-responsables et Solidaires en Région Sud (COFFEES) and a signatory of the Charte Éco-Festival, in 2020 the Festival d'Avignon created an interdisciplinary committee to draw up a wide-ranging plan of action toward reducing its environmental impact. It has made environmental sustainability one of the cornerstones of its governance structure, undertaking some specific actions such as using certified recycled paper, decreasing the use of paper materials or air-conditioning, recycling materials such as glass and plastic, choosing local suppliers, and other similar initiatives.

←
Joë Agemans and Marie Vinck in *The Land of Nod* by FC Bergman, Avignon, July 2016.

CREATING THE CONTEMPORARY — To summarize an artistic trajectory of over fifty years would be both an impossible and futile task, since this would overlap with the history of contemporary theater. We can state, however, that over these decades the Festival d'Avignon has been one of the main European venues of the aesthetic elaboration for the performing arts. It has brought together the most advanced levels of international artistic production, imagining formats and proposals capable of stimulating experimentation, as well as rethinking the function of the performing arts in relation to other artistic fields and theoretical knowledge in the transformation of reality.

Indeed, the Festival d'Avignon is one of the first examples of an event that provides an innovative and far-reaching model, a cultural offering beyond the promotion of a single discipline or art form that articulates a layered, high-level cultural mission that fulfills a precise public function. In this sense, the support of public funds and the participation of institutions and public bodies in its governance has guaranteed financial autonomy, a basic prerogative for an artistic project. Both the choice of performances to be produced, activities to be programmed, and the design of projects aimed at maximizing audience involvement are all activities to be conducted autonomously, as free as possible from box office earnings and with the liberty of being as radical as necessary.

Scrolling through the many titles and names of artists who have passed through Avignon's stages in more than half a century, we note the presence of some of the most relevant figures on the international art scene. We also see an ever-increasing presence of artists and companies from countries other than France, both European and non-European, bringing together both dance and drama and multidisciplinary formats (categorized under the term "indiscipline"), as well as artists from different generations. Some of these names are Jacques Lassalle, Angelin Preljocaj, Pina Bausch, Alain Platel, Romeo Castellucci, Sidi Larbi Cherkaoui, Sasha Waltz, Pippo Delbono, Jan Fabre, Thomas Ostermeier, Emma Dante, Christoph Marthaler, Boris Charmatz, Amir Reza Koohestani, and many others. Theater, dance, performance, and audiovisual fill the festival's multifaceted artistic program, with a marked tendency toward experimentation and encounters among different languages. Not surprisingly, one of the festival's now historic sections is *Sujets a Vis*, in which artistic creations are commissioned from two artists from different disciplines who are invited to collaborate in the creation of a short performance. Much energy is also dedicated to "collateral" activities, the living extension of the curatorial project that involves a program of films, talks, and meetings aimed at performing arts professionals, as well as concerts and audience engagement activities, and other initiatives for children.

Thanks to the incessant production and co-production of artistic projects, Avignon is one of the most important platforms for the debut of new works, a true showcase where curators in charge of playbills and other international festivals can discover the latest works by the finest international artists. To this end, the festival includes a specific program of activities for sector practitioners, with meetings, debates, and workshops, thus expressing its vocation as an all-round platform for the performing arts.

SPACES — The spaces designated to festival activities increase each year and are both publicly and privately owned, historic buildings as well as modern architecture, outdoor and indoor spaces, theater halls and "unconventional" venues especially set up both in Avignon and nearby areas: churches, gardens, gymnasiums, schools, cloisters, theaters, galleries, museums, arenas, public streets. Of the 20 or so venues used in the three-week-long festival, the two main ones are the iconic Cour d'Honneur du Palais des Papes, the square in front of the Palace of the Popes, an exceptionally beautiful medieval setting where the festival was born in 1947 and which remained its main venue until the 1960s, holding up to two thousand spectators, and La FabricA, an indoor location inaugurated in 2013 that, over the years, has become a pivotal place in the life of the festival, with a hall for 600 spectators and a stage the same dimensions as those of the Cour d'Honneur. This is particularly important, as it highlights a fundamental element of the Festival d'Avignon's artistic project—namely, its production function. Much of the programming is commissioned, conceived, and/or supported by the festival, thus consolidating its primary role of stimulating creation. In this sense, La FabricA has become invaluable precisely because it allows companies to take advantage of a production space with rehearsal rooms and accommodation available all year round and the possibility of interacting and rehearsing on a stage similar to the one that will be used during the summer debut performance. In addition to being a production space, La FabricA is also the venue for the public-oriented programming during the year and focused on the local region. These programs have become increasingly relevant over the years. In line with the militant spirit of cultural decentralization that has permeated the festival since its inception, La FabricA is located on the outskirts of the city and provides an important place of reference that is always open to the public and full of plans. The festival's institutional website reports: "In 2019, 6,300 people came to La FabricA to participate in panels, workshops, educational projects, tours, residency presentations, or training sessions (not including performances during the Festival)."

RELATIONSHIP WITH THE LOCAL AREA — The relationship with the public, interaction with the social reality of the area, and openness to spectators who are anagraphically, culturally, and socially distant from contemporary artistic production are the main objectives of the project envisioned by the festival's artistic director for almost a decade, Olivier Py. This led to the exponential increase of programming aimed at citizen participation and cultural mediation, expanding the mission created by Vilar. The lines of intervention are many and varied. Some initiatives delve deep into the festival's artistic programming, such as the creation of a printed guide for children, a publication presenting a series of initiatives aimed at them, as well as games and activities that help kids become more familiar with the festival's themes and languages. Then there are participatory art projects that are part of the official program, workshops, meetings, and masterclasses held by guest artists during the festival and aimed at both amateurs and professionals, as well as outreach programs implemented in local schools and universities. The festival also includes activities related to artistic practices but not directly connected to its programming, such as workshops held throughout the year at La FabricA and activities in partnership with the Ministry of Education, conducted in collaboration with associations and social centers active in the suburbs or in the city's prison. Regarding accessibility, the Festival d'Avignon has activated a specific program for people with motor and sensory disabilities, in collaboration with centers and associations dealing with these issues, by devising a series of actions aimed at making the artistic program accessible, including audio-descriptions of performances, tactile devices, subtitling, simultaneous translation, sign language, and so on.

THE "OFF" FESTIVALS — While initially it was mainly local artistic companies that performed around the city, taking over the streets or clubs with their shows, gradually more and more national and international artists started to flock to Avignon. Since 1966, what was a spontaneous practice grafted seamlessly onto the main festival has become one of the must-see events of the French summer, spreading throughout the city and enlivening it through highly diverse forms of entertainment. Companies take part in the "OFF" on a voluntary basis, independently finding funds and locations to perform. There is no selection or artistic direction, but in 2006 a nonprofit association, AF&C (Avignon Festival & Companies), was created to bring together companies and individuals, with the support of public bodies. The aim of this association is to "transmit information received from cultural organizations and institutions, ensure communication and coordination of the OFF through concerted action with all interested parties (companies, venues, audiences, partners, institutions, etc.), promote the artistic dimension and professionalization of live performance," thus providing communication and exploration tools of the "OFF" offer to the public, as well as a subscription that allows access to the various venues for a fee. ❡

EDINBURGH FESTIVAL FRINGE

EDFRINGE.COM

— Down with artistic direction!

↑ Zoe Ní Riordáin in *Everything I Do*, directed by Maud Lee, Edinburgh, August 2019.

Something important for the destiny of the performing arts was happening in Edinburgh in 1947. Something with many elements in common with what we have seen in Avignon, but with a different development. While in Avignon, Jean Vilar fostered his vision of an encounter between experimental theater and the population, in Edinburgh some companies excluded from the prestigious Edinburgh International Festival decided to earn their place on a program in alternative city venues, staging their performances independently, without any kind of support from institutions or official theaters, thus creating their own "OFF" festival. This is how the Edinburgh Festival Fringe was born. Indeed, Fringe Theater means "theater at or on the fringe," a type of theater that is created outside official circuits and now synonymous with "avant-garde theater."

Since then, for three weeks every year in August, Edinburgh is mecca to street performers, circus artists, actors, dancers, poets, musicians, stand-up comedians, contortionists, acrobats, puppeteers, you name it. They are all part of what is to date the largest theater and performing arts festival in the world. It is a huge event across about 300 locations throughout the city and its model has set the standard for many other similar experiences. What is special about the Fringe is that it does not have any kind of artistic direction; it is a festival where anyone can perform. From amateur groups to established companies, from the most irreverent shows to the most classic performances, the solid principle behind the Fringe—which has now lasted for more than 70 years—is precisely that no conditions are placed on the participation of artists. The only requirement is the willingness (and ability) to organize their own show independently, identifying venues and times, bearing the costs, and taking care of communication and promotion. This does not always prove simple, and success, or profit, for that matter, is not always assured. Indeed, often the opposite is true. So why does the Edinburgh Festival Fringe continue to attract more artists and audiences year after year? The reason is intrinsic to its essence. Being able to find a way to build one's own career within the global artistic environment, in which competition has become increasingly fierce, has become a titanic task. At the same time, it is increasingly difficult for curators to discover new talents, as they have become almost strangers in certain areas of artistic production and distribution, both nationally and internationally. Finally,

→→
Silence, Edinburgh, August 2019.

the possibility of enjoying truly diverse cultural programs has been reduced for the public in general due to the selection and exclusion mechanisms dictated by algorithms that now pervade contemporary society. Therefore, an opportunity as open, confusing, kaleidoscopic, and intense as the Edinburgh Festival Fringe is something truly unique and unmissable. The painstaking logistical and communications work of the Festival Fringe Society is omnipresent in the apparently chaotic self-management of the artistic programming. This organization, which began as a volunteer student association to support artists with food and affordable accommodation, has today become a full-fledged corporation. Indeed, its functions include managing box office ticketing of more than 3,500 events, providing the public and artists with publicity services scouting the vast array of shows provided each year, and organizing meeting spaces, refreshment stations, and programs to assist emerging artists. It's a vital support for an apparently autonomous machine, whose sheer entity requires some form of coordination, otherwise information and content would be completely dispersed.

A massive event with thousands of participants each year, some of which mix with other important festivals held in the city during the summer, the Edinburgh Festival Fringe transforms the medieval city into a hotbed of creativity, making every imaginable space—outdoor and indoor—a platform that promises success and glory to the most diverse artists from all over the world. A festival-monster that fascinates and frightens at the same time, where among flyers, posters, and promotional strategies new theater stars are born each year, while just as many are lost along the way.

LEARNING TO FUNCTION

In 1947, the city of Edinburgh decided to create an event to celebrate and promote the European cultural scene after World War II. This is how the Edinburgh International Festival—a festival of opera, drama, classical music, and ballet that brought together artists from around the world—was born. During that first festival, eight companies, not among those invited by the fledgling festival, decided to go ahead and independently stage their shows on the sidelines of the official event, creating the foundation for the future Fringe Festival. Since its inception, the Fringe's identity has been shaped by the principles of self-production and self-organization, regardless of

→ Ockham's Razor, *This Time*, St. Stephen's Theatre, Edinburgh, August 2019.

official invitations, and the use of unconventional venues. The current name would emerge in the second year of the initiative and was attributed—as is often the case when dealing with forms of counterculture or underground movements—by a critic who recounted how, on the fringes of the main festival, these spontaneous artistic manifestations were taking place.

No official organization would exist for several years, although the festival continued to expand and attract increasing numbers of artists and spectators. In 1951, students at the University of Edinburgh started an outreach center where participants could find affordable food and accommodation, but it was only in 1958 that the Festival Fringe Society was born. Its founding act enshrined the principle that any kind of censorship or control of the festival's artistic programming was prohibited.

In the late 1950s, the Fringe was still a manageable dimension for volunteers and students, with approximately 20 companies on its "playbill." As early as 1969, the number of companies reached 494, making the Fringe the largest arts festival in the world.

With no official artistic direction, the history of the festival progressed in parallel with the evolution of its organizational structure and various logistical adjustments, optimizing the conditions that guarantee the success of this sprawling event. Unconventional or unprogrammed activities put into practice by participants gradually

became part of the festival structure. One such practice that became popular in the 1970s was sharing performance venues and covering expenses jointly, so that some venues divided their spaces to make it possible to stage multiple performances. The early 1980s saw the emergence of "super-theaters" with several spaces that allow performances to take place simultaneously, such as The Assembly Rooms or The Circuit, a tent village located on a plot of land.

It was during the 1980s that the festival underwent a process of "professionalization," whereby the theaters began to make use of appropriate technical setups, and amateur shows—which are still held today—were flanked by other works that could appear in any other "IN" festival.

In 2000, a centralized computer system for ticketing was inaugurated; unfortunately, the Festival Fringe Society folded in 2008, initiating a crisis that led to the dissolution of its board of directors. A new chief executive officer was appointed who was tasked with closing the hole in the budget.

Despite the difficulties and controversies, today the Fringe Festival continues to be the largest performing arts festival in the world, with some 3,000 performances by companies, groups, and individual artists from around the world, held in more than 250 locations in Edinburgh, and with over one million tickets sold. Its free-access formula has been and continues to be emulated in many cities around the world,

←
CIRCA acrobats perform at Jupiter Artland, Edinburgh, August 2022.

transforming the name into a kind of traveling brand, or a model for a certain type of festival. Indeed, there are more than 200 Fringe Festivals scattered around the world—from Adelaide to Rome and Turin, from Milan to Istanbul—where the word "fringe" always comes before the word "festival." This tells us how much the notion of "fringe," previously an attribute to describe a specific initiative in Edinburgh and distinguishing it from the main festival onto which it was grafted, has, over time, become a name, a brand, an idea that is still exported throughout the rest of the world.

THE SPRAWLING FESTIVAL — In 2019, the Edinburgh Festival Fringe hosted more than 3,500 performances in some 300 venues—concert halls, churches, high schools, or even unconventional venues such as hair salons—across the city, but an important part of the festival takes place in the streets and parks of the city. With its free or otherwise low-budget street performers, performances that serve as "teasers" for ticketed shows, and other "festivals" that have sprung up as offshoots of the Fringe, such as the Free Edinburgh Festival Fringe, one of the most remarkable aspects of the Edinburgh Festival Fringe is its ability to attract both established and emerging artists from all continents, looking for an opportunity to make a name for themselves outside their home countries. More than 60 nations are represented on stage, while Scottish companies and artists (the greater part from Edinburgh) make up about 25 percent of the program with around one thousand performances.

According to the festival website, the Fringe offers a program covering virtually all theatrical genres and disciplines from live performance, theater, dance, physical theater, circus, cabaret, children's shows, musicals, opera, music, spoken word theater, exhibitions, and events. The largest space is perhaps dedicated to comedy, which makes up more than a third of the festival program and attracts the largest audience.

The Festival Fringe Society follows the original ethos of the theater companies that founded it in 1947 and is not concerned with nor involved in the festival program or lineup. There is no jury or selection committee for the Fringe, thus any artist or show can go on stage, including experimental performances difficult to present elsewhere. As we will see in more detail, the only requirement for participation is to be able to afford the rental of the hall and the cost of producing and staging the performance, arriving earlier than others to schedule the day and time of the show. Furthermore, there are no themes or key words to be used as input for companies when proposing their work. In the words of Shona McCarthy, chief executive of the Festival Fringe Society, "No theme is imposed on the artists, but in general, the festival reflects the ideas and issues that are in the air at the time. It's a way to keep abreast of what is happening in the world. Climate change is a recurring theme in the shows, as well as gender issues, migration, and minorities."

The Festival Fringe Society prints the official program containing information and brief introductions to the shows, manages the central box office and website, and promotes the events at a local, national, and international level. In 2019, an "Inspiration Machine" and an app were created to facilitate and improve visibility of festival events for all kinds of audiences, as explained in that year's program:

> Our approach was grounded in robust market research: 78 percent of respondents to our 2018 audience survey said they came to the Fringe to take a chance and see shows they wouldn't see anywhere else. However, with nearly 40 percent of audience members also struggling to navigate the program, there was a clear need to assist audiences in discovering work that was most relevant to them. We developed several new ideas to help audiences get the most out of their Fringe. Our Inspiration Machine was an interactive, arcade- style machine that delivered randomized show suggestions at the touch of a button—more than 600 artists enhanced their regular program listings with ten-second video promos for the machine, and it was spun more than 100,000 times by Fringe-goers over the course of the festival. The FringeMaker app rewarded audience members who explored different Fringe venues, with nearly 1,500 people taking part. This marketing approach was a great success, resulting in a 6 percent increase in tickets issued. Significantly, 56 percent of Fringe attendees lived in Scotland, with more than 850,000 tickets—just over a quarter of total tickets issued—booked by Edinburgh residents.

During the rest of the year, the Festival Fringe Society carries out an important support function for artists by providing programs and initiatives for their professional development, both within the festival setting and outside. These include the *Arts Industry Office* for artists planning to participate in the festival, where a range of professionals help them navigate one of the world's largest theater markets. At the last festival, some 673 artists and companies approached the *Arts Industry Office*, receiving personalized assistance on all aspects necessary to develop their artistic careers, from communication to promotion and distribution. The Fringe *Marketplace* is an online platform where artists attending the Fringe can connect with practitioners and other curators from around the world. The works featured on *Marketplace* are selected by some of the Fringe's venue directors and festival members, making the Fringe a valuable platform for artists seeking to build their foreign tours. The Festival Fringe Society curates a number of funding, mentoring, and networking projects aimed at young emerging artists, in collaboration with entities such as the Canada Hub, the British Council, and the Arts Council Wales.

During the festival, the Festival Fringe Society provides Fringe Central, where artists, producers, company members, and arts or media industry practitioners can access hands-on support or meet with one another during the entire month of August. In 2019, Fringe Central welcomed more than 8,000 artists. The main task of the Festival Fringe Society is to welcome audiences and artists, to accompany and support them on their journey through this artistic jungle. It seems that this organizational task has been mastered, as stated in *teatroecritica.net* on September 20, 2019:

> The organization is impeccable. The city is clean, orderly, and quiet despite the rivers of people and, of course, refreshing beer. Organizing about a dozen venues with street food and an open bar, with discounts for operators, tends to centralize affluence in the main places of interest and creates places of exchange and meeting to maximize the theatrical experience. At the festival headquarters—a place dedicated to operators and companies—opinions and points of view are exchanged, international realities are met, and dialogue is created . . . the main message seems to be: "relax, we have everything under control."

The Edinburgh Festival Fringe is, therefore, also an important opportunity to promote tourism for the city and Scotland in general. As for the economic impact on the economy of the country, the festival's over one million visitors generate about 173 million pounds each year.

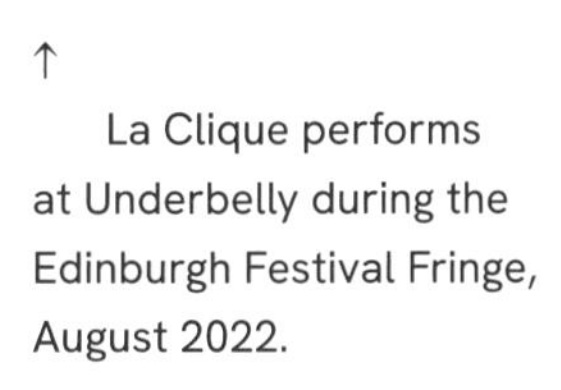

↑ La Clique performs at Underbelly during the Edinburgh Festival Fringe, August 2022.

ON THE ARTISTS' SIDE — Shona McCarthy, chief executive of the Festival Fringe Society, defines the Fringe as a platform: "The best way to describe the festival would be to compare it to YouTube. Anyone who registers can be part of it. We do not make any selection . . . The only condition to participate is to find a venue."

The Fringe is indeed open to all and is undoubtedly a great opportunity to make oneself known to the public, the press, and the many practitioners visiting the city. Participating, however, can also be very tough, both because it is not easy to navigate such an intense experience and because performing implies costs that need to be recouped while making your way through such a large number of competitors; this may scare off even the best promoter. McCarthy advises companies to set specific goals before performing in Edinburgh: "Why do you want to come to the Fringe rather than another festival?

This is very important to know. Some want to be in front of audiences who are not used to seeing performances, others want to perform on the street. There may be many reasons, but knowing them will help to find the best opportunity with respect to the location and not to get false expectations about the experience."

Artists who come here are actually agreeing to experience something very different from any other festival where the norm is that the artistic director selects and invites companies, pays a fee for the performance, covers the artists' transportation, food, and lodging expenses, and provides technical support.

While bringing a show to the Fringe means having the opportunity to showcase it to approximately 500 cultural industry practitioners, 77 journalists, and 1,661 international producers, programmers, and agencies participating in the Fringe (as reported by the festival website), it is equally true that one must be able to find the right location, arrange logistics, bear the costs of rental, technical setup, scenery, and performers on stage and, last but not least, effectively promote the show in the midst of such a dense and chaotic artistic competition. As we read in *teatroecritica.net* of September 20, 2019:

> Performers find the most diverse and absurd ways to promote their shows on the street, handing out postcards, flyers, and bumf of all kinds to weigh down the journalists' bags. People plastered with flyers, performers in deshabille with postcards in their underwear, whole troupes parading down the streets while dancing. Everywhere posters, playbills, with new additions every day, and then the glittering stars of some new newspaper.

Not everyone performing at the Fringe manages to bring in enough of an audience to make a profit or even recoup their expenses. This is also because many places such as theaters or pop-up venues (pubs, cafes, restaurants) are themselves trying to make a profit. At the Fringe, arrangements between performance venues and artists vary widely: the revenue generated by the show can be shared, a percentage of individual ticket sales can be agreed on, or the rental costs can be split by sharing the space with other companies; or the audience can be asked to contribute as well. The alternative is to perform in free-of-charge settings, provided the show does not require technical and stage setups, where "the hat is passed round" to take in any proceeds that the audience freely offers—or does not—as a contribution for the artists' performance.

Among the main goals of those who participate in the Fringe is to get reviews and meet some impresarios who will choose to invest in their artistic project and take it on tour. These goals, however, come with several obstacles and caveats. First and foremost, the ability to promote one's project by bringing audiences, press, and practitioners to see it, which is directly related to the number of days at the festival, the type of locations and times available, as well as the quality of the project itself. If a longer rental period implies higher costs but greater visibility, in contrast, being on the billboard only a few days radically decreases the chances of earning money and meeting with journalists or cultural practitioners. Again, the choice of location and timing can be decisive: if something more important or interesting is taking place at the same time, or if the distance to or from the venue is too great, it makes a difference. In short, it is a very delicate balance, the advantages and disadvantages of which must be considered with great thought, reasoning over a substantial investment and whether this would be best continued over time or spent all at once. Indeed, there are several companies that return time and time again to the Fringe, precisely for the purpose of rooting themselves within the soil of this festival-rainbow, slowly building a community or artistic path that can bear fruit over time.

Therefore, the Fringe represents a democratic, horizontal, and accessible model with no selection or filtering of artistic proposals. Be that for the better or worse, these are the ideal conditions to lay bare some of the worst vices of the performing arts market: ferocious competition, the double-edged sword of self-production and free labor, the need to independently carry out all aspects of artistic production (staging, communication, administration, public relations), and, finally, the overly powerful mechanisms of visibility and publicity, which do not always reward the most convincing projects but those that sell best.

On the other hand, it is impossible to deny the overwhelming appeal of an event such as this, which allows everyone to perform, to test themselves within a professional context, to meet colleagues, insiders, and professionals who can help develop an artistic career. There is no denying the enthusiasm and curiosity of audiences, who fearlessly throw themselves into this colorful carillon—sometimes brilliant, sometimes wacky—of expressive and artistic languages. They arrive *en masse* to the Scottish capital, which becomes the center of the world for three weeks, crisscrossed with a diversity of faces and stories. ❡

LONDON INTERNATIONAL FESTIVAL OF THEATRE

— *A thousand meanings of "festival"*

LIFTFESTIVAL.COM

↑
Elizabeth Streb's dancers performing *Human Eye* at the London Eye, London, July 2012.

Let's leave behind the medieval cityscape and Gothic architecture of Edinburgh, enlivened by the sounds and colors brought by the artists who take over the city during the Festival Fringe, and move to another English-speaking location, the nerve center of the United Kingdom, a fundamental ganglion for the birth and development of all artistic forms and cultures, a global political and economic hub: London. Despite what one might think, in the 1980s the art scene of perhaps the most cosmopolitan of European capitals experienced a period of stagnation. While punk-rock and its myriad offshoots disrupted music and fashion around the world, British theater remained tenaciously attached to its patriotic roots, compliant with Margaret Thatcher's conservative politics. This climate was closed to the stimuli and experimentation that were renewing the performing arts landscape in other countries. We must thank two fresh graduates from Warwick University who, returning from a trip to Portugal where they had taken part in a street arts festival, founded what was to become one of the most important platforms for contemporary experimental theater in the United Kingdom and Europe: the London International Festival of Theatre (LIFT). As David Benedict reported in *The Observer* in 2002, "Over the past 20 years, LIFT has radically, and sometimes roguishly, redefined what we think of as theatre and much of the experimentation in this country can be traced to its influence."

Created to draw the most innovative international artists to London and give space to narratives from continents such as South America, Asia, and India, LIFT has made its mark in the arts scene for its ability to produce experimental artistic formats, capable of renewing the conception of British contemporary theater. Now theater is hybridized with dance, performance, circus, and music in an operation meant to refocus the relationship between contemporary arts and the urban context, using performance languages as an opportunity for collective imagination, community interaction, and the regeneration of the city's private and public spaces. Originally conceived as a biennial summer program, then expanding to take over the artistic seasons of different spaces and venues in London, today LIFT has become both. In addition to the three weeks of programming taking place every two years between the end of June and the beginning of July in the most diverse and unimaginable places in London, LIFT also conducts a series of participatory and widespread projects in the city's neighborhoods—Tottenham first and foremost—involving schools, associations, local authorities, and individual citizens. This offers a platform for production and support of the careers of international artists and helps

→→
Luke Jerram's *Sky Orchestra*, London, September 2011.

to disseminate the performing arts, nurturing their narrative, and developing professional training programs aimed at the young. LIFT has always stayed true to a mission that over the years has often changed in form but not in vocation, to its desire to interact with today's changing reality. It is now particularly active in dialoguing with the myriad different identities across London, always finding new ways to contribute to community building thanks to its collaboration with artists and its trust in their ability to devise contexts and forms in which to express themselves collectively.

MILITANCY AND EXPERIMENTATION

In 1980, inspired by the street theater festival in Coimbra, Portugal, in which they had participated, Rose Fenton and Lucy Neal, recent graduates of the University of Warwick, decided to create something similar in London. As a result, initially the London International Festival of Student Theatre was born, which shortly thereafter was renamed the London International Festival of Theatre. From the beginning, the idea of its founders was to create an international festival that would welcome theater artists and directors from around the world, offering shows never before presented in the UK that had a common experimental and political approach. An article by journalist Lyn Gardner in *The Guardian* (February 25, 2004) reminds us that:

> Today's theatre-goers can catch directors and companies from all over the world in theatres across Britain. So it is perhaps hard to imagine what an insular place British theatre was in 1980, when Fenton and Neal arrived in London fresh from Warwick University with a dream of replicating an international student festival they had attended in Portugal. There they had seen young independent companies from eastern Europe and South America who offered very different visions of theatre . . . They were right. And yet the theatrical establishment was highly resistant, arguing that people wouldn't want to see theatre from abroad when everyone said that British theatre was the best in the world.

In 1981, LIFT was registered as a charity and the founders organized the first festival, which ran from August 3 to 16, welcoming theatrical groups from Poland, France, Brazil, the Netherlands, Malaysia, West Germany, Japan, and Peru, alongside British artists. It was indeed the UK's first international theater festival; its ambitious program was well received and, more importantly, it drew the attention of a number of sponsors and patrons, following which Rose Fenton and Lucy Neal decided to expand the team. Despite this, the first LIFT festivals were financially complex, so much so that the 1983 event—the second, being a biennial festival—was almost canceled.

Looking back on the festival's first 25 years, the founders recall putting together the opening program on a budget of £100,000, paying artists £5 a day and organizing picnics in London's parks, rather than providing actual hospitality.

The survival of LIFT was thus something that went against all expectations, defying established political mechanisms and trends in what was the conservative and Thatcherite London of the 1980s. An example to illustrate the level of adversity was that, in 1981, Arts Council England refused to fund the first festival on the grounds that it was not possible to allocate grants for an event with a program composed mainly of performances by foreign companies. Soon LIFT would become a political battleground, finding in Labour's Ken Livingstone—at that time head of the Greater London Council—an important ally who raised substantial public funding for its operations. LIFT's tenacity had an impact at a political level too, helping eradicate a kind of conservative attitude and generating international networking to pave the way for a new conception of theater programming. By demonstrating the high level of its cultural mission, LIFT was able to develop a different model of sustainability, which included private investment. A sponsorship campaign was launched in 1986, and a civic partnership followed in 1991. In addition, Julia Rowntree, head of the sponsorship campaign from 1986 to 1995, launched three initiatives that brought business and art together, the most important of which was the LIFT Business Arts Forum.

From 1981–2001, LIFT would host companies from more than 60 countries, also curating the Out of LIFT season, geared specifically to young people and playing an important role in renewing the conception of theater and performing arts in the British context. LIFT is credited with important debuts, such as Ariel Dorfman's *Death and the Maiden*, the production of experimental performance projects such as Deborah Warner's *St Pancras Project*, and Bobby Baker's *Grown-Up School*; it also introduced British audiences to key directors of the international art scene, such as Robert Lepage and Romeo Castellucci. Indeed, programs included the most disparate forms of expression, such as circus or pyrotechnic arts and a multitude of other art forms. LIFT is also credited with its innovative approach to the city's spaces: the festival has always used not only theaters and halls, but also streets, urban areas, unconventional spaces such as disused buildings, and schools, thus contributing to their reinvigoration. In 2011, the sky was the stage for the festival on its thirtieth anniversary, when *The Sky Orchestra* flew over London in balloons.

G-CGWW

BYHU
G-BY

LIFT was increasingly taking the form of an idea or concept capable of manifesting itself in different ways, whose specificity was not so much in the format, the aesthetics investigated, or the type of artistic language that was adopted, but in its adherence to contemporaneity. It demonstrated an ability to listen to new languages and the most innovative expressive urgencies, especially attracting those from different geographical or cultural contexts. On its twelfth anniversary in 2001, the founders decided to abandon the biennial festival format, launching the LIFT Enquiry season with the intention of opening a space for discussion about the purpose and possibilities of theater and festivals at the beginning of the new millennium. From that point on, and for the next five years, LIFT curated an annual program of events, hosting international and national artists in shorter seasons, and organizing workshops, conferences, residencies, and projects. To prove that change had to be something intrinsic to LIFT's mission, in 2004—after twenty-five years at the helm of the association—the founders left the directorship of the festival, which was passed on to Angharad Wynne-Jones until 2008.

In 2010, LIFT resumed its biennial format, providing seven weeks of programming but, in fact, surpassing its nature as a festival and increasingly becoming a platform for production, research, and debate in contemporary performing arts.

The revitalization of the festival involved a renewal in its mission, setting itself the goal of engaging a younger local audience from communities of diverse origins, socio-economic backgrounds, and cultural affiliations—groups London has in abundance. LIFT's vision of this celebration of community values, ideologies, and identities coincides with the very essence of a festival. This new trajectory has involved LIFT entering into a crowded landscape of arts organizations striving to maximize their cultural relevance in order to maintain financing from the government, to continue raising sufficient revenue from ticket sales and to engage new audiences while trying to package a thorough, valuable, and innovative program.

As of 2017, LIFT's joint artistic director and CEO is Kris Nelson, former director of the Dublin Fringe Festival, one of the "little brothers" of the Edinburgh Festival Fringe. His approach is characterized by a focus on multidisciplinarity and on emerging and iconoclastic artistic experiences.

In 2018—the last festival before the pandemic—LIFT staged 20 performances for about 40,000 spectators; it also engaged 400 Londoners aged six to 76 who participated in the creation of one of the commissioned works, and it provided more than 15,000 free tickets, which enabled greater accessibility to its program.

←
CIRCA acrobats perform in *Depart* at Tower Hamlets Cemetery Park, London, 2016.

INTERACTION AND TRANSFORMATION AS CURATORIAL LINES — From the very outset, LIFT's artistic project has had a very clear physiognomy, occupying a specific space in the artistic landscape in which it was located—that of the British theater scene of the 1980s—and fulfilling a public function that was unrecognized at that time, namely that of reconnecting the community through an emotionally and culturally dense experience such as artistic creativity. Internationality, multidisciplinarity, and a renewed relationship with the territory as community and as physical place are the key concepts to describe a cultural project that over time has been able to renew itself without ever losing sight of its goals and founding principles. In this sense, LIFT takes on the dual connotation of a curatorial and cultural project in the fullest sense. Far from being simply a platform for international performances or a showcase for new creations, it commissions works and produces site-specific projects. Thanks to an unceasing search for an active relationship between artistic works, spaces, and the city's inhabitants, the artistic direction continually interacts with the actors involved in its projects, helping to shape the content offered within the festival. This collaboration takes place as much between the artists—with whom themes, issues, and expressive needs are shared, together imagining formats and modes of fruition and working concretely in their realization—as with the audience, through a creative process in which they are no longer mere users but true activators.

The international component should be understood not simply as a vocation for foreignness, but as an openness to dialogue with new visions, even radically different from one's own and through which to interact with reality. Not surprisingly, once the international vocation becomes a common and structural modality in artistic programming, the focus turns back to indigenous communities, thus intercepting the diversity that runs through the same urban or local territory. In this context, performance art takes on an additional public and political role as a device for transforming subjectivities and, consequently, the ways in which they create society. Going back to the interview with the two founders in *The Guardian*, Lyn Gardner describes what LIFT has been since its origin:

> This was a festival that openly questioned whether we needed festivals at all. It regularly changed shape and content, and it constantly surprised. A LIFT show was just as likely to take place in a park, on the streets, in a derelict hotel or the back of a taxi as it was in a theatre. Embracing high art and low spectacle with equal vigour, LIFT brought to London work from around the world that made us examine our own culture more deeply. At times of momentous upheaval—the destruction of the Berlin wall, the war in Palestine, conflict in Tiananmen Square—it sometimes felt as if LIFT was bringing us dispatches from the front line, allowing people to tell their own stories. This wasn't entertainment, it was essential.

Today, LIFT is a platform dedicated to the arts and their relationship with contemporary society and is capable of functioning on multiple levels and through different actions. In addition to cultural planning and community involvement, LIFT plays a pivotal role in the development of the professional paths of international artists and companies; it conducts important activities such as in-depth studies, storytelling, and the dissemination of issues related to the performing arts and theoretical and philosophical questions that are intrinsically intertwined. This is seen in the various programs produced by the festival over the years and continues to keep the interest of its

↑
Lâcher de violons by Transe Express through the streets of Barking, London, August 2009.

community active, also outside the short but intense period of the festival through skillful use of technology, media, and social channels. LIFT weaves a medium- to long-term relationship with artists by supporting dramaturgical mentoring, production, and distribution of their shows, consulting and connecting with international networks, as well as curating meetings and artistic initiatives outside the festival weeks. In addition, LIFT is known to pay close attention to social media marketing strategies, and also develops digital performances as part of its communication strategy, allowing audiences to actively participate in the creation of performances designed for the digital dimension.

THE RELATIONSHIP WITH URBAN SPACE — The ethos of the festival is to commission, produce, and present the most radical avant-garde contemporary theater from around the world, generating additional significance through the choice of venues in which the performances are presented: halls and theaters as well as disused, insignificant, or forgotten places in a cosmopolitan metropolis like London. Thus, roads, parks, houses, industrial buildings, rivers, and canals are all potential venues. As we saw to a lesser extent in Avignon, since its first festivals LIFT has made the relationship with architecture and locations in the city one of its focal points, and through various editions of the festival it has managed to attract very different target audiences, as well as renewing the urban imaginary, thus contributing to the revitalization of different sites. For example, about seven years before Tate Modern took over its current premises at the Bankside Power Station, an abandoned facility, it was the site of the 1993 LIFT festival *Fireworks* show. Similarly, in 1999 British theater and opera director Deborah Warner presented *The Tower Project* in the Euston Tower skyscraper, ushering the public into a deserted office building from which they could observe city life from above. Again, in 2016, the Australian company Circa Contemporary Circus proposed *DEPART*, a performance in Tower Hamlets Cemetery Park, a nature reserve and monumental garden in London's East End; in 2018, 150 musicians and dancers performed in the Tower of London, directed by artist and choreographer Hofesh Shechter, in the opera *East Wall*.

The relationship with space not only helps disseminate the artistic proposal across London through contact with the city's various communities, but takes on a true artistic role by assigning a precise level of significance to the work that contributes in its own right to its overall artistic value, just as all other expressive components that are involved in its creation.

EDUCATION, LEARNING, AND CIVIC ENGAGEMENT — Community involvement and the educational function are two of the main poles around which LIFT's entire identity has developed, entering the social and cultural fabric of the city and playing an important role in promoting and providing professional training in the performing arts. Although present early on in the artistic project, this tendency gradually became more and more central and articulated, thus managing to maintain a direct and constant contact with the evolution of such a multicultural and diverse society as London.

In 1991, LIFT began experimenting with an educational and community program and also hired a specific education manager, integrating this line of activities into the main festival program from 1995. A series of workshops, lectures, forums, and discussions were launched, such as the *Daily Dialogues*, created in 1993 and curated by author Alan Read, with 21 daily public workshops with artists, theorists, and theater companies engaged in the festival program.

Other projects launched as part of LIFT's learning mission include Phakama, the International Youth Arts Exchange Project (started in 1996), as well as the previously mentioned Business Arts Forum (launched in 1995) and the Teachers Forum (created in 1999), or the Placement Program, part of LIFT's training package to help student trainees find employment in the arts and advance their professional careers. Available roles include Audiences & Evaluation, Development & Events, Marketing & Digital, Producing and Technical. LIFT trainees have worked at Dance Umbrella, Tate, Royal Court, The Yard, Battersea Arts Centre, Artsadmin, Jerwood Foundation, CASA Latin American Theatre Festival, and Cameron Mackintosh Ltd, and some have become successful freelancers.

LIFT TOTTENHAM — One of the projects in which LIFT's civic engagement particularly stands out is LIFT Tottenham. In 2015, LIFT decided to focus some of its work toward the youth and communities in the multicultural neighborhood of Tottenham, North London, a territory with one of the highest poverty rates in the country. A long-term program of activities was established, involving schools, associations, youths, and the local government, bringing them together with international artists and companies, building partnerships, and commissioning site-specific projects.

The UpLIFTers program was born within the framework of LIFT Tottenham. Since 2015, this program has supported an artistic collaboration between two schools in the neighborhood (Duke's Aldridge Academy School and The Vale School – LIFT) and a commission created specifically for this project. This is a five-year partnership that engages students in participatory art experiences, introducing them to arts-related languages and professions. The program continues to this day, involving more than 30 individuals, providing them with the basic skills of cultural event production (conception, planning, scheduling, budgeting, promotion, execution, de-briefing, and relations with local agencies and businesses) and accompanying them throughout their entire school careers.

As we have seen since its first festivals, LIFT has been able to set in motion pioneering initiatives in artistic practice, education, civic engagement, and professional development, becoming one of the leading contemporary performance festivals. This has helped renew first the British and then the international art scene, betting on experimental and innovative artistic projects and giving a voice to projects from other countries and marginalized cultural contexts. Thus, this is a top-notch artistic program accessible to a diverse audience, which can appropriate it and make it a tool for awareness and growth. ¶

SIBIU INTERNATIONAL THEATER FESTIVAL

SIBFEST.RO

— *A festival-universe*

↑
Călătoriile lui Gulliver by Jonathan Swift, directed by Silviu Purcărete, Sibiu, May 2012.

From multicultural London, a crucial hub for cultural and artistic production, we move eastward to the heart of Central and Eastern Europe, specifically to Sibiu, Transylvania, in the very center of Romania. Despite its small size (it has 161,480 inhabitants), Sibiu's history is distinctive and rich in culture. Founded in the Middle Ages by Transylvanian Saxons of German origin, its population would remain predominantly German and Hungarian until World War I, later becoming mainly Romanian. A terminus of the postal network to the east, over the ages Sibiu became an important commercial center, recording some significant events in Romanian cultural history: this is the city where the first book was printed in Romanian, the first hospital founded, the first pharmacy, the first school, and the first theater. It is no coincidence that here in 1993 the Sibiu International Theater Festival (Festivalul Internaţional de Teatru de la Sibiu, FITS)—one of the largest performing arts festivals in the world—came to life.

FITS is Central and Eastern Europe's first major festival dedicated to the performing arts. It is held annually, usually in the summer, with an average of 500 events from over thirty countries. Conducted with the patronage of the Romanian Presidency and with the support of the Sibiu Municipality and Local Council, FITS brings together great artists of the international stage each year, offering audiences the chance to enjoy some of the world's most highly regarded, globally recognized, and award-winning performances.

This is a small town in what might be considered the outskirts of the world, but instead it is a crucible of history and cultural transition that each year is transformed into a global hub for artists, spectators, and practitioners from around the world, including the United States, Canada, Iran, Japan, France, Georgia, Germany, Indonesia, Italy, Mexico, Russia, Singapore, South Korea, and Turkey.

Born as a brainchild of Constantin Chiriac—its founder and still the "face" of the festival today—the cultural project articulated by FITS is based on a few cornerstones: the prestige of the artistic figures involved; the international positioning built from collaboration with cultural institutes, embassies, and transnational entities; and the desire to condense the nation's broadest artistic and cultural offerings into its ten days of programming, in order to reach a culturally and generationally diverse audience.

→→
Călătoriile lui Gulliver by Jonathan Swift, directed by Silviu Purcărete, Sibiu, May 2012.

On a par with other major international festivals, such as the Edinburgh International Festival or the Festival d'Avignon, but concentrated in only ten days, the FITS model succeeds in accounting for how explosive and transformative a transient, fragile, and ephemeral form such as a festival may be. It provides an important stage and meeting place for artistic companies from around the world by giving form to an international scenario capable of shifting the center of gravity of artistic production.

AN UNSTOPPABLE EXPANSION

In 1992, inspired by the cultural program in Antwerp, the Cultural Capital of Europe that year, Constantin Chiriac—then an actor at the Radu Stanca National Theater in Sibiu—decided to collaborate with the city's House of Culture to start a student theater festival. After the first one, he decided to broaden the scope of the festival and make it international and professional, seeking to promote the development of the arts scene, which, during the period of Ceausescu's dictatorship (he was executed in 1989), had seen a drastic reduction in the number of performing arts professionals. Thus, in 1993, the first Sibiu International Theater Festival was born, hosting eight performances from three countries and staging them in conventional venues, namely theaters.

Initially, the festival was held to coincide with National Theater Day, March 27, but as it grew, the organizers decided to change the time period, shifting the festival dates to late May and early June, thus making it easier for audiences to attend thanks to the more favorable weather conditions. Without having to worry about the possibility of bad weather, Constantin Chiriac had the idea of using unconventional urban spaces, primarily churches, historical buildings, pubs, industrial sites, and outdoor spaces such as parks, to embrace the history and life of the city and enhance its heritage. The history of the Sibiu festival coincides with its expansion in terms of the number of artists involved and performances programmed, as well as with the expansion of the network of international relations, which each year brings new companies to Sibiu. In 1994, the number of participating countries rose to eight from the three for the first festival; the following two years the city received artists from 21 and 24 countries, respectively. The name of the festival was soon changed; in its early years, in order to express its more professional approach, and again in 1997, it became today's Festivalul Internațional de Teatru de la Sibiu. The duration has also increased from year to year to make room

↑ *Vangelo*, directed by Pippo Delbono, November 2017.

for the ever-increasing number of scheduled events: the first three festivals lasted three days; then, in 1995, four days; in 1999, a ten-day duration was decided.

In 1997, the festival launched the Sibiu Performing Arts Market, an associated structure that aims to "ensure equal opportunities for all artists, cultural workers, performing arts institutions or cultural networks to meet with important producers from around the world." Each year, the important Marketplace network facilitates meetings and future collaborations among 300 international participants from various cultural organizations (arts management agencies, NGOs, public institutions, independent companies, etc.), developing partnerships with artistic and cultural entities around the world.

Over the years, the festival has grown steadily to become a key event on the Romanian political agenda, invaluable in consolidating the country's international standing. The 2005 festival totaled 68 participating countries involving about 2,000 artists. This was crucial groundwork for the 2007 edition, when Sibiu was the European Capital of Culture (together with Luxembourg). The figure of Constantin Chiriac was decisive in this cultural achievement and international recognition. The year 2007, therefore, marked a turning point in the history of the festival and thus, the project continued to expand, later involving 2,500 participants from seventy countries.

In 2010—for the first time in the festival's history—all tickets were sold out in advance, and the program included a "Heritage" section, presenting the repertoire of the most representative performances of the Radu Stanca National Theater in Sibiu, also directed by Constantin Chiriac.

Festival after festival, FITS has continued to persevere by following the logic of prestige, offering in a small town off the major cultural circuits a combination of large-scale public events scattered throughout the urban territory, prestigious theater and dance performances by major international companies, more experimental and contemporary artistic formats with popular performances, street art, and classical works, as well as a multidisciplinary program made up of concerts, opera, films, book presentations, workshops, lectures, and seminars.

A crucial aspect of FITS is its ability to establish networks and connections with a wide range of cultural realities, from associations to large public bodies, companies, cultural institutions, and embassies, continuing the drive to bring recognition and prestige to the project.

The result has been to bring to life one of the largest theater and performing arts festivals in the world. According to the European Commission, the Sibiu Festival is the third most important festival in Europe after the Edinburgh Fringe and the Festival d'Avignon. Over the years, several prominent international figures have participated, from the great protagonists of contemporary theater such as Eugenio Barba, Bob Wilson, Peter Brook, and Mikhail Baryshnikov to important institutional figures, including Ursula von der Leyen and many others. As confirmed by the international recognition during the festival's twentieth anniversary in 2013, Constantin Chiriac gave important insight into the festival's financial strategy: "This year's edition relied mostly on corporate and foreign financial contributions rather than support from Romanian authorities, as only 15 percent of the €6 million budget is covered by public funding."

MULTIFORMITY AND COMPLEXITY — The artistic and design framework of FITS is, to this day, tied to the vision of its president and founder, Constantin Chiriac. A theater and film actor, a specialist in cultural management in the United States and the United Kingdom, a tireless weaver of relationships with leading international directors, academics, politicians, presidents, and diplomats, it is thanks to his intuition that today Romania is home to one of the most topical theater events in Europe. His work as director of FITS and the Radu Stanca National Theater has been honored with numerous awards (the most recent being the Order of the Rising Sun from Japan and Chevalier of the Order of Arts and Letters from France) and professorships he holds at various international universities. The vision of a single person was powerful enough to create a vast field of relationships and collaboration, transforming a small Transylvanian town, dense with history, into a world platform for performing arts, theater, and beyond. The following is a brief outline of the history of FITS.

Since the first festival, some of the most representative international theater companies, directors, actors, and set designers have been in Sibiu. This has led to a transformation not only of the community's openness toward other mindsets, worlds, and cultures, but also to a greater professionalization of Romanian artists and students of the performing arts, who have been invited to Sibiu to present performances and participate in workshops, lectures, and other activities. During its first 27 festivals, FITS presented more than 1,500 performances (theater, dance, circus, music, opera, musicals, concerts), of which more than 1,000 were theatrical performances. World-renowned directors and young filmmakers with great potential have contributed to the festival's reputation: Rimas Tuminas, Andriy Zholdak, Hanoch Levin, Lev Erenburg, Eugenio Barba, Yuri Kordonsky, Pippo Delbono, Eimuntas Nekrosius, Masahiro Yasuda, Levan Tsuladze, Lars Norén, Peter Brook, Armin Petras, Joël Pommerat, Declan Donnellan, Hideki Noda, Ivan Vîrîpaev, Peter Stein, Wajdi Mouawad, Krystian Lupa, Lev Dodin, Angélica Liddell, Emmanuel Demarcy-Mota, Data Tavadze, Kazuyoshi Kushida, Yoshi Oida, Monika Strzepka, Christoph Marthaler, Thomas Ostermeier, Luk Perceval, Jarosław Fret, Alvis Hermanis, Tim Robbins, Tang Shu-Wing, Philippe Genty, Akihiro Yamamoto, Jernej Lorenci, Robert Wilson, Hideki Noda, Eric Lacascade, Lisa Peterson, Eirik Stubø, Timofey Kulyabin, and many others.

It is almost impossible to review one of Europe's most extensive art programs, which has made heterogeneity and the ability to speak to a wide audience its veritable trademarks. Theater was undoubtedly the starting point for this great cultural enterprise, but soon the program opened up to different artistic forms and activities related to other artistic disciplines, including performing, visual, and literary. "We are a multifaceted and complex festival of all the arts," as we read in the website. This statement should be understood not only in its wider significance, but also in a somewhat intensive perspective: FITS not only ranges "in width," to encompass many types of artistic disciplines, but also "in depth," in the sense that its program aims to "reach the core" of the many genres embraced by a single discipline. If we examine dance featured in the festival program, for example, we find contemporary dance, traditional dances from different cultures (Flamenco, Kathak, Kabuki, Butoh, Noh, Dervish, African, Balinese), hip-hop, etc. Some of the most important contemporary and traditional dance choreographers participated in the Sibiu festival, such as Karine Ponties, Gigi Căciuleanu, Lia Rodrigues, Marie Chouinard, Sasha Waltz, Paco Peña, Rocío Molina, and Olivier Dubois.

Then we have circus performances, both in theaters and in the streets, Romanian and international musicals, operas, free concerts in the squares, and musical performances by ensembles and orchestras in churches, from fado to gospel, from organ to symphonic music. The offerings are truly vast and varied, and it is impressive to think that it all takes place in just ten days. Each year, the festival has a title to help the audience navigate through this rich artistic program.

These are the titles of the various editions of the festival: *Tolerance*, 1995; *Violence*, 1996; *Cultural Identity*, 1997; *Links*, 1998; *Creativity*, 1999; *Alternatives*, 2000; *Challenges*, 2001; *Bridges*, 2002; *Tomorrow*, 2003; *Legacies*, 2004; *Signs*, 2005; *Together?!*, 2006; *Next*, 2007; *Energy*, 2008; *Innovations*, 2009; *Questions*, 2010; *Community*, 2011; *Crisis. Culture Makes a Difference*, 2012; *Dialogue*, 2013; *Uniqueness in Diversity*, 2014; *Growing Smart, Smart Growing*, 2015; *Building Trust*, 2016; *Love*, 2017; *Passion*, 2018; *The Art of Giving*, 2019; *Empowered*, 2020.

↑

Le sorelle Macaluso, directed by Emma Dante, April 2014.

THE INTERNATIONAL DIMENSION AND OTHER LINES OF PROGRAMMING — The international impact of the festival is evident on many fronts: in the names of the artists in the program, in reports on the websites of various cultural institutions—Spain, France, the United Kingdom, Italy, and many others—with which FITS conducts its activities, in the words of personal greeting from distinguished personalities who participated in the festival (in the "Testimonials" section of the institutional website), in the participation in various European projects, and in the activation of training and international exchange programs.

Indeed, each year Sibiu hosts about 500 volunteers from all over the world who contribute in the implementation phase of the festival, activating various cultural exchange and professional training programs with international partners.

Since 2005, the festival has initiated relationships with entities and institutions in Canada, Iran, Japan, France, Georgia, Germany, Indonesia, Mexico, Russia, Singapore, South Korea, Turkey, and Hungary for the selection and exchange of interns. One of the main partners is the EU-Japan Fest, with which Sibiu has been cooperating for ten years, facilitating the arrival of more than 130 young Japanese who completed an educational experience in-situ, making the organization of the festival possible.

Since 1997, FITS has curated Performance Exchange, a structure associated with the festival since its first edition to promote the creation of a network connecting festivals and artists, independent companies, and state institutions in the field of performing arts. Performance Exchange organizes a program of specific meetings to generate future possible connections and partnerships. Precisely because of its "peripheral" location with respect to other European cultural circuits, distant from the world's great capitals, one of the traits that embodies FITS's identity is the desire to attract prominent figures from the international theater scene and to focus on the prestige of an event that has grown year after year. The Celebrity Alley project—launched in 2013 at the initiative of FITS management and the Radu Stanca National Theater—goes in this direction with the creation of a Sibiu Walk of Fame. This was installed in the Parcul Cetății and is dotted with stars dedicated to important personalities who have participated in the festival. The first to receive this accolade were Ariane Mnouchkine, Declan Donnellan, Eugenio Barba, Silviu Purcărete, Georges Banu, Nakamura Kanzaburo XVIII; to date, there are about 50 stars in place. Although far from Hollywood, this initiative witnesses the city's relationship with the most important personalities in international contemporary arts.

During the ten-day event, the festival becomes a catalyst for possibilities and artistic and commercial experiences for the benefit of the entire city. There are several "collateral" activities that take place during the festival. As already seen in other cases, although not part of the official program, these play an important role in defining the cultural project and positioning of the festival in general. The first is *Applause*, the free magazine produced each year in collaboration with professors and students from the Humanities and Theater Studies specialization of Lucian Blaga University, Babeș-Bolyai University in Cluj-Napoca, and the National University of Theater and Cinema

Arts in Bucharest; it is the result of a critical writing workshop that contributes to the dialogue around the works featured at the festival. *Therme Forum - Theater and Architecture,* established in 2018, engages world-renowned performing artists and architects in a three-day meeting and debate on the relationship between community, architecture, and the performing arts. Additionally, there are meetings where guest artists are requested to dialogue with critics, scholars, or other artists around theoretical issues related to their artistic trajectories, or on the role of the arts in society. A series of workshops are also organized for artists-in-training, which focus on specific practices and issues of artistic craft: playwriting, choreography, Stanislavskian theater, No and Kabuki theater, directing, set design, and so on. A film section was also inaugurated to delve further into the works or thoughts of artists who have left their mark on the artistic landscape. Films, documentaries, and audiovisual works by figures such as Peter Brook, Ariane Mnouchkine, Pippo Delbono, Robert Wilson, and Ohad Naharin have been screened during past festivals.

FITS is an opportunity to interweave theatrical discourse with literary and theoretical issues. The festival publishes books—studies, essays, albums, and anthologies on artists, performing arts history, management, author's books—that are presented during the festival season. Since 1997, FITS has also published an anthology of plays presented in the *Reading Shows* section, which includes contemporary texts by Romanian and international playwrights, published in different languages. Finally, since 2012 and in cooperation with the Sibiu Chamber of Commerce, Industry, and Agriculture, the festival has hosted a book fair where Romania's leading publishers present more than 4,000 publications.

With one of the most extensive offerings in a multidisciplinary perspective, and most layered investigations of individual genres and disciplines, FITS is one of the largest theater festivals in the world. Its ability to attract the most prominent figures in the performing arts, but also its focus on collaboration, exchange programs, and partnerships with international entities, have made the festival a cultural and economic opportunity for the entire city, transforming a small town in Transylvania into a European cultural capital (officially in 2007, but reconfirming this accolade each year of the festival), such is its scope in terms of artistic mission, audience, and related activities. ❡

→→

Faust, after J. W. Goethe, directed by Silviu Purcărete, original music by Vasile Şirli, Sibiu, 2008.

SANTARCANGELO FESTIVAL

SANTARCANGELOFESTIVAL.COM

— *Radical and popular*

↑

Giovanfrancesco Giannini and Gianmaria Borzillo in *Save the Last Dance for Me*, choreography by Alessandro Sciarroni, Santarcangelo di Romagna, September 2022.

The great changes that swept through the 1970s in the world of theater reached Italy as well. In addition to large urban centers, such as Rome and Milan, one of the hotbeds of elaboration and rethinking the theater sector was actually a small village, Santarcangelo di Romagna, in the hinterland of the region, just a few kilometers from Rimini and the Adriatic Riviera. This is where one of the very first festivals dedicated to theatrical experimentation and live arts in Italy has been held since 1971. Indeed, this has had a particular impact on the Italian and international performing arts scene, nourishing the link between art and politics that had been at the center of cultural reflection since the 1970s. For more than fifty years during the first fortnight of July, the squares, streets, and any other space in the small town that can accommodate an audience are filled with shows, concerts, performances by street artists, and crisscrossed by artists and spectators from all over Europe and beyond.

Taking place in the summer in one of the historically highly touristed areas of Italy, the Santarcangelo Festival maintains a relationship with the region that is evident both from the point of view of the management structure—with various local municipalities including Santarcangelo participating in its governing body—and from that of the cultural mission. It is an avant-garde event but offering forms of accessibility for highly diverse audiences through a program of free events, participatory projects, and services, including bars, public drinking fountains, campsites, and many other initiatives. One of the characteristics of this festival is its ability to stir up controversy. Indeed, the issue of the festival's relationship with the region ignites bitter local political disputes almost every year and often strong criticism has been raised against some of the festival performances, considered as being problematic or harsh. In any case, Santarcangelo remains one of the most beloved festivals for the Italian contemporary theater community, which comes together every summer for a gathering where it can link up with the work of the most innovative international and emerging artists. For the last pre-pandemic edition in 2019, 12,200 tickets were sold for the 11 days of programming: 251 performances of which 111 were free in 33 performance spaces and involving 196 performers.

Santarcangelo is a particularly relevant event for sector specialists, so much so that it attracts more than 150 national and international operators and 94 accredited journalists. These are important numbers for a festival of artistic creation and experimentation, even more so for a small town of 22,000 inhabitants that has become one of the international hubs of contemporary live arts.

→→
Tamara Cubas, *Multitud*, Santarcangelo di Romagna, July 2018.

pp. → 276 | 277

Santarcangelo is the first Italian festival dedicated to theater and other performing arts, which in part follows the model of the festivals seen in the previous chapters, and which paved the way for the long tradition of summer festivals that still enliven the Italian summer from June to September. As pointed out earlier, Romagna represents a true cradle of Italian and international performing arts, thanks to a mix of economic, political, and cultural elements. Not coincidentally, the initial impetus behind the festival was political, in the wake of the 1968 movement, which we could summarize as a desire to reconnect art and society within a new vision of culture. The festival was an idea of the then-mayor Romeo Donati and his forward-thinking municipal council, and of the Santarcangelo-based screenwriter Flavio Nicolini, who then involved the Rome lawyer and filmmaker Piero Patino. The idea was for a festival of theater in the square because at that time there were no local theaters and there was a strong belief that art should be at the service of the community, "thus emphasizing the social and political character of scenic art, as opposed to a theater that has become a commodity." The first edition was organized in 1971, and in the early years leading names in theater and music such as Dario Fo and Franca Rame, Giorgio Gaber, Giovanna Marini, as well as emerging companies and groups from Eastern Europe, Brazil, and the United States were hosted.

In the late 1970s, the theories of Eugenio Barba's Third Theater, Living Theatre, and Jerzy Grotowski's approach to theater were making headway in Europe and reached Santarcangelo. Indeed, this approach characterized the years 1978–83, when the festival direction was under Roberto Bacci, Antonio Attisani, and Ferruccio Merisi, directors, authors, and theater performers who were close to these artistic trends. These proved to be formative years for some initiatives that would later remain in the festival's history, such as the organization of a free camp aimed at young festivalgoers, and a certain tendency to stir up controversy among the Santarcangelo community. That five-year period saw the appearance of a number of companies that would become central to the history of Italian theater, such as Danio Manfredini's, Teatro dell'Elfo, and Teatro Valdoca. The festival also became an opportunity for the creation of a link between practice and theory through collaboration with a number of DAMS professors, thus expanding the network of the artistic community in Romagna.

One of the most debated issues in those years was the future of the festival and its role vis à vis the artistic community, but also, and perhaps more pressing, its relationship with the region and its community. In 1984, the direction was entrusted to Roberto Bacci alone, under whose direction Santarcangelo dei Teatri was born,

↑
Silvia Calderoni and Ilenia Caleo, *Kiss*, Santarcangelo di Romagna, July 2019.

an expression of the desire to give life to a project that would go beyond the festival and continue throughout the year. Meanwhile, the best of experimental, increasingly performative, and radical theater of those years continued to pass through Santarcangelo. The performance *Genet in Tangier* by Magazzini Criminali, which was staged in the abattoir in Rimini and involved the slaughter of a horse (already destined to be put down) on stage was from those years, and aroused much controversy. Bacci was followed by Antonio Attisani, who focused on the festival as being a place for artists to meet and exchange ideas, broadening the horizon from research theater to other languages and different cultural and countercultural phenomena, with performances by a group of Tibetan monks, a cycle of seminars on cyberpunk by the Milanese publishing house Shake and its magazine *Decoder*, the parades of the Mutoid Waste Company, a group of British sculptors and performers who wandered through Europe in the late 1980s, some of whom have remained permanently in Santarcangelo since the 1990s. In 1994, Leo de Berardinis was appointed director and under his tenancy the festival strengthened its relationship with the public, looking at popular public theater, dialect theater and participatory projects: workshops, meetings, open rehearsals. The festival website names the following personalities as having participated in various editions.

> The protagonists in recent years have been Enzo Moscato, Claudio Morganti, Alfonso Santagata, Giorgio Barberio Corsetti, Moni Ovadia, Sanjukta Panigrahi, Giovanna Marini, Antonello Salis, Steve Lacy, Ivano Marescotti, interpreting Raffaello Baldini's first theatrical text, Marco Baliani, the Kismet, Judith Malina who with Lorenza Zambon for the Alfieri company interprets Doris Lessing, then we have Albe, Valdoca, Socìetas Raffaello Sanzio, and for dance Sosta Palmizi, Enzo Pezzella, Enzo Cosimi, Virgilio Sieni, Solari Vanzi. During the de Berardinis years, artists from the then new Italian theater—from Motus and Teatrino Clandestino to Fanny & Alexander and La Nuova Complesso Camerata—also appeared at Santarcangelo.

In 2005, the direction of the festival was passed on to Silvio Castiglioni, an actor and cofounder along with Ferruccio Merisi of Teatro di Ventura; and then it passed to Olivier Bouin, a cultural attaché at the French Embassy in Rome, who directed the festival until 2008 alongside Paolo Ruffini, but then unfortunately left following disagreements with the local administration. From then, something unique was introduced, different from all the other examples seen so far: the launch of a three-year (2009–11) directorship composed of a trio of artists: Chiara Guidi of Socìetas Raffaello Sanzio, Enrico Casagrande of Motus, and Ermanna Montanari of Teatro delle

Albe, accompanied by a critic/organizational coordination board composed by Silvia Bottiroli, Rodolfo Sacchettini, and Cristina Ventrucci. The festival then resumed the name of its early editions—Santarcangelo Festival Internazionale del Teatro in Piazza—and continued to attract leading names from the new art scene, such as Alessandro Sciarroni, Teatro Sotterraneo, Menoventi; established figures of the Italian scene including Mariangela Gualtieri and Roberto Latini; the experimental generation of the early 2000s, now-consolidated companies such as Fanny & Alexander, Kinkaleri, and Cristina Rizzo; and international names from different disciplines and crossover genres, such as Richard Maxwell, Arto Lindsay, Alvin Lucier, Burroughs, and Fargion, Zapruder Film Makers Group, Public Mouvement, Kornél Mundruczó, Ivo Dimchev, and Oriza Hirata.

From 2012 to 2016, the festival was led by Silvia Bottiroli (initially flanked by Rodolfo Sacchettini, then on her own), who aimed to make the relationship between the festival and the city even closer, curating several participatory projects and free offerings in public spaces; she also reinforced the international dimension of the festival. The final three-year period before the pandemic was under the direction of the Finnish curator of Belarusian origin Eva Neklyaeva, together with Lisa Gilardino, a curator, manager, and producer who would direct the festival in an even more multidisciplinary direction with an emphasis on performance, music, and visual arts.

MAKING COMMUNITY — Santarcangelo Festival is the latest name it has taken on over the years and now synonymous with one of the leading centers of conception and imagination in the field of performing arts. As already seen in part by tracing its history, it is evident how the festival has built its strategy through the succession of artistic directions, opening up to previously unseen experiments. This appears remarkable, especially when compared to the conservative trend that other festivals and cultural centers have demonstrated in terms of governance, and shows how the identity of the festival is something as deeply rooted in the audience as in the participating artists and the various curators and directors, and how it is something that persists over time. This is a kind of taking charge of the festival by all the parties involved, which allows its principles to be transmitted while changing direction, but it is also rooted in the immersive experience made possible by the Santarcangelo festival and its continuous experimentation and transformation. The association that organizes the festival has among its founding members

the City of Santarcangelo and other municipalities in the area, thus making the festival an administrative priority and giving stability to its staff. Although there is a skeleton staff during the year, this is reinforced before and during the festival period. The location and time frame is strategic: the festival is part of a dense summer calendar of cultural and entertainment events that crisscross the Romagna Riviera, contributing to enhance the appeal of the territory for tourism. Not surprisingly, in addition to the ministerial funds and the support of other regional and municipal public institutions, the festival is backed by a number of private and primarily local partners and a series of conventions and agreements with local hotels and accommodation facilities. This strong relationship with the local territory is also a result of the activity that the Santarcangelo dei Teatri association, which organizes the festival, carries out during the year. In fact, it manages Il Lavatoio, Santarcangelo's only theater, which is owned by the Municipality, and curates a program of performances, artistic residencies, workshops, and projects for schools.

← Stefano Ricci in *Madre* by Ermanna Montanari, directed by Marco Martinelli, Santarcangelo di Romagna, July 2021.

This continuous remodulation of the relationship with the audience, implemented by placing the acme of artistic radicalism in the middle of the Romagna summer, is perhaps one of the cornerstones of the festival's cultural project. Take, for example, one of the works that has most marked its course in recent years, namely *Azdora*. Conceived by the Swedish artist Markus Öhrn, *Azdora* is a project extended in time and space that combines black metal aesthetics and a crude investigation of the repressive mechanisms of bourgeois society, with the traditional figure of the "sfoglina" from Romagna. For about three years, a group of women from Romagna were involved "in a gothic ritual trajectory of liberation. Over a few years, these once devoted housewives became the hardened members of a collective, now even known abroad."

The festival's internationality, experimentation, imagination, projects related to sustainability, free outdoor events, DJ sets, and concerts attract the widest range of audience possible. Throughout the year, and significantly more so in July, when the festival is held, Santarcangelo is known worldwide as one of the gathering places for the contemporary performing arts community, where new artistic works are produced and new forms of interaction and cultural approach are explored. ❡

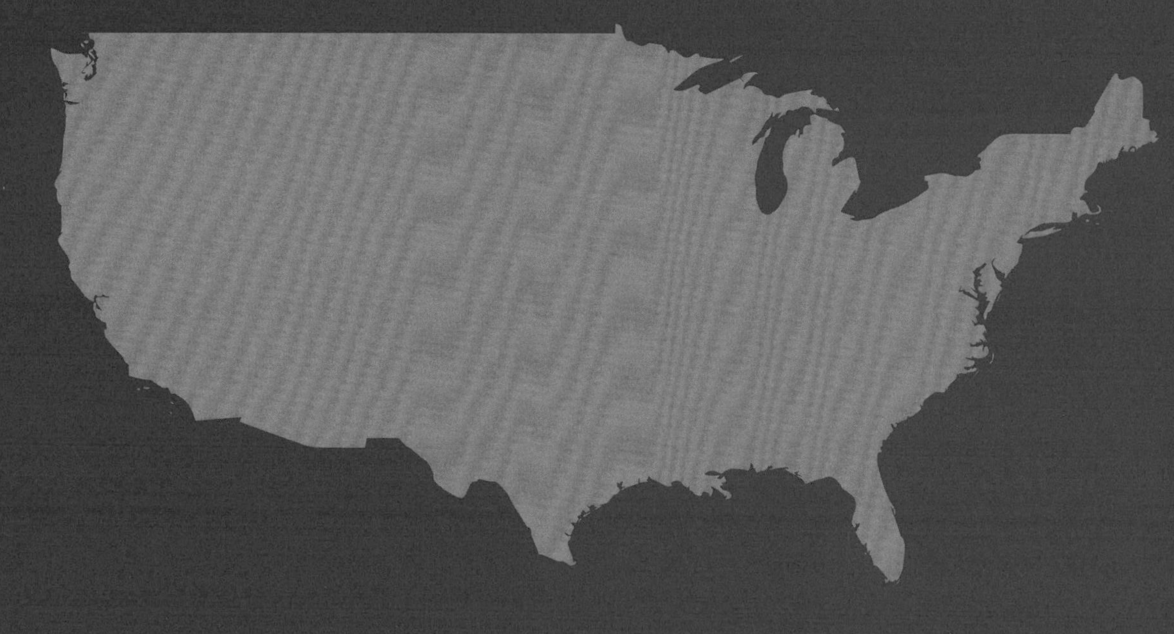

USA

GERMANY

ITALY

BELGIUM

COLOMBIA

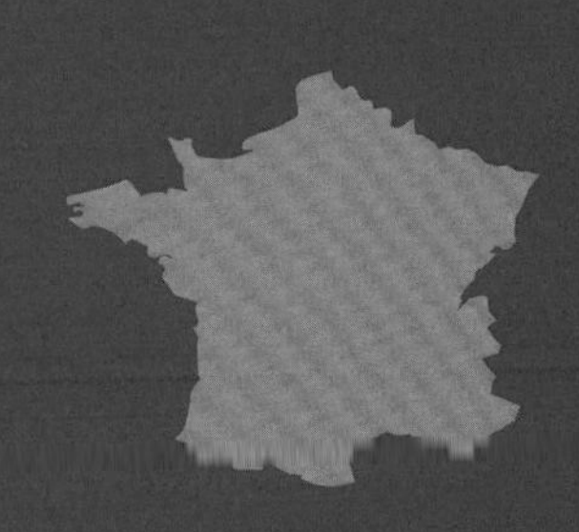

FRANCE

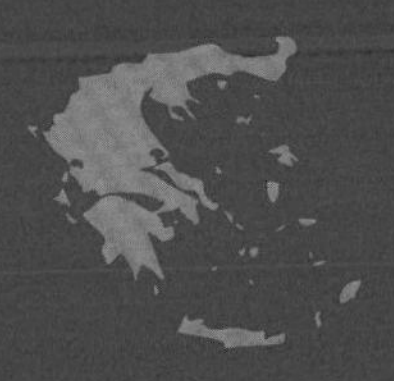

GREECE

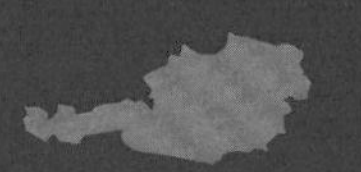

AUSTRIA

48° 51′ 40″ N 2° 20′ 27″ E

FESTIVAL D’AUTOMNE

PARIS / FRANCE

↓ Elsa Dorlin, *Travailler la violence #2*, Festival d’Automne, Paris, November 2022.

Created by Emile Guy in 1972, the Festival d’Automne is a multidisciplinary festival dedicated to contemporary performing arts. Theater, dance, music, and visual arts are the backbone of an itinerant festival that takes over Parisian performance venues between September and December each year. The festival is a completely open event for experimentation, free from any geographical limits, and is now a benchmark for avant-garde creation.

→

Théo Mercier, *OUTREMONDE The Sleeping Chapter*, La Conciergerie, Festival d'Automne, Paris, October 2022.

→→

Alice Ripoll, *Lavagem*, Festival d'Automne, Paris, October 2022.

4° 35′ 57″ N -74° 6′ 8″ E

IBERO-AMERICAN THEATER FESTIVAL

→ Danish company Teater Republique and British band The Tiger Lillies present *The Tiger Lillies Perform Hamlet*, Bogotá, March 2016.

BOGOTÁ / COLOMBIA

← A festivalgoer, 16th Ibero-American Theater Festival, Bogotá, March 2018.

The Ibero-American Theater Festival was born in 1988 thanks to Colombian actress Fanny Mikey, and every two years it takes over various performance venues in the Colombian capital. Theater, dance, and cabaret fill the two-week event that fosters a close and direct relationship with the audience by abandoning conventional theater venues and venturing into the city's neighborhoods and squares, creating closeness and proximity with the spectators.

37° 3′ 44″ N 15° 17′ 35″ E

ISTITUTO NAZIONALE DRAMMA ANTICO (INDA)

SYRACUSE / ITALY

The Istituto Nazionale Dramma Antico (INDA), an Italian foundation created in 1998 by an institute of the same name, has organized cycles of classical plays held in the Greek Theater in Syracuse since 1914. Born following an initiative of Count Mario Tommaso Gargallo and inaugurated with the staging of Aeschylus's *Agamemnon*, over the years INDA has become a worldwide institution and its program an international benchmark for classical theater.

↓ *Prometeo incatenato* by Eschilo, directed by Luca Ronconi, Palazzolo Acreide, May 2017.

BREGENZERFESTSPIELE.COM

47° 30′ 16″ N 9° 44′ 16″ E

BREGENZER FESTSPIELE

BREGENZ / AUSTRIA

↑
Madame Butterfly by Giacomo Puccini, Bregenz, July 2022.

The Bregenzer Festspiele is a festival dedicated to opera theater and classical music. Established in 1945, it is held on the shores of Lake Constance. Known for its floating stage, the Seebühne, and the spectacular lake settings, the festival takes place in various venues throughout the city of Bregenz: the Festspielhaus, the Kornmarkt, which stages rarely performed operas and operettas, and the Werkstattbühne, used for modern drama and contemporary musical theater performances.

51° 18′ 44″ N 9° 29′ 57″ E

DOCUMENTA

KASSEL / GERMANY

↓

Baan Noorg, *The Rituals of Things*, Fridericianum, Kassel, June 2022.

Documenta is a contemporary art festival created in 1955 by artist and curator Arnold Bode in Kassel, in the North Hesse region of Germany. It was inaugurated with the intention of placing Germany back at the center of European cultural discourse in the post–World War II period. To date, the festival—which runs every five years and lasts for 100 days—is a true benchmark for contemporary art in the world, outlining a cutting-edge snapshot of the trajectory art has taken in recent years

52° 29′ 55″ N 13° 19′ 43″ E

BERLINER FESTSPIELE

BERLIN / GERMANY

The Berliner Festspiele is an institution that each year hosts several festivals, exhibitions, and multidisciplinary events in two venues: the Haus der Berliner Festspiele and the Gropius Bau. The annual program of events focuses on contemporary cultural production and hosts major international artists. The festivals that are part of the Festspiele program are: MaerzMusik for contemporary music, Berliner Theatertreffen for theater, Musikfest Berlin for music in general, and Jazzfest Berlin for jazz music.

← *LOVETRAIN2020* by Emanuel Gat Dance, July 2023.

↓

Kateryna Ziabliuk performs at Berliner Festspiele, November 2022.

MANIFESTA

↓
Masbedo at Manifesta 12, Sala delle Capriate – Archivio di Stato di Palermo, 2018.

Manifesta is a biennial traveling exhibition dedicated to contemporary art. The first edition was held in 1999 in the city of Rotterdam with the aim of decentralizing contemporary art hubs. Focused on the reflection and study of the development and evolution of contemporary art, over the years Manifesta has chosen cities such as Pristina, Palermo, or Marseilles as its venues, emphasizing its quest to identify a new artistic geography.

45° 25′ 56″ N 12° 20′ 11″ E

BIENNALE DI VENEZIA

VENICE / ITALY

↓

Anne Imhof, *Faust*, German Pavilion, 57th Venice Biennale, 2017.

Initiated in 1895 thanks to a group of Venetian intellectuals who hoped to stimulate art and its market in the city, the Venice Biennale is one of the world's largest exhibitions of contemporary art and architecture. Alternating yearly, Biennale Arte and Biennale Architettura are held in the magnificent spaces of the Arsenale and Giardini in Venice. For more than a century now, the festival has presented major national and international artistic creations in its numerous pavilions, each reserved for a different nation.

50° 51′ 23″ N 4° 20′ 51″ E

KUNSTENFESTIVALDESARTS

BRUSSELS / BELGIUM

Born in 1994 from an idea of Frie Leysen and Guido Minne, the Kunstenfestivaldesarts focuses on theater, dance, film, and plastic arts. Closely linked to the city's urban structure, the festival not only presents major international art productions, it also offers an educational program, *Free School*, focusing on the sharing of and reflection on artistic practices.

← *Buster* by Romeo Castellucci, Brussels, May 2021.

↑ Lina Lapelytė, *What Happens with a Dead Fish*, Brussels, July 2021.

42° 44′ 9′′ N 12° 44′ 6′′ E

FESTIVAL OF THE TWO WORLDS

SPOLETO / ITALY

↓

The Old Woman by Daniil Kharms, directed by Robert Wilson, Spoleto, August 2013.

Inaugurated in 1958 with Giuseppe Verdi's *Macbeth* directed by Luchino Visconti, the Festival of the Two Worlds is a theater, music, dance, and performing arts festival created by the composer Gian Carlo Menotti. Every year the town of Spoleto hosts works from both the classical repertoire and avant-garde theater that dialogue with the city's historic theaters and the Piazza del Duomo, weaving a close relationship between the past, present, and future of the performing arts.

38° 7′ 7″ N 13° 22′ 14″ E

MORGANA FESTIVAL

PALERMO / ITALY

↑ Morgana Festival, organized by Museo internazionale delle marionette, Palermo, November 2022.

Established in the mid-1970s, the Morgana Festival is dedicated to the art of puppets and marionettes and is held annually in the streets of Palermo. During the festival, the entire city is transformed into a widespread theater in which the art of puppetry becomes the star. In addition to Sicilian and Mediterranean traditions, every year a multitude of international performers bring to life their artistic creations.

37° 58′ 27″ N 23° 42′ 37″ E

ATHENS EPIDAURUS FESTIVAL

ATHENS / GREECE

Founded thanks to the intervention of Minister Georgios Rallis in 1955, Athens Epidaurus is an annual festival dedicated to theater, dance, and music. It comes to life on the stages of two ancient Greek theaters, the Odeon of Herodes Atticus and the Ancient Theater of Epidaurus, offering each year the finest classical repertoire and experimental performance art, while encouraging the promotion of Greek artists on the international stage.

↓
Sir Peter Hall, *THE OEDIPUS PLAYS*, Royal National Theatre Production, Athens, September 1996.

40° 44′ 34′′ N -73° 59′ 35′′ E

PERFORMA

NEW YORK / USA

↓
Kia LaBeija, *Untitled - the Black Act*, New York, November 2019.

Performa is a performance art festival held once every two years in various New York locations and institutions. Founded in 2004 by curator and art historian RoseLee Goldberg, Performa aims to showcase the development of live art in all forms and through different cultural perspectives. To date, the festival is in its tenth year and fuels reflection both locally and globally by experimenting with new directions for performance practices.

4

MUSIC FESTIVALS

MUSIC FESTIVALS

The most emblematic of festivals in the collective imagination is probably the music festival, which we deal with in the last chapter of this volume. Large gatherings of people united by a common passion, ready to wait in endless lines to find their way among crowds of bodies, ready to vibrate in unison the moment the music begins. The music festival is a concentration of emotionality and sharing, able to crystallize the idea of community into something physically concrete and, therefore, performative. In the United States, modern music festivals grew along the model of the Woodstock Music & Art Fair, commonly known as Woodstock, held in 1969 in New York State. Although it was not the first such event (it was preceded by the Monterey Pop Festival), Woodstock holds a mythical place in the history of American—and world—pop culture. More than 150,000 tickets were sold, but half a million people came to the festival grounds. Tickets for the three-day event cost $18 in advance and $24 at the gate (equivalent to about $120 and $160 today). Woodstock, however, is commonly known as the "free festival," as the fences were never completed and people could attend freely. Initially planned to last only three days, the festival eventually lasted for four days, with shows held at all hours of the day and night.

Since then, the communal, revolutionary, and anarchic spirit of festivals has become the fuel that keeps huge money machines running, giving rise to a mainstream business that reaps profits and embraces countless corporate sponsorships. In Europe, Barcelona's Sónar Festival and Belgium's Tomorrowland demonstrate how music festivals affect industries across the board, from retail to tourism, and the region in general. Positioned at the intersection of visual arts, technology, and electronic music, Sónar has transformed the city's dynamism and atmosphere every summer since 1994, positioning Barcelona as the continental epicenter of electronic music and one of its main attractions in cultural tourism since its early years. The Barcelona City Council calculated that in 2015 Sónar's contribution to the GDP was 124.8 million euros, generating 1,200 jobs. In 2016, together with Sónar+D (a series of conferences on creativity and technology), the festival drew in 115,550 visitors from 104 different countries. According to *Billboard*, in 2014 more than 32 million people attended a festival in the United States. Coachella, one of the country's most popular festivals, grossed $114.6 million in 2017, setting an important record for the first recurring festival franchise to have a turnover of more than $100 million.

In the course of this chapter, we will explore different types of festivals: the larger, "mainstream" ones, which contribute to the creation or global affirmation of certain styles, imagery, and cultural phenomena, forging a significant relationship with what is happening in urban subcultures; and those directed toward a select audience of enthusiasts, looking at the quality of music production, especially of more cultured or traditional genres. Looking into each of these festivals will bring us into contact with the changing demands of society, touching on decisive contemporary issues such as the environmental impact these major events entail, or the inclusiveness of artists and audiences with respect to disability, gender identity, or cultural belonging.

The music festivals we are going to describe will give us insight into the current relationship that links cultural production to the market, as well as the ways in which marketing and communication are structured in a historical moment where most forms of life are essentially determined by these factors. Passion for a certain genre of music seems to increasingly imply adherence to a specific way of being, which involves a certain imagery, a certain way of dressing, a certain way of interacting socially, both live and online, and even a certain style of eating. Companies have long understood how to intercept these trends, but thanks to the advent of social media and their capacity of profiling users, they are now not only able to predict our behavior but also to direct this in increasingly effective and profound ways. The major mainstream festivals we will explore reveal how the collective dimension that audiences experience are closely linked with profit and the mechanisms needed to produce it today.

It is no coincidence that we end our partial journey into the universe of the performative in an ideal place where we approach the threshold of what separates and yet simultaneously binds together the domain of art and that of entertainment, social gathering, ritual, and collective debate. Here the artistic language—in this case, music—is certainly fundamental, but it becomes, above all, the trigger for something to do with ritual, with the creation of multiple subjectivities, with belonging to and recognizing oneself within a specific social sphere. Through these great windows of contemporary society, we can thus observe how performativity that characterizes the artistic dimension multiplies into a myriad of forms of human expression and sociality, affecting the individuals as such. Their desires, values, and idiosyncrasies are translated into discourse the moment they relate to others, rather like tools, objects, and actions that transform this space and all those who pass through it. Our analysis stops here, because to continue, we would need to map all forms of human aggregation, trespassing into the universes of sociology, psychology, anthropology, and politics. It will suffice for us to give a partial insight into that transitional zone in which performance exits the ordinary and the routine to become art.

→→
Crowd at Glastonbury Festival, Pilton village, UK, June 1986.

GLASTONBURY FESTIVAL OF CONTEMPORARY PERFORMING ARTS

— *England's gathering*

GLASTONBURYFESTIVALS.CO.UK

↑ Glastonbury Festival, June 2022.

Over 360 hectares of grounds, more than 20 stages and thematic areas, about 200 musicians and bands encompassing the best-known names in world pop and rock, and 250,000 bodies and souls experience what will perhaps be the most intense five days of their lives. We are at Glastonbury in Somerset, an English county characterized by rolling, picturesque green hills, remnants of medieval towers, and pastures. This is the setting for Worthy Farm, a vast dairy farm that has hosted one of the world's most important music festivals since 1970.

The Glastonbury Festival of Contemporary Performing Arts (the official name of what is better known as the Glastonbury Festival, or, for loyal visitors, simply Glasto) has gone through many phases in its life, changing names and ways to find enjoyment, and helping shape the evolution of pop music from the 1970s to the present. It is a veritable city of music and the arts, rising from almost nothing every year, and where, around the summer solstice, spectators take the place of placid dairy cows. The city then becomes equipped with solar panels, its own waste recycling center, bars, restaurants, shops selling sustainable products, and drinking water stations.

The origin of the Glastonbury Festival can be traced to the hippie movement that created a stir in the United States and Europe through the late 1960s and '70s, spreading values such as community life, pacifism, and love. A counterculture in which music and sociality—combined with the use of soft and psychedelic drugs—were the two fundamental pillars on which the experience of its followers was built. Indeed, we owe these alternative and subcultural movements , which are some of the most significant musical gatherings and collective events in recent history. The symbolic significance of these happenings, as well as the memories of those who participated in them, left their marks on the collective imagination and the evolution of tastes, musical and artistic genres, popular customs and habits. We mentioned Woodstock at the beginning, but actually many of the festivals we will deal with highlight a specific cultural mechanism, namely the transmission of ideas, concepts, aesthetic traits, and stylistic features among diverse strata of society. Initially, these musical festivals were perceived as innovative on the horizon of artistic or cultural landscapes, but over time they started to creep into the interstices of society and reach social contexts very different from where they originated thanks to a porous, permeable, and non-unequivocal mechanism of transmission and exchange between the underground and mainstream—something that has become more radicalized in recent decades through the impact of the Internet and social media.

pp. → 318 | 319

Glastonbury is no exception. From a small, self-managed festival organized by the Worthy Farm owner's son on his own grounds, mostly free and aimed at an "alternative" audience, involving musicians unknown to most (such as a very young David Bowie at the beginning of his career), it has become a mass event attended by thousands, broadcast by the BBC, and capable of generating a turnover on a par with that of a multinational corporation. The stage hosts world-famous names, from Billie Eilish to Kylie Minogue, from The Cure to The Chemical Brothers, Oasis, The Smiths, Velvet Underground, Radiohead, Robbie Williams, The Rolling Stones, Jay-Z, Adele, and many others.

After nearly 50 festivals, Glastonbury is an event that has entered the annals of history, one of the most important stages in the international pop scene, the place where young, up-and-coming bands and independent musicians make themselves known to the general public to then climb the charts. A place where the festival community comes together to celebrate a great collective ritual officiated around music. Glastonbury is also one of the settings where British pop culture, so rich in musical subcultures, is best expressed. Between the Sunday roast, beer, psychedelic drugs, green meadows, and the ever-rainy weather, some of the bands that have marked the British popular imagination, such as Oasis, The Cure, Pet Shop Boys, Coldplay, and others have performed. This is also the place where one of the icons of British punk, Joe Strummer, lead singer and guitarist of The Clash, returned each year to animate the legendary nightly bonfires, around which political and social issues were discussed and music played, as told in the documentary film *Joe Strummer: The Future Is Unwritten* by Julien Temple.

MILK AND FREEDOM

Back in the early 1900s, the town of Glastonbury was already known to English bohemians and lovers of the arts and music. It was here that in 1914 the opera composer Rutland Boughton founded a summer music school and festival along the model of Bayreuth, the German city chosen by Wagner as the venue to perform his operas, one of the earliest examples of festivals similar to those of today. The Glastonbury Festival presented works by contemporary composers until 1926, helping to build an image of a town associated with contemporary music and culture. Interestingly, the history of that first Glastonbury Festival was marked by misfortunes and historical events that, as we shall see, will also recur to a lesser extent in the turbulent history of the contemporary festival. The first festival was hampered by the outbreak of World War I, but Boughton decided to go ahead anyway. Instead of an orchestra, he used a grand piano, and in place of the theater, he used the local Assembly Rooms, which would remain the central performing space until 1926, when Boughton's backing of the miners' riots marked the end of the support he had received from Glastonbury's citizens, which brought an end to the festival.

About 50 years later, upon his father's death, Michael Eavis inherited the family farm of 150 acres and 60 cows, and in 1970 decided to start a festival there. He followed in the footsteps of the Bath Blues Festival, an alternative rock and progressive music event held in Somerset, where Led Zeppelin, Jefferson Airplane, and Frank Zappa had performed, among others. With the help of his wife, the first Glastonbury Festival (which in this first year was called the Pilton Pop, Blues & Folk Festival) was held in September 1970 and welcomed 1,500 people who paid £1 sterling for a ticket that included milk from his cows, a space to camp, and concerts by Marc Bolan, The Kinks, and seven other rock and blues bands. In *The Guardian* of May 23, 2021, *FRoots* magazine editor and folk singer Ian Anderson recalls the Pilton festival fondly:

> [It was] nicely ramshackle, not many people, Afghan coats, loon pants, minimal security . . . very simple, amateurish, in the nicest sense, and hospitable. A few bemused-looking bikers, the odd burger van, lots of grass—the green sort, and the other kind!

The 1971 festival was decisive in several respects. In fact, the festival was brought forward to June, close to the summer solstice—a period that would later become the tradition for Glasto. The first version of the famous Pyramid Stage, the iconic structure resembling a pyramid, was then built and would become one of the symbols of the festival, rebuilt as a permanent structure in the 1980s. In winter it was a hayloft and barn, in summer a legendary stage for world-famous pop and rock stars. Also in 1971, the Pyramid Stage welcomed a young and little-known David Bowie, helping to launch what would become an unparalleled artistic career.

Throughout the 1970s, the Glastonbury Festival was held intermittently as an informal and spontaneous event, to become an annual fixture (with occasional years of inactivity) only during the 1980s. In 1981, for the first time, it promoted a major humanitarian cause. Indeed, that year the festival was entirely dedicated to the campaign for nuclear disarmament, so much so that the logo was also reproduced on the poster and proceedings were donated to the sponsoring committee. In addition to the charitable aspect, the 1980s saw the festival's metamorphosis from an

→→
A man has his face decorated, Worthy Farm, Glastonbury Festival, June 2022.

independent, semi-spontaneous event to a mass event of international significance. This was when Glastonbury began to come to terms with its size and the necessity to regulate its entrances more tightly in order to meet national security standards. The issue of managing the number of spectators and activating systems to prevent access to the ticketless public would accompany the entire history of the festival, together with the consequences of bad weather and ground conditions. Several festivals were beset by bad weather and heavy rains, which turned the entire site into an expanse of mud (and not only, since prior to the festival the land was used for grazing dairy cattle!). This was the case in 1985, when Eavis decided to purchase the land of the nearby Cockmill Farm to increase the area available for the public.

In 1985, something happened about 50 miles from Glastonbury that foresaw another event that would take place five years later at the festival. For several years, the annual gathering of the New Age Travelers had been held at nearby Stonehenge, an iconic archaeological site in England. The New Age Travelers—also called New Travelers or simply Travelers—was an alternative community that emerged in the 1980s in the United Kingdom. Founded on New Age principles and heir to the hippie movement of the 1960s, the Travelers crisscrossed the country moving from festival to festival, rejecting the rigidities of bourgeois society and choosing to live collectively and nomadically. In the 1990s, the phenomenon became intertwined with that of illegal raves to such an extent that repressive actions were taken. Indeed, in 1985 there had already been a violent outburst known as the "Battle of the Beanfield." In their attempt to prevent an illegal gathering from taking place at Stonehenge, the police charged and arrested participants in what was the largest mass arrest since World War II at that time. Although these caravans did not have a good reputation in British public opinion, in the wake of Glasto's hippie origins, Eavis decided to give hospitality to the Travelers driven out of Stonehenge, allowing them to camp next to the festival area and start their own self-managed festival. In Eavis's words, "I put them in the field next door and they ran their own thing, with their own music. And it was free, even though I was doing a paying event on my farm. You had all these lovely posh girls from Hampstead coming down, and they all ploughed off to the hippie festival next door . . . I quite enjoyed the hippies' music and they did make me laugh."

The Travelers' "off" festival considerably increased the numbers as well as the level of anarchy, and the same situation repeated with each festival. The twentieth anniversary of the festival in 1990 was decisive in the complicated dynamics of audience management, as well as in the history of underground movements, and affected the direction of the festival's development. In addition to the Travelers, the 1990s were also the years of illegal raves and of tribes traveling from place to place autonomously, setting up sound systems and gathering their followers in the thousands. This extensive cultural phenomenon characterized the spirit of the times, reviving and updating the hippie and underground tradition, the very same one that had given birth to Glastonbury. The exponential growth in popularity of the festival, which each year sold more tickets, hosted more spectators, and invited more prestigious artists, implied an improvement in organization and logistics. This caused conflict with part of its public, which continued to consider the festival as something totally anarchic and free. Tension erupted at the end of the 1990 festival in what became known as the "Battle of Yeoman's Bridge," a full-blown guerrilla battle that broke out between the police and the community of Travelers, ravers, and hippies who camped around

↓ Hippies celebrate the summer solstice, Glastonbury Festival, June 1971.

the festival grounds each year. The uproar broke out on Monday, just after the festival had finished. Unlike at Stonehenge five years earlier, the police were forced to stand down, but the consequence of it all was that the following year's festival was canceled; furthermore, in 1992, security regulations became stricter and fencing was erected.

There are two reasons 1990 was a year of transition: first, the festival changed its name, taking on the current one of Glastonbury Festival of Contemporary Performing Arts; second, it was the last festival in which proceeds were donated to the Committee for Nuclear Disarmament. The world was transforming. With the fall of the Berlin Wall, nuclear threat was no longer on the agenda, while new humanitarian issues, such as poverty in African and Asian countries, and environmental conservation, were taking center stage. In the 1990s, the festival consolidated its role as a massive and politically engaged world event, actively collaborating with organizations such as Oxfam, Greenpeace, and WaterAid. This trajectory would be developed further by Emily Eavis, Michael's youngest daughter. Similarly, the resonance of the festival at the musical and artistic level also took on a more definitive form. These were the years of memorable performances by groups such as Oasis, Pulp, PJ Harvey, Jeff Buckley, and The Cure. In addition, programming began to give space not only to rock, pop, and indie but to the new genres that were emerging on the music scene, namely electronic and techno music. A dedicated area of the festival was inaugurated with performances by artists such as Massive Attack and Carl Cox. Proof of the popularity that Glastonbury had achieved was that in 1994 it began to be televised by Channel 4, and then from 1997 by the BBC.

Since 1992, the festival has been held every year, except for one year every five, when a festival is skipped. These are the "fallow" or "off" years when the terrain—and the local community—can recover. Today, the Glastonbury Festival is one of the largest and most important in the world in terms of lineup, attendance numbers, and revenue. It has grown from 1,500 visitors in the first year in 1970 to about 203,500 in 2019, and today, it is committed to experimenting with innovative models, such as the abolition of the use of plastic on-site.

BEYOND CONTRADICTIONS — Music has always been an important part of my life . . . I'd rigged up a very primitive sound system to play music to myself and the cows . . . It was a nine-foot-long pipe connected to a speaker and it made a hell of a sound. I used to play *Lola* by the Kinks a lot—that was our big milking song. One day in 1970, our baker lady who used to deliver bread to the farm arrived late. She told me it was because she'd been held up in all the traffic going to the Blues festival. I had no idea what she was talking about. She told me it was this big event happening at the Bath & West Showground, a few miles from the farmhouse . . . Jean and I agreed that we should go there on the Sunday, after chapel, and it was absolutely incredible. They had Led Zeppelin and Moody Blues and all these West Coast American bands. It was the whole flower-power era, and all the girls and blokes looked amazing. It was a very lovey-dovey affair, and emotional, too. I'd never seen anything like it before—it just hit me for six. We were watching Moody Blues, who were playing *Question*, which is a belter of a song, and I turned to Jean and said, 'I'm going to do one of these on the farm!' (*The Guardian*, June 26, 2020).

These words are by Michael Eavis, discussing his book that celebrates Glastonbury's 50 years, written with his daughter and festival co-organizer Emily Eavis. Therefore, we owe the world's largest outdoor festival of music and performing arts simply to the founder's desire to repeat one of his most intense experiences and to recreate this for others. The spontaneous, family-run nature of the festival still remains one of its defining characteristics, even though it is now a multimillion-pound event, and this is not the only contradiction that one might notice. We will see later that the festival seems to live in a delicate balance between opposing forces, managing so far to reconcile what might seem to be irresolvable contradictions. We could summarize these by citing the relationship between inclusiveness, spontaneity, sense of belonging, and the mass dimension of the event; the risk of staging a large-scale event highly dependent on variables such as weather; attention to social and humanitarian issues; experimentation with innovative models and best practices; and then the impact on the region from both an environmental and social perspective.

While in the previous chapters we described several examples of enterprises straddling the public and private sectors, here we are dealing with a completely private organization. More precisely, there are two private companies, Glastonbury Festivals Limited (GFL) and Glastonbury Festival Events Limited (GFEL), that are responsible for the festival and are able to generate sufficient profits not only to meet the costs of each festival—about £40 million pounds, including artist and guest fees, staff fees, staging, communication, logistics, and so on—but also a substantial sum donated to charity each year: in 2019, about £3 million pounds were donated to Oxfam, WaterAid, and Greenpeace as well as thousands of local charities and projects.

We have seen how the growth of the festival has involved tighter regulations and increasingly strict access control, as well as the exponential increase in the cost of tickets. The area on which the festival is held—now so much larger than Worthy Farm with as many as 21 other property owners letting out their own land during the festival—is bordered by an eight-mile-long, 20-foot-high barrier that includes two lines of fencing, specifically to prevent squatters from unauthorized entry to the area. Tickets that now cost about £240 usually sell out less than an hour after going on sale. In short, the festival is a huge money-making machine that generates an equally large economic payoff since it also involves shops, markets, bars, and restaurants. Despite the revenue that Glastonbury is able to generate, the second contradiction it faces every year is unpredictability: bad weather, first and foremost, but also accidents and global events. More mundanely, the festival has to factor in rapid changes in musical trends and increasing numbers of competing events catering for specific or evolving tastes; all of this can jeopardize the success of the festival, which needs high audience participation in order to make a profit.

Despite its size and need to generate profit, Glastonbury remains strongly attached to specific ethical and political principles. Its "activist" nature is seen not only in the charitable actions or collaboration with humanitarian organizations, large and small, but also in its focus on issues such as inclusiveness, environmental footprint, and the respect of workers' rights, which the Eavis father and daughter have translated into innovative initiatives and best practices. From some statements published on the official Glastonbury website we can infer the attention that the organization pays to such matters. We find an "Anti-Slavery Statement," giving an account of how workers are hired, and the practices in place to ensure acceptable working conditions; or a "Diversity Statement," acknowledging the need to monitor and do more to be inclusionary on the basis of race, gender, disability, sexual orientation, religion, age, and social class, and expressing the willingness to increase accessibility and transversality in the festival.

Among the various documents available on the official Glastonbury website there is also an "Ecological Policy" page, perhaps the issue for which Glastonbury invests most through its innovative tools and best practices. Glastonbury's priority over the years has always been to become a "green" festival while facing the complex

task of staging a massive event in a rural area lacking adequate services and infrastructure to accommodate large numbers of people for such an energy-intensive activity.

Glastonbury's focus on environmental issues and the climate crisis is implemented through two distinct approaches. On the one hand, it has adopted a policy of reducing environmental impact through specific actions; on the other, it seeks to become a platform for practical and theoretical elaboration, a sounding board for environmentalist discourses. It is sufficient to say that, in 2019, the guest speakers included David Attenborough, the celebrated British scientist and naturalist, a well-known personality in the world of nature documentaries, and the environmental collective Extinction Rebellion.

In addition to an area—The Green Fields—dedicated entirely to environmental issues and powered by wind and solar energy, a program of environmentally related issues is organized.

↓ Festivalgoers walk at the Unfairground during the Glastonbury Festival, June 2022.

Furthermore, the festival also does several things to reduce its environmental impact: the installation of thousands of recycling bins and the total elimination of plastic by providing water dispensers and reusable cups, a wide range of biodegradable products (from tableware to glitter) and recycled materials; the use and sale of zero-mile, organic and fair-trade foods; as well as continuous efforts to increase public awareness. In line with the festival motto, "Love the Farm, Leave No Trace," all spectators entering the festival area must sign a "Green Pledge" in which they agree to fulfill a series of actions, including not urinating on the green areas of the farm, which when the festival ends revert to pastureland. Furthermore, no plastic or disposable containers are used and only locally sourced wood is used for campfires.

Images of recently concluded festivals are well-known, with the area looking like a sort of open-air trash site when the public leaves. Cleanup operations on the farm and the neighboring fields where the festival is held take weeks each year and involve about 400 people, not to mention the waters of the surrounding rivers that are often contaminated by chemicals, drug residues, sewage, and other materials. The soil itself undergoes considerable erosion, suffering the weight and footsteps of tens of thousands of people over a very few days, which is why the festival skips a year once every five years. It is important to remember that Eavis is first and foremost a dairy farmer who manages a fully working farm. Most of the year, Worthy Farm is home to about 500 dairy cows, most of which are moved during the festival to allow them to graze free from disturbance. Despite some fines received for contamination, Eavis said that the grass grows back fairly quickly after reseeding, and during the fallow year when there is no festival, the cattle can graze year-round.

To further limit environmental impact and ease the burden on local waste-disposal facilities—with quantities that in three days reach that of an entire city—Glastonbury Festival has its own recycling center where waste is manually disposed of by hundreds of volunteers and festival staff, thus achieving high percentages of recycled and composted waste. Autonomy and sustainability seem to be the organizers' choice for energy consumption: 1,500 square meters of solar panels have been installed at Worthy Farm, while biofuels are used to power the stage generators. Like other similar major events,

↑
Kendrick Lamar performs on the Pyramid Stage, Glastonbury Festival, June 2022.

the environmental impact of a festival of this magnitude must be weighed against the capacity of the land to withstand such stress. In this sense, Glastonbury's location is rather peculiar. The site is sufficiently isolated and sparsely populated and there is no lack of space, but it is surrounded by small towns (Glastonbury has about 10,000 inhabitants, corresponding to 4 percent of the festival's total audience) and therefore, the roads and accommodation facilities are unsuitable to accommodate such massive numbers.

Reflection on environmental sustainability and the impact such events have on the territories in which they take place is a vast and complex issue that affects music festivals as well as other cultural and entertainment events—an issue that urgently needs to be addressed at all levels. By virtue of its political vocation and ethical sensibility, partly a legacy from the hippie culture in which it was born in the 1970s, Glastonbury Festival has the merit of being one of the first major events to pose these questions and provide actions that are feasible and replicable elsewhere. For Glastonbury, this involves achieving concrete goals in waste reduction, recycling, the use of renewable energy, as well as the dissemination of a culture of respect and care for the environment.

CREATING THE CONTEMPORARY — It is like going to another country . . . Coming to Glastonbury involves a fair amount of travel, and probably a queue to get in but, when you get past these impediments, you enter a huge tented city, a mini-state under canvas. British law still applies, but the rules of society are a bit different, a little bit freer. Everyone is here to have a wild time in their own way.

These lines from the *Introduction to Glastonbury* section on the festival's official website confirm that one of the main characteristics of Glastonbury is its ability to build a community, creating a hub where people of different generations and cultural backgrounds spend three or four days immersed in a collective dimension where music, sharing, and fun are the common traits.

The musical programming, now quite different since the first years, has gradually become increasingly diverse, including not only big stars but also emerging artists, thus offering an eclectic array of events to satisfy different audiences.

There is no escaping a certain "British" flavor in the lineup of the various festivals. From the 1960s onward, the UK has been a veritable hotbed of musical trends and subcultures, with various musical genres connected to aesthetics, reference imagery, and fashions that spread into groups of young people to become actual community lifestyles, with their own fetishes or quirks (certain clothing brands, accessories, etc.) and rituals (from specific venues to dance styles). Cities like London, Manchester, and Liverpool were endlessly churning out music bands, first the Mods, then Punk and Rocker, the New Romantics in the 1980s, the Spiral Tribe in the 1990s, and so on. Although involving mainly younger generations, music and subcultural styles are still a defining feature of British pop culture at the moment. Since its first edition, Glastonbury Festival seems to have been able to seize on these movements and act as a sounding board for the subcultures of the time, coinciding with and defining communities, and in so doing, helping to affirm their existence and spread their values globally.

The "headlining" band of the first Glastonbury Festival in 1970 (at that time still Pilton Pop, Blues & Folk Festival) was T. Rex by Marc Bolan, considered to be the founder of Glam Rock, an extremely popular musical genre in the UK and widespread among the different strata of British society. Then, the "second" edition of Glasto in 1971 hosted David Bowie, just when his name was starting to be heard in the world pop and rock scene, and before he entered the pantheon of music stars. Another significant example is the 1995 festival, which helped establish Brit Pop as the genre of the moment thanks to Oasis's performance, which went down in history as one of the band's most important; but it also launched Pulp, an alternative band from Sheffield destined to become one of the icons of Indie Rock. By studying the changing lineups at Glastonbury and comparing them with the evolution of international music and pop culture, we note two specific trends: first, the dominant role that UK-branded music production, and its related aesthetics, have played in recent decades, setting the standard and influencing trends around the world; second, the gradual homogenization and paradoxical fragmentation of the cultural landscape in the last few years when the dynamics between underground and mainstream has become completely blurred. This has created a decidedly complex and diverse scenario in which styles multiply at an increasingly rapid pace and the distance between pop icons and emerging forms of expression is gradually shrinking.

If until the early 2000s Glastonbury maintained a certain image linked to Indie music, in recent years the festival's lineup has definitely shifted toward pop, R&B, electronic, or more popular and generalist styles by hosting the biggest stars in the industry: from Shakira to Beyoncé, Kylie Minogue to Jay-Z, and the rising stars of today such as Billie Eilish or Charli XCX. Despite its size, the festival is still very diverse, with the participation of many musicians of different genres and from diverse artistic backgrounds. Thus, the strongest names attract a wide audience who also have the opportunity to discover or learn more about lesser-known artists.

While Glastonbury is certainly famous for music, there are regular performances of comedy, dance, theater, and circus. These activities are gathered under the title of the Glastonbury Festival of Contemporary Performing Arts, emphasizing the multidisciplinary and performative nature of the event. Indeed, the festival space is divided into stages and pavilions that are autonomous in terms of programming and operation: Shangri-La, where the late-night parties are concentrated, Silver Hayes, which features a program of dance, drum b bass, garage, Afrobeat, hip-hop, bass, neo soul, and jazz; Kidzfield, intended for children; Babylon Uprising, dedicated to reggae and dancehall music; Theatre and Circus, an area designated for theatrical and circus performances; Pilton Palace Cinema, the "cinema corner" of the festival with screenings of various film genres.

Born as a spontaneous gathering, today Glastonbury accommodates all types of audiences and needs that may arise during the marathon that the festival has turned out to be. In this sense, it resembles a contemporary city-world: varied, multifaceted, inclusive, and most certainly expensive. It is a place to always respectfully practice coexistence and the utopia of a community based on pleasure and the sharing of passions. It is an event that, to continue attracting the most effervescent trends in pop culture, has had to multiply internally, perhaps making compromises with the mainstream but continuing to ensure an authentic and unique experience for those who choose to attend. ❡

TOMORROWLAND

TOMORROWLAND.COM

— A twenty-million-euro fairy-tale

↑

The Reflection of Love, 16th Tomorrowland festival, July 2022.

Leaving behind the mud, ramshackle tents, and Cockney accents of the Glastonbury Festival attendees, we now immerse ourselves in an atmosphere of colorful confetti and sequins, lights, fireworks, water fountains, impressive fairy-tale sets, and over 17 stages ready to host more than 1,000 DJs. Very aptly, the name of the place is Boom, a Belgian municipality of 17,166 inhabitants in Flanders, midway between Antwerp and Brussels—more specifically, inside the De Schorre Park, a green area that was originally a clay quarry. The site was purchased in the 1980s by the Boom Municipality and the Provincial Authority, which transformed it into a recreational park for various outdoor activities such as walking, climbing, and many other sports, as well as a venue for events large and small. Since 2005, initially once a year, then twice (and even three times in 2022), the park has been transformed into that magical place better known to electronic music fans worldwide as Tomorrowland.

If pop music takes the center stage at Glastonbury, Tomorrowland is entirely dedicated to EBM (Electronic Body Music), or simply electronic music, with great DJs such as David Guetta, Steve Aoki, and Tiësto and different musical genres, many of which are excellently represented in the lineup of what has been described as the best music festival in the world.

Founded by the two brothers, Manu and Michiel Beers (again, an apt name) during their college days in 2005, it was a place to throw parties and invent new formats. Working with ID&T, a Dutch company that has been organizing music events and festivals since 1990, they launched Tomorrowland, the Belgian answer to the cult festival Mysteryland, established by ID&T in 1992 and held on the outskirts of Amsterdam.

Among the spearheads of the European summer festival season (but here the term European seems far too reductive), Tomorrowland takes place annually in Boom on one or two weekends in late July. Since 2013, it has spawned a series of international spin-offs: TomorrowWorld in the United States (until 2015), Tomorrowland Brasil (in 2015 and 2016), and a winter edition in Alpe d'Huez, France, since 2019.

If compared to Glastonbury, Tomorrowland seems to belong to a different era, although chronologically they are not so distant: indeed, the inspiration here is less close to the 1960s and 1970s counterculture model and more related to the Central European club culture of the 1990s, not without a touch of a certain business-oriented hedonism typical of capitalism of that time.

→→
The Reflection of Love, 16th Tomorrowland festival, July 2022.

Its numbers seem in a different range with respect to Glastonbury and are almost unrivaled in the world. While the first festival had about 10,000

spectators, today about two million people try to get hold of one of the approximately 200,000 tickets available per weekend. In 2019, tickets sold out within 45 minutes. As pointed out by *Forbes*, "only Glastonbury sold out quicker, in 36 minutes, but that festival hosted 'only' 267,000 attendees." Even on social media, Tomorrowland reaches unparalleled numbers: 14.7 million followers, compared to Coachella's 2.7, 210,000 live-stream views, and more than 718 million impressions.

Tomorrowland's strength, besides the quality and breadth of its lineup, is undoubtedly due to the powerful identity it has created based on specific imagery and aesthetics, with the fairy-like setting serving as the common denominator of the general concept: an oneiric world detached from reality, in which "the people of tomorrow" can find themselves immersed in an extraordinary experience, a fairy-tale-like utopia in which the ordinary is suspended.

While Glastonbury lives on the myth of an experience in which authenticity, spontaneity, freedom, and sharing are at the center of a vision where the mud, dirt, and even small recklessness represent a concept of alternative living and the sense of community that the festival generates, Tomorrowland depicts an atmosphere that operates on a completely different plane. Acting as a living (and therefore performative) brand, everything in Tomorrowland hints at sunshine, beauty, dream, and wonder. Participating in Tomorrowland is to enter a parallel world, an impeccably organized and staged space where a multitude of people have the opportunity to feel they belong to a certain magic, united under the motto PLUR (Peace, Love, Unity, Respect).

THE PARTY BUSINESS

Brothers Manu and Michiel Beers from Antwerp were studying at university in the early 2000s and loved to throw parties all the time and invent ever-changing formats, such as "Antwerp Is Burning," one of the best-known among young people in town: it was a diffuse party spread across five different venues with a single ticket, and ran from 2000 to 2004. Later, their work spawned festivals and other similar events and was eventually taken over by ID&T. Building on their experience in the Antwerp clubbing scene and the success of their formats, the two brothers decided to discontinue their studies and devote themselves entirely to the events company they had just established. In 2003, they came up with the idea of launching an electronic music

festival; looking to the Netherlands to orient themselves in the complex universe of stage sets, light design, and sound systems, they found the inspiration "that permitted Tomorrowland to take off." So, when they approached ID&T in 2004, the company thought their idea was excellent and decided to buy 50 percent of the festival shares. This joint venture enabled the first edition of Tomorrowland to take place in 2005 in Boom, a city transformed for one day, August 14, into the setting of a fairy-tale. The lineup of the first festival was that of a first-rate electronic event, including the big names of the period: Sven Väth, Sasha, Armin van Buuren, Justice, and Erol Alkan. There were 10,000 attendees who reached Boom and participated in the birth of what would become a major musical and commercial project.

By word of mouth, news of the festival spread throughout Belgium and the audience increased dramatically. The next year, the setup included eight stages and enough space to accommodate an additional 15,000 visitors; a camping area that could hold 3,000 attendees was also created. The year 2007 marked an important moment of transition: for the first time, the festival was held over two days, welcoming about 20,000 spectators from the Netherlands, France, Germany, and the United Kingdom.

↓
Tomorrowland Winter, a magical experience in Alpe d'Huez, France, March 2022.

The real turning point in the festival's history, however, was the year 2008, when as many as 50,000 spectators (including 15,000 campers) reached Tomorrowland: a true record for a Belgian festival. The first sold-out event took place in 2009; this would be commonplace for subsequent festivals—the main hurdle for potential attendees being to beat the rush for tickets. The importance of sets and staging became even more central when the goal was to make the festival experience increasingly immersive and engaging: in 2010, Dreamville was inaugurated, an area designated for camping but also for daily life within the festival, with bars, restaurants, and stores.

In 2011, the festival received more than two million requests, so the organizers decided to add a third day. In less than 24 hours, 180,000 tickets were sold. In 2012, Tomorrowland was awarded the Dance Music Award for Best Music Event, becoming a festival of global resonance and beginning to stream DJ sets, interviews, and behind-the-scenes footage online, thus increasing the visibility of its program. In 2012, ticket sales were opened to Belgian citizens first, and only later to the rest of the world. In 2013, more than 200 nationalities were registered among the festival attendees, in part due to the "Global Journeys," travel packages that Tomorrowland introduced for its visitors. Starting in 2017, the organizers added a second weekend, thus expanding the capacity and reaching 400,000 spectators, eventually leading up to the 2019 edition, which involved more than 1,000 artists on 18 stages spread over a huge 90-plus-acre ground. In reference to that edition, *Forbes* (September 6, 2019) questioned: "Is Tomorrowland the best music festival in the world?"

> Over 15,000 members of staff (none of whom were volunteers) worked there, which is more than many music festivals, with over 500 members of international media who took part. Over two million beer pints were sold during the two weekends, paid with Tomorrowland's own currency, Pearls . . . And then there is the famous Tomorrowland Aftermovie, which are over 20-minute-long movies that seem to be put together by a Hollywood-level production team and consistently pull in millions of views. According to several insiders, all DJs earn the exact same amount, which makes it even more fascinating, when taking into consideration that global superstar DJs such as Armin van Buuren and Tiësto would earn the same as the upcoming first time DJ playing on the smallest stage.

The success of Tomorrowland inspired the founders to start an international business, creating a format that could be exported to other countries. Unfortunately,

Tomorrowland soon ran into several problems. In 2013, the Beers brothers decided to partner with the American entertainment giant SFX, which had acquired ID&T specifically to develop Tomorrowland internationally. To ensure the independence of the Belgian-European festival from SFX's projects in the Americas, they purchased the old shares of ID&T. Later, they became partners with SFX, creating a dedicated subsidiary to develop the format in the Americas (TomorrowWorld, 2013) and Brazil (Tomorrowland Brasil, 2015). The 2015 edition of TomorrowWorld held in Atlanta turned out to be a bitter failure for SFX. This is how *Vice* magazine (September 28, 2015) tells the story:

> What happened at Whitelake this weekend may have been more than an uncontrolled outpouring of hip young people, struggling as they did to survive . . . Scattered showers throughout the festival turned the 8,000-acre farmland into a giant mud pit, and the festival organizers' decision to limit transportation services on Saturday left many people stranded, with some shelling out hundreds of dollars to pay for surge-price Ubers, and others forced to sleep on the side of the road with no water or food . . . The festival canceled Sunday to non-campers, who formed the majority of attendees . . . This was the third year of the EDM festival's US edition—the original Tomorrowland in Belgium was founded in 2005—and unless there's some major damage control to assuage the livid masses vowing never to return, it may have been its last.

In 2016, SFX applied to be placed under the protection of US bankruptcy law. The company's stock fell nearly 95 percent in six months, and after the catastrophic TomorrowWorld edition in 2015, SFX lost $52 million. In March 2016, the organization confirmed the cancellation of the 2016 edition of TomorrowWorld. Meanwhile, in Belgium, the Beers brothers sought to reassure the market and the public by issuing the following statement:

> Chapter 11 proceedings [a provision of US bankruptcy law that allows companies to restructure following a major financial failure, ed.] will not affect Tomorrowland. The festival held in Belgium is 100 percent created, organized, and managed by the Belgian team. Tomorrowland Brasil will also take place as planned in two months in Itu (São Paulo). Tomorrowland Brasil is organized in close consultation with the Belgian team by a motivated local team that is able to work independently from SFX in North America for all aspects of the event.

↑
Dancers during the opening show of Tomorrowland, July 2022.

The following year, the third edition of Tomorrowland in Brazil was canceled. In November 2016, Luiz Eurico Klotz, founder and director of Plus Talent, the agency responsible for organizing Tomorrowland in Brazil, announced that the following year's festival would not take place due to the difficult financial situation the country was going through. In December 2016, SFX emerged from bankruptcy, reducing its debt by $400 million. Renamed LiveStyle, the society's promoter announced that TomorrowWorld might return to the United States, Brazil, and other locations outside Europe. In addition, Tomorrowland spokeswoman Debby Wilmsen commented on the corporate developments, saying that the festival was working to expand abroad again.

In 2019, the first edition of Tomorrowland Winter was held in France's Alpe d'Huez, which welcomed 30,000 visitors amid heavy controversy regarding the festival's environmental impact on the mountain's fragile ecosystem and public subsidies worth of 400,000 euros.

DESIGNING A UNIVERSE — With about 12 hours of music per day, Tomorrowland's lineup is clearly its biggest strength, but not the only one. The choice underpinning the festival's programming is clear and comprehensive: to be heard on the various stages of Tomorrowland is the finest of international electronic music in all its forms. Providing several stages helps differentiate the programming of the festival, thus engaging with a range of electronic music genres. If the Mainstage—the most filmed and photographed, the one that each year presents the most impressive set design and becomes the guiding image of the festival—hosts important names of the world star system, there is no shortage of space for emerging or less-established artists, and, above all, there's no lack of space for underground movements. By scrolling through the lineup, we detect a bias toward the European scenario, particularly of central and northern Europe. If you manage to grab one of the much-coveted Tomorrowland tickets, as music journalist Damir Ivic wrote in *Redbull.com* (June 2019), suggesting eight tips to best enjoy the 2019 festival,

> . . . you will find yourself immersed in a festival where, over the course of three days, there really are a lot of different genres of music passing by when it comes to the dance floor, and always with top performers . . . if you're into techno there's Dave Clarke, Chris Liebing, Rødhåd, and many others, as well as a whole stage curated by Nina Kraviz with Helena Hauff, Paula Temple, and a live-set by Karenn or the stalwart Richie Hawtin himself, Charlotte de Witte, a live-set by Monoloc, Sam Paganini. Just one of these names would make a pretty big and important techno festival.
>
> And that's just techno. Because Tomorrowland is that place where you go from A$ap Rocky to Paris Hilton (hey, not just two random names: they really are going to be there, on the first weekend) but in between there is techno, and then "historical" house, drum'n'bass, happy hardcore from the '90s, more experimental affairs, various oddities, as well as being the "harbor" where Diynamic (read Solomun & friends), Afterlife (Tale Of Us & friends), Cocoon (Sven Väth and friends) end up docking in full force.

→→

Fireworks at Mainstage during the set of DJ Tiësto, Tomorrowland, July 2019.

But when dealing with Tomorrowland, we cannot just mention the art project. Indeed, what gives life to the largest electronic music festival is an all-round composite and articulated commercial

project in which each element contributes to consolidate its position in the panorama of major global events on the one hand, and the relationship with its audience on the other. This generates countless revenue opportunities that ensure its economic sustainability, as well as continuous development and innovation that has never stopped, one festival after another. Although the whole machine remains entrenched in the original concept and inspiration behind Tomorrowland, the festival—in the words of its own founders—has become for all intents and purposes a business. In an interview, Manu Beers stated that at some point, one realizes that more than organizing an event, it is like running a business, and that a more professional approach is needed, with someone who can provide the business side of the company with a solid backbone.

Tomorrowland is a distinct universe that has very specific characteristics compared to the cultural enterprises described in the previous chapters, namely a business-oriented company that has made entertainment and dancefloor culture its core business and main activity. What is interesting to note is the marketing strategy used to carry this out. The Tomorrowland people bring to life a trickle of seemingly minor activities, details, and operations, which help nurture the festival's image and reinforce its identity and brand: organizing travel packages; branding the tents in the festival's camping area; using an internal currency in place of cash; and projecting the famous Tomorrowland Aftermovies, short films that are released each year when the festival is closed. Everything in Tomorrowland is aimed to enhance the fairy-tale imagery of the festival, to create expectation about the promised experience, to articulate a rich and multifaceted framework that captivates viewers not only during the festival but also before and after, even if they have never attended in person.

Let us explore some of the "side" operations animated by Tomorrowland. In DreamVille, the "residential" area of the festival, participants can sleep—with a range of accommodation solutions—in a simple igloo tent, obviously branded with the Tomorrowland logo, or in a luxury bungalow, or in a "camp" complete with air-conditioning, swimming pool, spa massage, and so on. Visitors can eat at various food outlets, bars, and delicious restaurants; they can buy groceries, practice yoga, and go shopping, and also make use of a series of basic services for daily life.

The festival also has a tour operator, Global Journey, that organizes all-inclusive trips not only to bring people to the festival site, but also to allow them to enjoy the experience during the journey. From virtually every country in the world, planes, trains, and Tomorrowland-branded buses depart, ready to transport the "People of Tomorrow" toward Boom. Visitors can purchase packages that include travel costs, festival entrance fees including an overnight stay in DreamVille, gadgets of various kinds, and, in some cases, additional travel stops or activities such as a "Detox Day."

Tomorrowland stays true to its roots, keeps the community and festive perception of its mission intact, and refuses to "sell out" to sponsors. Beyond the alcohol or certain products available at the festival, the only omnipresent brand is that of Tomorrowland, even when the stages are funded by large multinationals that line up each year to secure a spot in the festival's prestigious list of partners.

THE IMAGERY OF TOMORROWLAND — Another crucial aspect comes into play in the construction of the "Tomorrowland universe," one that interacts with and underpins all the operations described above—namely, communication strategy. This does not merely involve the selection and planning of communication and promotion strategies, but something more abstract and conceptual. We are dealing with the notion of a homogeneous yet internally articulated image that embodies the very essence of Tomorrowland and is developed in an integrated fashion at all levels. This also affects the artistic programming, setting, and collateral operations, which are all bound by a common visual identity, different modes of storytelling, social strategy, and the production of digital content to amplify or complement what takes place live. All these elements are single components of a larger, more comprehensive design that holds together communication, programming, marketing, and business development.

In a quick comparison with Glastonbury, which is also a "commercial" festival, very involved in constructing its own identity, the Belgian festival excels in its ability to disseminate effective images that create leverage on the exceptional nature of the experience that it is able to deliver. If Glastonbury's Instagram profile teems with peace symbols, tents surrounded by green meadows, cows, and Michael Eavis's good-natured smile set in his thick white beard, Tomorrowland's is an explosion of saturated colors, young bodies, and faces bathed in the light of the setting sun (Boom is no less rainy than Somerset), fireworks, water fountains, and light games. Then there are the glittering and impressive sets of the Mainstage with its crowds always radiating a general sense of coolness. The fairy-tale atmosphere envelops and captures everything, managing to make the camp tents look cozy and the faces of the thousands of participants look fresh, even at the end of a three-day-long musical and physical marathon.

This somewhat cosmic fantasy world is evident in the titles that characterize the festivals each year, providing an imaginative key to access the kind of event that will be experienced during the festival days. Indeed, since 2011 Tomorrowland festivals have been titled: *The Tree of Life, The Book of Wisdom, The Arising of Life, The Key to Happiness, The Secret Kingdom of Melodia, The Elixir of Life*. On the one hand, these titles interact with the scenic main "theme," which characterizes the iconography and images of the Mainstage sets as well as other minor stages. On the other hand, these titles help create a narrative of the festival, both within the single events and throughout the years, drawing on the magic, fairy-tales, and fantasy sagas typical of central and northern European culture, but also on the ritual—thus performative—dimension of the festival itself. This is conceived as a gathering of dispersed yet "chosen" people who, finding themselves in this exceptional context, give birth to something prodigious that reconnects humanity with nature, life, love, and joy. Festival attendees are both knights, called on to officiate at this annual collective ritual, and witnesses. When they return home, they will spread the word about the out-of-the-ordinary experiences at Tomorrowland. It is no coincidence that the title *The Book of Wisdom* was repeated for two festivals, in 2012 and 2019, and that the festival encourages its audiences to photograph, film, and share their moments at Tomorrowland on social media. Indeed, the website contains numerous references to this: "Keep sharing these magical moments with your friends!" or "Tomorrowland would like you to make as many photos and videos as possible and put loads onto your social media accounts!" or "Charge your phone so you can reach your friends and share your experience on social media."

While Tomorrowland delegates to its attendees the live storytelling of what happens during the festival, thus expanding the range of people reached by its channels, there are also several communication strategies—whether live or not—managed directly by the festival. This multiplies the possibilities of interaction and participation by focusing on those who are not present but can nevertheless be reached by digital and other content formats, which also circulate outside the festival period or as side projects of the festival itself. Such temporal continuity generates anticipation through the memory of the lived (or missed) experience, as well as expanding the possibilities to tap new audiences. At the time of writing, Tomorrowland's YouTube channel has as many as ten million subscribers, achieved thanks to the festival's focus on video production and documentation, as well as the creation of live streaming clips broadcast via social channels. These are high-quality, professional products, as seen in the Aftermovie (the now famous short films that are released following each festival) and in other long video clips in which images and music narrate the festival and nurture the imagery around it to encapsulate the spirit that animates it.

The desire to fix, narrate, and celebrate what is consumed in the two summer weekends of Tomorrowland has led to the creation of cultural products that use the festival itself as content. The Aftermovies can be placed somewhere between promotion and documentation, aimed at the festival community (including the potential one), and released for free and online circulation. A different case is the documentary film *This Was Tomorrow – The Tomorrowland Movie*, made in

2015 for the festival's tenth anniversary. It takes viewers on a journey of discovery of the main participating artists in the various editions, while also investigating what festivals and electronic music represent for the people who take part, as well as for the development of the music business.

Recently and in collaboration with Virgin Music, Tomorrowland launched its own music label, Tomorrowland Music, with the intention of working even more closely with artists and labels and supporting their recording and publishing activities. In addition, there is an entire line of Tomorrowland-branded products developed in collaboration with various labels and manufacturing companies: clothing, snowboards, Bluetooth speakers, various accessories, jewelry, vinyls, and even a limited-edition sparkling wine. With its branched business, which not only offers an out-of-the-ordinary experience to the 400,000 people who attend the festival but also insinuates into their consumer habits, into music and film production, and into the imagination of people who will never attend, Tomorrowland represents an excellent example of an event that has built a solid community over the years. It has continued to keep the quality of its musical offering very high, as well as that of the event itself, while remaining true to the passion that inspired, and continues to inspire, its founders. This is the base on which the Beers brothers have been able to develop a large and efficient economic machine, which not only ensures the sustainability of the event but also generates profit, thanks to the wager renewed year after year on innovation, quality, and effectiveness. ¶

↓ *The Reflection of Love*, 16th Tomorrowland festival, July 2022.

COACHELLA VALLEY MUSIC AND ARTS FESTIVAL

COACHELLA.COM

— When music becomes cool

↑
The Chemical Brothers perform at Coachella, April 2011.

If there is one festival that has gained a special place in the collective imagination of the younger and older generations in recent years, it is undoubtedly the Coachella Valley Music and Arts Festival. Palm trees, sunsets, merry-go-rounds, beautiful young women and men with sunglasses and flowers in their hair, pastel colors everywhere, a dreamy and effervescent atmosphere. It is like the feeling of spring when the cold winter has just gone. We are in the middle of the California desert, specifically at the Empire Polo Club in Indio, a 78-acre park dedicated to sports such as polo and field hockey, halfway between Los Angeles and San Diego and close to the Joshua Tree National Park. Every year since 1999—with a break in 2000—and normally for two weekends in a row in April, one of the world's most celebrated pop music events comes to life. This event stands as a benchmark for fashion and youth styles throughout the West.

Following the example of the great European festivals, including Glastonbury, and the wave of gatherings that populated California's West Coast in the 1960s and 1970s (and that inspired Woodstock), slotting into the wake of the rave phenomenon that reached the United States in the 1990s, Coachella was founded between the late 1990s and early 2000s by Goldenvoice, a small Los Angeles–based promoter agency that dealt mainly with emerging bands from the new US punk, grunge, and indie scenes. After twenty festivals, Coachella is today one of the most iconic pop culture venues, a paradise for influencers and fashion bloggers who can show off their "Instagrammable" outfits against the backdrop of the desert sunset, but also a gathering where big brands hunt for up-and-coming trends.

If its cool and fashionable side is perhaps the one most characteristic of the festival today, the music lineup continues to be no less significant, including the top names of world pop music, whose shows are discussed for months on social media and in magazines. The biggest names in indie, electronic, and experimental music have performed on the Coachella stage just before (or just after) becoming stars of mainstream pop, changing the fortunes of music and popular culture. While in the early years the billing was mainly alternative, indie, and rock, inviting bands such as Jane's Addiction, the Pixies, Weezer, as well as experimental or electronic music artists such as Radiohead, Chemical Brothers, Bjork, Sigur Rós, or Tricky, over the course of the festivals the lineup has gradually widened. Now the leading names of the star system, such as Madonna, Beyoncé, Jay-Z, Ariana Grande, Billie Eilish, and Childish Gambino feature regularly. This list of names confirms how the search for

→→
Madonna performs at Coachella, April 2006.

diversity and a balance between major pop figures and more experimental and avant-garde bands is a constant at Coachella. The festival has witnessed important moments in music history over the years, such as its famous reunions—from Bauhaus, the historic British post-punk/new wave band, to Destiny's Child, the group with which Beyoncé became known.

Yet even Coachella has not been immune to failure and controversy over the years. The very first festival faced the risk of bankruptcy, which was eventually followed by its takeover by AEG, a large company headed by Philip Anschutz, a businessman who donates to anti-LGBTQA+ organizations. Despite the controversy and criticism, for a great many Coachella still remains synonymous with "festival" and has yet to stop shaking up the world's pop culture.

THE VALLEY OF THE INDIE

Coachella's brand of "indie" is rooted in its DNA, as seen in the musical background of its founders and the scenario inspiring the very idea of the festival. In the 1980s, Goldenvoice was a small but vibrant California booking agency managed by its founder Gary Tovar, a surfer, promoter, and punk concert organizer on the West Coast. In true California dreamin' style, he also financed his business through income from the trade in marijuana. He was undoubtedly an almost mythological character and instrumental in the development of the underground music scene. Accused of dealing drugs, in the early 1990s Tovar sold Goldenvoice to Paul Tollett and Rick Van Santen, two young California promoters who were his friends and already active in organizing underground concerts. The California punk scene was changing, and Los Angeles was the epicenter of the emerging alternative rock movement in those years. Goldenvoice was close to the new bands (Nirvana, Jane's Addiction, Red Hot Chili Peppers, Pixies), promoted their work, and ended up playing a key role in establishing this new sound and beginning to compete with the big booking agencies. Goldenvoice's "militant" approach, however, is its distinguishing characteristic: its promoters are first and foremost fans of the groups they work with, and the collaboration between the agency and the artists they follow is based on mutual empathy, as well as an affinity of tastes and visions.

The idea for the Coachella Valley Music and Arts Festival was born in 1993, when the music group Pearl Jam broke its agreement with Ticketmaster, the US event ticket sales and distribution giant, which at the time had an exclusive with almost every venue in the United States. As might be expected of a true indie band, in disagreement with Ticketmaster's refusal to lower ticket prices in order to meet the needs of their audience, Pearl Jam refused to play at venues run by the company. Goldenvoice then decided to support the band in their search for a new venue to perform, thus scouting out what would be the future home of Coachella: the grounds of the Empire Polo Club in Indio, a two-hour drive from Los Angeles and at the gateway to the California desert. A rather crazy idea, but one that turned out to be a winner, implying new development possibilities for Tollett. However, it was the example of large European festivals (such as Glastonbury) and the impetus of the nascent US rave scene, which was beginning to gather thousands of people for long collective sessions of techno and dance music, that would shape the Coachella concept in Tollett's mind. His idea was a stage large enough for the Goldenvoice bands (whose popularity was now growing exponentially) to perform, giving rise to a dimension of live music fusion that was not practiced in the United States at the time.

Tollett had to wait until 1999 to open the first festival, with a lineup that included Beck, Morrissey, and the Chemical Brothers. Everything took place over a single day that proved to be quite successful, but it was not enough to cover the costs of the event: on that occasion, Goldenvoice lost a lot of money—between $850,000 and $1,000,000—and Tollett was forced to sell his own home and car.

↓
Harry Styles on stage at Coachella, April 2022.

Yet, the agency was no stranger to economic hardships and risk. The good reputation of Tollett and his associates, as well as the affection and friendship that bound them to the artists, ensured that Goldenvoice was not isolated and was helped financially by other festivals, such as Lollapalooza. Two years later AEG bought Goldenvoice, with the idea of investing again in what seemed like a good idea—namely, Coachella itself. Thus in 2001, two years after its initial economic flop, Goldenvoice launched the second festival, which continued until the forced stop caused by the pandemic. The entry of AEG was a turning point in the life of the festival, but also a change in its general outlook and attitude, marked by bitter controversy with the figure of Philip Anschutz.

The mix of alternative, indie, electronic, and experimental pop is what has distinguished Coachella's lineup since the very first festivals, combining big names with up-and-coming and lesser-known bands while continuing to focus on independent and experimental musical genres. If 2004 was the first year Goldenvoice made a profit from the festival, the 2006 edition marked the point of no return regarding its size and the entity of its artistic programming. The "big names" became ever bigger—from Madonna to Daft Punk and Kanye West—and the musical offering more layered, bolstering electronic and dance music as well as hip-hop and Black music, genres that over the years would take over from indie and rock.

The year 2011 paved the way for the festival's explosion thanks to the advent of social media and online platforms. Indeed, it was during that festival that Coachella began to be streamed on YouTube, allowing millions of people to learn about it and follow live performances by the best-known artists in global music. As a result, in 2012 public demand increased exponentially and Tollett decided to add a second weekend to the festival, with the special feature of repeating the exact same lineup and thus allowing the audience to enjoy the same concerts twice; it was also the year of the incredible show by Dr. Dre and Snoop Dogg, who literally brought Tupac back to life in an uncanny performance in which a hologram of the rapper (who was killed in 1996) took the stage. But the festival that definitively set the course for Coachella and established it as one of the world's largest and most influential music festivals was in 2018, when it opened up to pop by hosting a historic, nearly two-hour performance by Beyoncé.

If even before there had been little doubt that Coachella was one of the events with the greatest impact on styles, musical trends, and the collective imagination, capable not only of witnessing their development but also of changing their course, the latest festivals have definitely elevated it into the pantheon of the world's most impressive musical and commercial events. With some 250,000 spectators over the two weekends of programming, each year is a sell-out within hours of the launch of ticket sales and despite the cost for the basic ticket of around $400. In addition to attendance numbers, box office, and the relevance of its lineup, Coachella has established itself as a landmark in the development of youth trends, insinuating itself into the viral social dynamics thanks to the imagery it has constructed, and today has become the Instagram festival *par excellence*.

TRANSFORMING THE HORIZON — The eclecticism of Coachella's artistic mission is one of its strengths: as we mentioned, the festival lineup caters to diverse audiences, involving both avant-garde artists and pop stars, spanning genres from electro to pop and rock to hip-hop, techno, and many others. This is how writer John Seabrook described Coachella in a 2017 *New Yorker* article:

> In creating Coachella, Tollett took the best aspects of the indie-rock, jam-band, and SoCal rave/dance nineties festivals, added the large art installations of Burning Man, and grafted this new festival hybrid onto the original hippie rootstock—the sixties-era longing for a new world which three days in the desert helps satisfy.

Paul Tollett was and still is a key figure in the festival. In addition to curating the lineup, he personally selects all the artists on the bill and negotiates fees with their agents in a process that takes no less than six months. Seabrook wrote, "Coachella is a delicate ecosystem of the grand and the intimate. Tollett creates the biosphere that sustains it."

Another key figure in the festival is Paul Clemente, Coachella's artistic director. We must remember that the festival's full name is Coachella Valley Music and Arts Festival, since visual art has been from the very outset an important component in the development of its artistic project and has grown step by step with the festival's growth. Quoting again from Seabrook's article:

> "We're designing these pieces so hopefully they're having an impact on you, even peripherally, from sometimes as much as a quarter of a mile away," Paul Clemente, the festival's art director, told [Seabrook]. "As the Coachella venue has been growing over the years, the art has had to grow with it." Mr. Clemente started working for Goldenvoice in 2007, after more than 15 years working in film visual effects, including on *The Matrix*. He said taking on a role with the festival was a natural transition, since both gigs involved using a variety of tools and media to

make pieces that are specific to one site and one context. Though some of the Coachella installations will eventually become permanent public art pieces in desert communities, Mr. Clemente said most of the pieces will be displayed only once. The rise of Instagram, he said, has added another layer to that calculation. "These are fleeting moments, here: To experience these shows and this art on this scale, you have to be here at Coachella. And people want to take away those images."

Part of the failure in 1999 was due to some mistakes in communication strategy. Tollett acknowledged that announcing the line-up of the brand-new festival too soon was "financial suicide," just as suicidal as launching the announcement of the festival the same week as Woodstock, which would be remembered as a disastrous three days of violence, sewage spills, and Jamiroquai, severely judged by the US public. Today, Goldenvoice aims to release the celebrated festival poster "as close to New Year's Eve as possible," in order to make space for itself in the highly competitive festival calendar by announcing the main guests first. This is also because they will most likely be the same as in other big festivals such as Glastonbury, Bonnaroo, Electric Daisy Carnival, and Lollapalooza. Looking at the festival billboards—whose graphics have remained the same for about 20 festivals, changing only the color palette—we notice how the artists' names are not all the same size. There is a definite hierarchy in their dimensions and position: a simple criterion to identify the entity of the fee paid for the engagement.

The early billboards already presented that mixing of genres mentioned previously, with space left for the most significant names of the alternative scene, such as Jane's Addiction, Weezer, Red Hot Chili Peppers, but also experimental pop and electronica such as Chemical Brothers, Bjork, Fatboy Slim, Beastie Boys, as well as new wave and post-punk names like The Cure, Siouxsie & The Banshees, New Order, and Kraftwerk. One of the special features of these early years were the reunions: starting with Jane's Addiction, then Bauhaus, Siouxsie & The Banshees, Pixies, Stooges, Rage Against the Machine, The Jesus and Mary Chain, The Verve, Guns N' Roses, Destiny's Child, and all the way to NSYNC; the reunion operation was undoubtedly a perfect strategy to draw audiences and enrich the

→→
Beyoncé performing at Coachella, April 2018.

↑
The *Spectra* installation by the UK studio Newsubstance, Coachella, April 2022.

Coachella billboard by differentiating it from other major festivals. By surveying the lineups of the various festivals, it is possible to follow the evolution of pop music: Sonic Youth, The Strokes, LCD Soundsystem, Franz Ferdinand. Before long, the latest New York indie scene began to make itself heard and, from the underground genre that it was, within a few years it was raging on stages (and in advertisements) throughout the West, and beyond.

The year 2006 was pivotal in this regard, as the overall design of the festival's musical programming took on a definitive and accomplished format, reserving equal space and visibility for different musical genres: not only alternative, indie, and experimental pop, but also electronica, dance, and hip-hop; then, about twelve years later, mainstream pop was also included. This continuous shift in focus to attract genres and artists would become a prominent feature, in that it anticipated and helped to shape new global trends in music.

In the early 2000s and until at least 2010, Coachella was undoubtedly the American Mecca of the indie scene. Just by reading the names featured on the posters of the various festivals we can see a gradual increase in the presence of DJs, producers, and musicians active in electronic and dance music. In addition to the Main Stage, the Sahara Tent—the pavilion dedicated to electronic music—has gained importance and has become relevant in the Coachella musical horizon, so much so that it led to the inauguration of a second spot, the Dew Lab, dedicated to dance music. 2006 was also a pivotal year in this regard due to Madonna's celebrated performance in the Sahara Tent and the equally famous performance by the two Daft Punk "robots." These two shows definitively sanctioned the entry of electronics as a fundamental element in Coachella's artistic trajectory, and the Sahara Tent as a place of imaginative and technological experimentation, thanks to the powerful sound systems and amazing lights that accompany the performances of DJs and producers.

While electronica and electronic dance music (EDM) made their presence felt through the 2000s—culminating, in 2007, in the DJ and producer Tiësto's performance on the Main Stage—2006 was also the year that hip-hop entered the festival with Kanye West's performance, which attracted the largest crowd in Coachella's history until then. This was an important milestone for the attendance of Black patrons, who finally found their place in a festival that, until then, had a predominantly white identity. Hip-hop reached its climax in 2012, the year of the already mentioned performance by Dr. Dre, and Snoop Dogg, but would continue over the years, coming to attract today's new trap scene.

→→
Festivalgoers watch DJ Snake performing at Coachella, April 2017.

Through alternative, indie, electronic, and hip-hop, Coachella actualizes its role as a true transformative agent of musical culture, capable of intercepting new trends and attitudes of the younger generations and shifting them from an underground dimension typical of specific urban centers to a widespread and global phenomenon.

In 2018, the festival finally opened up to pop, challenging its "indie" audience, which has considered the word "pop" as something derogatory. This operation facilitated greater mixing of audiences and musical genres. In 2018 Beyoncé—the undisputed queen of pop—took the stage, being thankful for having the opportunity to "be the first Black woman to perform as a headliner on the Main Stage of Coachella." The road is now marked out: after Madonna, Jay-Z, and Beyoncé it will be the turn of Ariana Grande, Billie Eilish, the South Korean girl band Blackpink, and many others.

pp. → 360 | 361

Over these "twenty years in the desert," the Coachella stage has hosted one of the major musical events of the year, where the world's most celebrated stars perform, confirming their celebrity and offering their music to a vast and diverse audience.

COACHELLA AS A STYLE (OF LIVING AND CONSUMPTION) — According to the UK edition of *GQ* magazine (April 2019), "From the perspective of its partners, Coachella's most profitable asset is its audience. 'At Coachella, you have north of 100,000 people into everything from tech to music to art to fashion,' Daryl Butler, HP's head of US Consumer Marketing tells me. 'And then the advent of social media has allowed what happens in a narrower experience to be broadcast around the world.' A hive of celebrities and influencers, the reach of Coachella extends far beyond the festival grounds, it's broadcast around the world in real-time through Instagram posts and Twitter feeds."

It is precisely its hipster attitude and ability to seize on trends "before they were cool" (to mention the expression used by young hipsters to testify their independence from fashion and their exclusive taste) that has made Coachella the ideal place to observe the emergence of new styles and cultural and social phenomena in general. Indeed, the major brands monitor this in order to effectively orient their business according to the new market segments that emerge. What Coachella has been able to create—similar to what happened with Tomorrowland, but here at an even deeper level—is not just a brand but a true cultural hegemony that affects fashions as much or perhaps more than what is seen on the catwalk of a major fashion show. Its strong aesthetic component is probably the key to this phenomenon. By aesthetic component, we do not mean something only exterior such as clothing, makeup, and the attitude with which the participants experience the festival, but something to do with belonging and distinction. Indeed, this phenomenon was explored by the French sociologist Pierre Bourdieu in his *Distinction: A Social Critique of the Judgement of Taste*, published in 1979: a mechanism whereby the enjoyment of certain cultural products becomes synonymous with social or intellectual distinction. Again, it is interesting to note the trajectory of the names that appear in the various festival billboards. Coachella has been a point of reference for audiences who like to discover musicians and learn about new music genres less familiar to the general public (or at least, perceive themselves as such); this attitude then becomes a mass phenomenon, facilitated in part by the advent of social media. Thus, the new challenge for the indie sector is to re-evaluate pop, adding an extra layer of complexity. Perhaps, then, it is no coincidence that from a certain point on, the Coachella lineup becomes unabashedly pop. A veritable cultural short-circuit: if, due to the Internet and the use of social media, alternative culture no longer exists as such since its codes are now attainable by everyone, then everyone becomes "alternative," and "alternatives" begin to appreciate the mainstream instead. The result of this phenomenon is what we see today and also what takes place on the lawn of the Empire Polo Club in Indio during Coachella: the dizzying multiplication of trends, lifestyles, and forms of subjectivity, united by certain tastes and, in each case, brought together in a commercial space promoted by large corporations.

Thus, the affair that jeopardized the festival's image a few years ago, namely the acquisition of Goldenvoice by AEG, owned by Philip Anschutz, appears definitive. He funded some anti-LGBTQA+ organizations, such as Alliance Defending Freedom, the Family Research Council, and the National Christian Foundation. Despite the denials, this could not but negatively affect the reputation of a festival that makes diversity and eccentricity its keystones, triggering a kind of persistent boycott against Coachella. In 2020, the question still continued to burn; according to *Vice*, "Coachella is still an ethical dilemma for many progressive artists." If on the one hand Coachella represents the true place to be both for the audience and for the bands, and more so for emerging bands, given that it has become a logistical and economic behemoth capable of attracting sponsors of all kinds, it risks coming into contradiction with its own roots and, therefore, alienating parts of its grassroots communities. Indeed, these communities have since expanded and become much more influential, both politically and commercially. In this sense, it is interesting to acknowledge the festival's policy regarding inclusiveness and accessibility. In true American style, where the focus on certain issues is definitely greater than in other countries, the institutional website includes several pages dedicated to projects through which Coachella declares its radical anti-sexism, anti-racism, anti-colonialism, and anti-ableism policies, placing itself at the forefront in the condemnation of certain discriminatory, aggressive, and violent attitudes. Indeed, several festival initiatives go in this direction.

Yet in the vast ocean of influencer audiences attending Coachella, often more interested in taking selfies at sunset with the Ferris wheel as a backdrop than in the music, incidents of discrimination have been noted, even recently. The Anschutz controversy is not the only political criticism that has arisen around Coachella. As of 2017, one of the main accusations leveled at the festival has been that of cultural appropriation in relation to the style and aesthetics the festival offers; incidentally, its title is a Mexican word for Mexico City's symbolic snake. The fact that its geographical location is close to the desert, in the vicinity of the Mexico/US border, gives Coachella a specific imagery made up of palm trees and *camperos*, as well as references to hippie psychedelic aesthetics. And then we also have feathers, Indian headdresses, bindis, and body painting that immediately evoke the repertoires of other cultures, often oppressed by white Westerners (Native Americans *in primis*, and in the very territories where colonization of land was perpetrated) and flaunted by the festival audience, which was and still is predominantly white.

Beyond personal opinions around these important controversies, what we must emphasize is—even in the case of cultural appropriation, homo-, lesbo-, and transphobia, and ableism—that Coachella imposes itself as a kind of cultural laboratory, bringing out what are now the most accessible and fruitful debates that are sweeping through the West in recent years, which, after having spread among communities of scholars and activists, now have a wider audience at Coachella, which acts rather like another sounding board. ❡

MONTREUX JAZZ FESTIVAL

MONTREUXJAZZFESTIVAL.COM

— *The art of making and disseminating music*

↑
Grace Jones at Montreux Jazz Festival, July 2017.

Back to Europe now, to the town of Montreux on the placid shores of Lake Geneva, in the French-speaking part of Switzerland. The delightful landscape, nestled between the mountains and the waters of the lake, and the architectural beauty of its surrounding villages and castles, make Montreux one of the best-loved tourist spots in the area, as well as a magnet for artists, especially musicians. Despite its population of under 30,000, Montreux became well-known during the second half of the twentieth century for being an international art center. It famously hosted the celebrated Mountain Studios, owned by Queen, where the albums of several important bands, including Queen, the Rolling Stones, David Bowie, and many others were recorded. A number of competitions, art awards, and festivals of various kinds are held here.

Let's leave behind the dust, mud, and endless lines for Coachella chemical toilets and visualize instead a romantic break on the lakefront: concerts, elegant deck chairs, the beautiful view from the main stage, and the thorough arrangements for the live shows held in the town's theaters and concert halls. Although it formally falls into the same category as the festivals we described previously, which involve practically all existing genres, the Montreux Jazz Festival presents a completely different model from Glastonbury, Tomorrowland, and Coachella, both in terms of the style and audience it addresses and the manner in which it is organized. Founded in 1967 as a festival devoted entirely to jazz, one of the most relevant and long-lived musical genres of the twentieth century, which has spawned a myriad of musical subgenres and derivations connected with some of the political, social, and artistic issues that have marked contemporary times, today the Montreux Jazz Festival presents an eclectic program of concerts and live sets spread over three weeks in July. The huge stages with their throngs of fans that gather in the vast spaces of Glastonbury, Tomorrowland, and Coachella are replaced here by venues scattered throughout the town of Montreux, including indoor spaces with decidedly different capacities from those seen so far. The 250,000 people who reach the festival each year are distributed over various dates in a three-week-long schedule, planning their participation at the festival in an autonomous and personalized way.

If the festivals described so far are large collective events, in which music is undoubtedly at the center but also becomes the pivot for an immersive and total experience in which to lose oneself among thousands of strangers, Montreux's image is one of intimacy, of proximity between

pp. → 366 | 367

audience and international artists, which is made possible precisely by the dimension of the location. And again, if the target audience of the previous three festivals was mainly the young and very young, the Montreux Jazz Festival is more a gathering for melomaniacs, enthusiasts, connoisseurs, practitioners of more or less cultured or experimental music, from a wide range of age groups. Undoubtedly, this festival positions itself at a higher level of cultural production and fruition, where pop also belongs but only when it can demonstrate its artistic and experimental potential.

In addition to the big names in jazz and rock music who have passed through here, more overtly pop star system figures have also taken part in the festival in recent years: Muse, Radiohead, Kendrick Lamar, Pharrell Williams, Ed Sheeran, Alicia Keys, Adele, Lady Gaga, Tyler The Creator, Lizzo, and Rita Ora. This presence is a sort of validation of their musical production as a true artistic expression. Thus, the prestige of the Montreux Jazz Festival is given primarily by the quality and "artistry" expressed by the lineup; aesthetics, lifestyles, and fashions are all present in the overall picture but remain in the background. What is at the core here is the love of music and the exceptional musicians who perform here.

MUSIC HISTORY ON THE SHORES OF THE LAKE

After training as a cook, Claude Nobs—also known as Funky Claude—worked for some time as an accountant at the Montreux Tourist Office. Passionate about music, in 1964 he began organizing his first concerts, one of which included the Rolling Stones' first performance outside the United Kingdom. The following year, he flew to New York to meet Nesuhi Ertegun, codirector of the Atlantic Records label, who decided to support the idea of a festival. In June 1967, having become director of the city's Tourist Office, and with the help of journalist René Langel and pianist Géo Voumard, Nobs put together the first Montreux Jazz Festival, which immediately met with wide acclaim in Switzerland and abroad thanks to the participation of a number of prominent musicians such as Charles Lloyd and Keith Jarrett, involved through their links with Atlantic Records.

Merging a passion for music and the intention to revitalize tourism in Montreux, the Jazz Festival represented from the outset a meeting point for the international jazz community. The Swiss town already had a musical heart. One episode that speaks well of its connection with the 1970s rock scene is that of the famous 1971 Montreux Casino fire, which was the inspiration for Deep Purple's celebrated *Smoke on the Water*. It was December 4, 1971, and the band was in their hotel where they were recording thanks to the Rolling Stones' Mobile Studio (the first mobile recording studio in music history, conceived by Ian Stewart, tour manager of the Rolling Stones, and built in 1968). Suddenly flames began to consume the Montreux Casino, where a concert by Frank Zappa and his band Mothers of Invention was taking place. What had happened was that during a solo by guitarist Don Preston, flames from a flare gun had caught some curtains, and in an instant a fire had broken out. Some young men were trapped in the flames and the director of the Montreux Jazz Festival, Claude Nobs, succeeded in rescuing them. Then the structure collapsed in on itself and Deep Purple witnessed everything from the outside. The image of smoke and flames reflecting off the waters of the lake inspired one of the most famous songs in rock history, which is also one of the most vivid accounts of that night.

We all came out to Montreux
On the Lake Geneva shoreline
To make records with a mobile
We didn't have much time
. . .
Smoke on the water
A fire in the sky
Smoke on the water

→→
Jam session with Janelle Monáe at Montreux Jazz Festival, July 2019.

The figure of Nobs is thus central to the development of the Swiss music scene and its relationship to the wider international context: in 1973 he became director of the Swiss branches of Warner, Elektra, and Atlantic, helping to organize concerts of the best-known US bands in Switzerland.

Some of the finest personalities in jazz, soul, and blues have taken to the Montreux Jazz Festival stage since its earliest years. In 1969 Ella Fitzgerald performed for the first time, while Les McCann & Eddie Harris recorded the live album *Swiss Movement*, the first jazz record to sell over a million copies; the following year Carlos Santana flew to Switzerland to perform, just a few months after playing at Woodstock, while in 1976 Nina Simone gave one of the most unforgettable performances in her entire career.

In short, while running up against the wrath of jazz purists, Claude Nobs decided to open the festival program to other musical genres as well, making Montreux an increasingly important *rendezvous* for lovers of blues, pop, and rock, as well as,

UPOLE

ACCOR

of course, jazz. From 1990 to 1993, Nobs was joined in artistic direction by Quincy Jones, one of the cornerstones of Black music. In those years, one of the festival's top artists was Miles Davis, so much so that in 1993 the two made a live album together, *Miles & Quincy Live at Montreux.*

The fame and size of the festival continued to grow, hosting the likes of David Bowie, Prince, and Elton John. Although he delegated the operational side of the event so that he could focus on special projects, Claude Nobs continued to play a central role in the life of the festival until 2013, the tragic year in which, at the age of 76, he lost his life in a skiing accident. Following the sudden death of Nobs, the direction of the festival, as well as the Montreux Jazz Artists Foundation and Montreux Jazz International SA, passed on to Mathieu Jaton. Passionate about music and a graduate of Lausanne Hotel School, Jaton was hired by the festival in 1999 at the age of 24 as marketing and fundraising manager.

Another central figure in the festival is Stéphanie Aloysia Moretti, artistic director of the Montreux Jazz Artists Foundation, who acted as Claude Nobs's artistic coordinating assistant since 1989. It is to her that we owe the festival's famous piano, voice, and guitar competitions, which started in 1999 and gave birth

to the Montreux Jazz Talent Awards. Her goal was to mix pop with avant-garde and traditional genres.

Another significant element in Montreux Jazz's history is its relationship with the visual arts. As early as 1967, the festival started the custom of commissioning Swiss and international artists to create its official poster. The artists were given complete freedom and allowed to influence the musical imagery through visual languages. It was, however, the 1982 poster created by Swiss sculptor Jean Tinguely that left a meaningful mark and gave birth to the festival logo, which is still highly recognizable today. In 1983, it was the turn of Keith Haring, who created a triptych of posters, and in 1986 of Andy Warhol. In addition to these leading figures, there are several other artists who have contributed to the festival's visual identity: from Niki de Saint Phalle, David Bowie, Max Bill, and Yoann Lemoine (Woodkid) to the contemporary artist JR, who in 2020 created the poster for the 54th Montreux Jazz Festival.

MONTREUX: THE CITADEL OF MUSIC — Unlike the three major festivals described previously, the Montreux Jazz Festival thrives in a realm somewhere between the public and the private, the commercial and the cultural, between the intimacy possible in a small town nestled in the hills of French Switzerland and the internationality of its lineup, which ranges from emerging artists and others active in niche music scenes to top stars from pop, rock, and jazz music. During the 16 days in July when the festival comes to life, the city of Montreux is literally transformed into an exceptional location hosting performances both outdoors and in various indoor venues. Although not among the event's official funders, the Municipality of Montreux cannot but play an important role in the festival's success. In an interview, the festival director Mathieu Jaton stated that Montreux somehow gives over its identity for a fortnight and all the city's institutions back the festival and collaborate in finding solutions—which is something invaluable.

While the festival was originally held at Montreux Casino (with a pause from 1971 to 1975 due to renovation work after the previously mentioned fire), in 1995—and until 2008—the venue was doubled in size through the addition of the Convention Center, which, as of 2007, houses two main stages, the Stravinsky Auditorium (capacity of 3,500) and the Miles Davis Hall (capacity of 1,800).

←
Claude Nobs, founder and general manager of the Montreux Jazz Festival.

In all, the festival has 11 stages, six of which are free and five ticketed, including the Stravinsky Auditorium, the Montreux Jazz Club, and the Montreux Jazz Lab, which are the most important showcase venues of the festival. Festivalgoers can access some 55 eateries, bars, and outdoor areas, making the festival experience a continuous exploration of both the town of Montreux and the artistic program. The festival alternates between larger events with high audience numbers and myriad smaller live shows, jam sessions, acoustic performances, workshops, and meetings, aimed at smaller numbers. In addition to the main stages, other venues include the Petit Théâtre, with its fine acoustics, that hosts jazz and soul concerts, with a capacity of 300 people; Les Jardins, a small outdoor stage for acoustic showcases, improvisations, and DJ sets, where up to 300 spectators can relax on lounge chairs scattered on the lawn, drinking beer and cocktails until late at night; Music in the Park, an open-air stage set up in Parc Vernex, where concerts by Swiss and international artists and big bands take place from the early afternoon; and the brand new Lake Stage, an atmospheric venue opened in 2020, located on a platform built directly on the water, with a capacity of 500 people.

FREE-OF-CHARGE ACTIVITIES OF THE MONTREUX JAZZ ARTISTS FOUNDATION — To date, between free pool parties, silent discos, outdoor concerts, jam sessions, workshops, and night events, about 250 of the 380 concerts are free. After years of mixed economic results, the increase in free-of-charge activities over the various festivals is a direct result of Nobs's willingness to invest in the cultural function of the festival rather than its commercial dimension.

By recognizing the important role played by festivals as a center for music dissemination and promotion, in 2006 Claude Nobs began to apply for public funds to finance the many free events and ensure the sustainability of a cultural project continually under pressure from rising fees and the organizational unpredictability typical of a summer festival. As Jaton states in *Bilan*, June 28, 2019, "With a budget of 28 million, 70 percent of our revenue comes from ticket sales and food and beverage and is not guaranteed. This in turn depends not only on the lineup but also on the weather . . . but if we have two weeks of rain, then obviously we are in the red . . . even five days is enough of a problem . . ."

To develop and enhance the public function of the festival, the Montreux Jazz Artists Foundation (MJAF) was established in 2007 to oversee most of the concerts associated with the free stages. As these are declared to be of public benefit, they are entirely funded by public grants and private donations. MJAF aims to promote new talent, support creativity and career development of artists, and make music

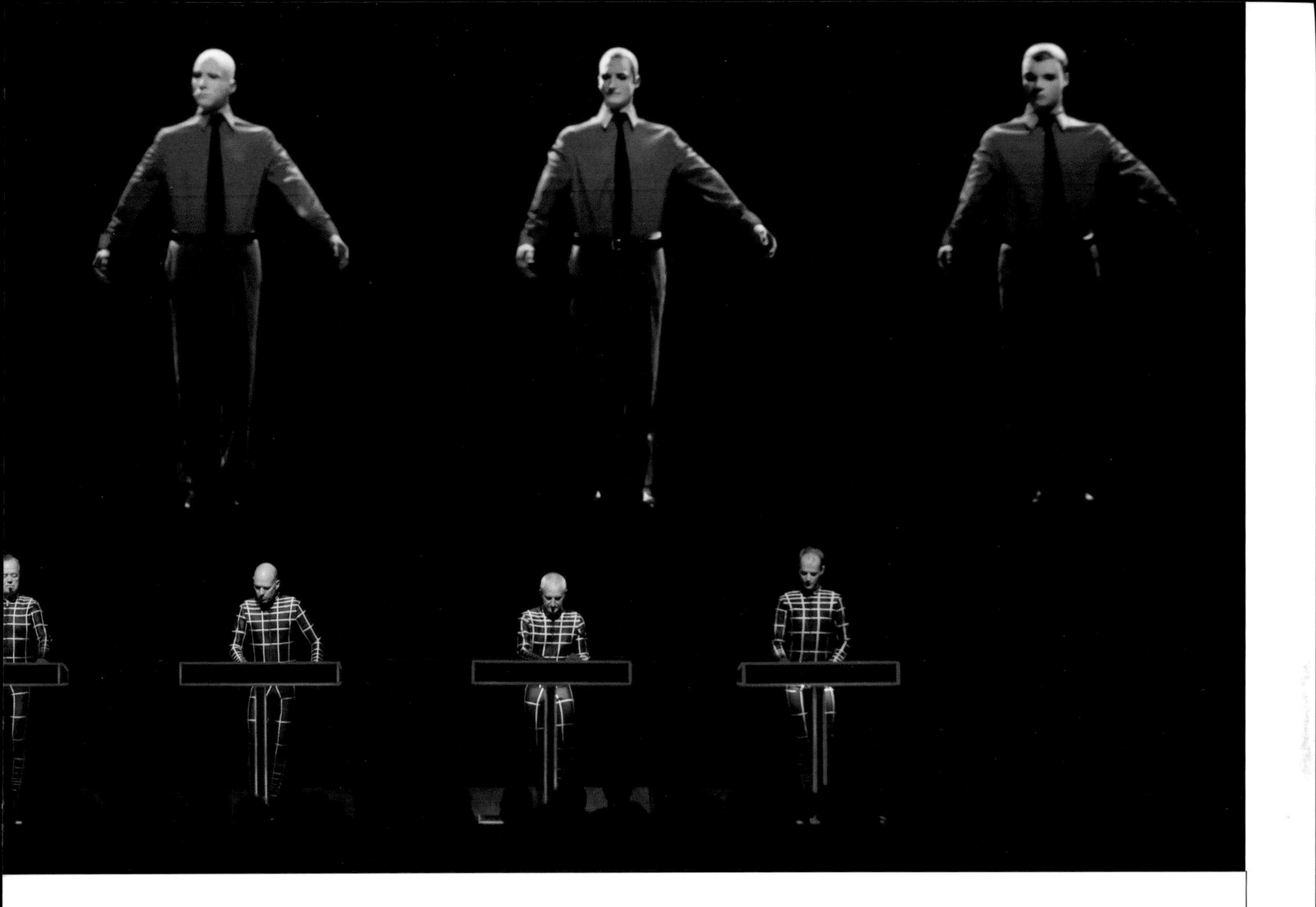

accessible to all audiences. Its function is to strengthen music culture and the development of live music by maintaining free access to cultural mediation activities and concerts.

Part of MJAF activities take place during the Montreux Jazz Festival to provide services to musicians and audiences and safeguard the diversity inherent in the jazz music scene. MJAF's main activities also include the Talent Awards, whereby each year 16 young talents are selected and judged by a panel of experts for the categories of best band and best soloist; the Montreux Jazz Academy, a residency and mentoring program that provides space and tools for the career development of emerging artists; a program of free and educational activities planned during the festival, from free-of-charge stages for performances to workshops, meetings, film and documentary screenings, and jam sessions.

During the rest of the year, the Montreux Jazz Artists Foundation organizes various concerts in Switzerland and abroad to promote and support its selected artists.

The centrality of music and its cultural function are the basis of the relationship with sponsors, referred to as "partners" precisely because they are primarily companies active in the music and arts sectors. Indeed, the festival's relationship with its partners is not only economic, since the latter are also involved in the planning phase. Again, Jaton stated that certain old systems, such as check in exchange for visibility, do not exist in Montreux.

↑ The German band Kraftwerk performing at Montreux Jazz Festival, July 2013.

↑ Pier Arnoldi, 1994

↑ Jean Tinguely, 1982.

↑ Marylou Faure, 2021.

EXPORTING THE MONTREUX JAZZ FESTIVAL — In addition to the main event held each year in Montreux, the festival has created a kind of brand, a sort of "quality label," exporting the name and its formula to several other locations in the world: The Montreux-Detroit Jazz Festival, The Montreux-Atlanta Jazz Festival, Montreux Festival On Tour, and The Montreux Jazz Festival in Monaco. For years now there has been a Montreux Jazz Festival in Tokyo, one in Rio, and soon there will be one in Hangzhou, China.

In an interview Claude Nobs remarked that it was difficult for the Montreux festival to continue growing due to restraints such as seating capacity and traffic in the city. One option was to market the name, which means supporting other festivals while advertising Montreux and Switzerland. Both the name and the model work well as they offer a mixture of paid and free concerts, workshops given by musicians, competitions, access to archives, and involvement of local groups.

SUPPORT, STIMULATE, TRANSMIT

Over the course of its more than 50 festivals, Montreux Jazz has earned a special place in the music festival scene, establishing itself early on as a prestigious stage for top international musicians. Being invited to play at the festival is tantamount to receiving specific recognition for the value of one's artistic journey: "Montreux Jazz is the original prestige festival. If they invite you here, it is your duty and an honor to come and perform," says American drummer, DJ, and producer Questlove. Thanks to its high-profile artistic programming, the acoustic excellence of its halls, and the beauty of the location, the festival has based its success on building an identity of quality, professionalism, and dedication to music. If the origin of the festival was the desire to promote jazz, soul, and blues, soon the lineup began to include many other genres, presenting artists from different inspirations, backgrounds, and professional pathways but all united by the fact that they represent the best in their genres.

Looking at the evolution of its lineup, the element that perhaps returns most to characterize the festival's musical offering is the strong presence of what we can call Black music: from jazz to blues, soul to R&B, funk and rap to hip-hop, including a specific focus on Brazilian music. In this sense, the blending of these genres with more popular ones, such as rock and pop, as well as the juxtaposition of names known to the community of music connoisseurs, with more famous ones such as David Bowie, Elton John, or Deep Purple, has allowed the musical styles that are more historic or followed by experts and aficionados—such as jazz or blues—to meet a wider audience, find terrain for experimentation and innovation, and continue to evolve and stay in touch with contemporaneity.

The promotion of live music, the stimulus toward musical experimentation and hybridization, and the continuous search for quality are the axes on which the festival's artistic program takes shape. These are grafted onto its cultural project and are translated into a commitment to protect, transmit, and disseminate the highest level of music, as well as to support the artistic careers of young musicians from around the world. These two aspects are what gave rise to two specific lines of activity, which intersect the main one of the festival and amplify its work: the creation of a video archive of concerts, led by the Claude Nobs Foundation, and MJF Spotlight, a project that adds to the music promotion activities of the Montreux Jazz Artists Foundation in discovering and supporting new and emerging talents.

YAMAHA

MONTREUX MEDIA VENTURES — In the eyes of Claude Nobs, the cultural and artistic worth of what was happening on the stages of the Montreux Jazz Festival was evident from the very beginning. From the first festivals, he wanted to record all the concerts using the best technology available, thus setting the basis for the creation of "one of the world's largest private collections of 'live' music recordings," as stated on the Claude Nobs Foundation website. Today, this archive includes not only the historical memory of the festival's evolution, but also the musical history of jazz and other musical genres, from blues and rock to rap, soul, Latin, and many others.

To achieve this goal, in 1973 Nobs founded Montreux Sounds, which has been documenting the festival ever since and today is the owner of an archive of 5,000 "Live at the Montreux Jazz Festival" recordings, as well as a number of co-productions with the Swiss National Television (RTS) of early festivals. Montreux Sounds works for and together with artists, broadcasters, producers, filmmakers, documentary filmmakers, journalists, and cultural institutions. Not surprisingly, the Montreux Jazz Festival boasts a long list of albums released with the title "Live at Montreux." From Alanis Morissette to ZZ-Top, there are many artists who have benefited from the teams and documentation tools of Montreux Sounds, recording their own performances at the festival and releasing them on their own.

Under the guidance of the Claude Nobs Foundation, this unique collection of audiovisual archives has been included in UNESCO's Memory of the World Register. Thanks to a partnership with EPFL, the Federal Polytechnic School of Lausanne, the archives, which include more than 11,000 hours of live music, have been fully digitized and conserved since 2017. This initiative, Montreux Media Ventures, is the latest offshoot of the Montreux Jazz Festival and a source of additional income: thanks to the materials in the collection, many albums, documentaries, reports, and services are produced in addition to the media partnerships and collaborations initiated with TV stations, production houses, and other organizations.

At the heart of MJF's activities is a focus on music education and support for young talent. Against this backdrop, the pandemic saw the emergence of an additional youth promotion project, namely MJF Spotlight, an initiative conducted in partnership with TikTok and aimed at raising the visibility of up-and-coming young artists. Ahead of the 2022 edition, 20 young artists were selected who would be under the festival spotlight. These musicians perform during the course of the year and are then involved in the summer festival. Each month the festival devotes an in-depth feature to one of them with video interviews, live streams of their performances, and a playlist on Spotify with a compilation of their works.

Thanks to the attention to its artists, a real passion for music, and the highest quality in its every aspect, the Montreux Jazz Festival has been a venerated location for musicians from all over the world for 55 years. Here, the experiential dimension and the ability to create community go hand in hand with the fundamental cultural function of stimulating the creation, experimentation, and dissemination of music, and playing a fundamental role in the preservation and transmission of its repertoires, which are as ephemeral as all the various performing arts. ❡

←
Jamie Cullum performing at Montreux Jazz Festival, July 2018.

BURNING MAN

BURNINGMAN.ORG

— *An appointment in the desert*

↑

A crowd of thousands cheer as the Burning Man is burned and falls to the ground, September 2004.

We close this chapter with the case of a special event that struggles to fit into the categories we have used so far and, in some ways, encapsulates many of the aspects that characterize the festival as an aggregative form of artistic fruition and sharing. Burning Man is first and foremost a gathering that brings together thousands of people in the middle of the Black Rock Desert in Nevada, an area once occupied by a prehistoric lake and now commonly referred to by the "Burners" as "la playa."

What comes to life each late August in Black Rock City—the transitory town set up in the desert to host the festival and which, once it is over, disappears—is the materialization of a community utopia, where thousands of people gather in a climatically hostile place in conditions of pure survival. Indeed, there is no running water, no telephone reception, no housing, no money used: these are the ingredients to experience a different form of collective life, based on self-expression, self-determination, self-sufficiency and care, both of the place and of the community that inhabits it.

The element around which Burning Man brings people together is precisely artistic expression: some 114 large works of public art —created with environmental sustainability at the forefront—occupy "la playa," where participants can more or less interact with the installations. There are also DJ sets, concerts, fires, and other types of performances; group body practices such as yoga and meditation; and, of course, the final bonfire of the effigy after which the festival is named. Burning Man has initiated a true artistic movement that has spread throughout the world, carrying forward the principles and aesthetics born within the annual event.

Burning Man, however, is also a huge economic enterprise, with a budget of about $45 million and more than 100 employees. The primary intent is to avoid any commercial implications: "Burning Man is not a festival! It is a city where almost everything that happens is entirely created by its citizens, who are active participants in the experience," as the event website reports. Forget the bars, shops, and nightclubs of Glastonbury or Tomorrowland—money is practically nonexistent here; participants are expected to bring food, supplies, shelter, and whatever they may need. Everything else is bartered. Yet, there is an interesting

→→
The Burning Man festival happens every year at Black Rock Desert in northern Nevada. It starts on the last Monday in August and lasts a week.

musical lineup, which also draws in important names from the electronic, trap, and rock scene (in 2019, for example, Australian Flume, DJ Diplo, trapper Mr. Carmack, the Sacramento indie duo Hippie Sabotage, and French producer CloZee) to account for a ticket price ranging from $425 to $1,400.

AN ALTERNATIVE WORLD

Burning Man was born in 1986, when Larry Harvey and his friend Jerry James burned the first "Man" on a San Francisco beach; but at that time it was hardly an event. They lit it, and a curious crowd gathered around them to watch it burn, interacting with the wooden figure, singing, and dancing. As that crowd grew, they soon had to move from the beach to the Black Rock Desert. That crowd now consists of 70,000 people, the maximum allowed by the authorities. The founders of Burning Man define this event not as a festival but as a "global cultural movement based on ten practical principles" that define its distinct value and ethical universe: Radical inclusiveness, Gifting, Decommodification, Radical self-reliance, Radical self-expression, Communal effort, Civic responsibility, Leaving no trace, Participation, Immediacy.

> We have ten principles that people have to agree to follow. We didn't start with these. It basically was something that came about because of what we noticed was happening. It was about inclusivity, it was about leaving no trace, because we're guests on that desert. It was about self-reliance. You had to take care of yourself. Basically you end up helping your neighbors as well. It's about participating. There are no velvet ropes in front of the artwork. There's no standard that keeps you back from experiencing it. A person interacting with the art means that they are part of the artwork, not separate from it . . . Burning Man is also radically creative. It has no stage. It is an experiment in a temporary community. We ask participants to bring themselves.

This is how Crimson Rose, one of the founders of the Burning Man Project, expressed herself in an interview with the *LSE Business Review* (November 30, 2017). Rose is one of the key figures in the event, together with Larry Harvey, Jerry James,

Marian Goodell, Harley Dubois, Michael Mikel, and Will Roger Peterson. As co-founder of Burning Man, the Black Rock Arts Foundation and the Burning Man Project, Crimson Rose has been a part of the project since 1991. She also conceived the Art Department, which is in charge of everything that goes into making the large-scale participatory artworks for which Burning Man is famous. The official event website reports that under Crimson's guidance, Burning Man functions as an unlimited canvas of inspiration, whose works now find public placement in cities around the world and serve as catalytic sparks for community collaboration.

↓
A woman sits in a shelter during a dust storm on the playa of Black Rock Desert, August 2007.

↓
The sun rises behind a wood and neon statue, the centerpiece of the annual Burning Man festival, August 2002.

Another key figure is Marian Goodell, also among the founders and CEO of the Burning Man Project, part of it since 1995, and cofounder of the organization that later became Black Rock City LLC, which produces the event. She served as director of business and communications, leading the development of the Burning Man Regional Network, now streaming in six continents, with more than 300 representatives in 40 countries. Although originally designed as a for-profit business, Burning Man is now run by a not-for-profit organization called the Burning Man Project. As reported in *LSE Business Review* of November 30, 2017.

We started as Black Rock City LLC and then, leading up to 2012, we created the Burning Man Project. It is the not-for-profit umbrella for the subsidiaries . . . we actually gifted our ownership over to the Burning Man Project, for the whole community. We pay taxes. We pay a lot of money in taxes. And it has to be that way . . . For many years we made no profits. Whatever there was went right back into the business. We had to become a real organization and be real.

The element of rejecting commodification is one of the hallmarks of the entire project, even though this is an initiative that requires very high costs and generates equally high revenues.

Precisely because of this, and thanks to its iconicity, Burning Man attracts many technology leaders, including Elon Musk, CEO of Tesla, Sergey Brin and Larry Page, the founders of Google, and Mark Zuckerberg of Facebook/Meta. Yet, paradoxically, while most of the festivals described in these pages are highly receptive to social media, Marian Goodell deplores their use, stating how they pollute the spirit of an event, without any connection to the founders' idea, and emphasizing the core element of an event like Burning Man: "What is important is finding your community there, not checking a box and showing it on Instagram."

FROM SPECTATOR TO PERFORMER — In a radical and amplified fashion, Burning Man offers us a concrete example of the elements on which the cultural action of festivals is modeled. These are processes such as the creation of community, cohesion, sociality, and the construction of an experience around artistic languages that are capable of having an impact both on the subjectivities at play and the very dynamics of artistic creation—and so, transform them. In essence, a mechanism that expansively reproduces the very

→→
Burning Man festival, August 2003.

pp. → 386 | 387

objective of the artwork. Wendy Clupper explains it well in the 2007 book *Festivalising! Theatrical Events, Politics and Culture*:

> Burning Man as a festival-space offers participants a landscape that is vast and, like the theatrical art forms it hosts, hybrid in nature and seemingly unlimited in vision. Part of the Burning Man experience is the inability of participants to really explain what Burning Man is and is like, and that for one to know they simply must go. This moment of recognition represents the initial awareness of the cultural experience of Burning Man, one that turns spectators into performers . . . Inasmuch as it is a transformative experience it must be emphasized that it does offer participants the opportunity to break free of not only the social roles that are imposed on them and that they play out every day, but also the chance to interact with others in a uniquely performative way.
>
> As the escapist alternative to mainstream society in America, the festival culture of Burning Man rejects commodification, encourages radical self-expression and subverts the usual social order by providing participants the opportunity to explore change in social behavior away from economic competition . . . Burning Man inspires this community-making both on site and off, as it has established its culture beyond the immediate theatrical experience through regional and online communities, thus creating a collective identity. Participants are culturally significant as artist collectives because they represent through their flamboyance, exhibitionism, and transgressions, a new social category for cultural performativity.

Burning Man is, therefore, the place where the distinction between spectator and performer is blurred, because every aspect of the event is "to be done": all are called on to participate in the creation of the conditions for a unique and unrepeatable experience to take place, one that is completely independent from the festival lineup. While it is true that any manifestation of performance culture would be stunted if the audience were not there to actualize it, here the performing DJs are as much protagonists as the colorful and extravagant participants who dance, create, and interact for eight days, heedless of the temperature changes, dust, and having to share out-

door showers with thousands of people. Here, miles away from the nearest urban center, we concretely experience a different form of society, based on altruism and sharing, which is the other side of the coin of radical self-acceptance. A utopia that goes on stage for eight days every year, made possible thanks to the contribution of thousands of people, where art is the binding agent, the means of self-expression, and communication with others. Burning Man is something that profoundly marks those who experience it; one shared wish is that it's taken farther afield than the isolated perimeter of Black Rock City to give rise to a global network of artists, performers, and enthusiasts who—through their own practices—seek to translate the change experienced in that isolated place in the middle of the Nevada desert. ❡

↓ The Flaming Lotus Girls of San Francisco, *The Serpent Mother*, August 2006.

CANADA
INDIA
FRANCE
ITALY
HUNGARY
ATLAS OF PERFORMING CULTURE

USA
BRAZIL
AUSTRALIA
SPAIN
JAPAN
MALAYSIA
PORTUGAL
SWITZERLAND
PUERTO RICO
MUSIC FESTIVALS

-22° 59′ 59″ N -43° 21′ 58″ E

ROCK IN RIO

RIO DE JAINERO / BRAZIL

Rock in Rio is one of the world's largest music festivals dedicated primarily to rock music. Since the first festival held in Rio de Janeiro in 1985, it has hosted, among many others, top bands and performers such as AC/DC, Queen, James Taylor, George Benson, Al Jarreau, and Yes, highlighting the non-exclusively rock matrix that the event has adopted over time. Since 2004, the festival has also been held in other locations such as Lisbon, Madrid, and in Las Vegas in 2015.

↓ Favela's Espace, Rock in Rio, September 2022.

→ Black Pantera & Devotos performing at Rock in Rio, September 2022: Fernando Schlaepfer's "All Power to the People" tattoo.

45° 30′ 53″ N -73° 31′ 58″ E

OSHEAGA MUSIC AND ARTS FESTIVAL

MONTREAL / CANADA

Every summer on Île Sainte-Hélène, thousands of visitors take over the green lawns of Parc Jean-Drapeau to attend one of Canada's leading music events, the Osheaga Music and Arts Festival. Between well-known names and up-and-coming artists, the festival (which is named after the former denomination of the region) is known for the diversity of its audience and featured artists.

↑ Machine Gun Kelly performs at the Osheaga festival at Parc Jean-Drapeau, Montreal, July 2022.

41° 53′ 5″ N -87° 39′ 53″ E

PITCHFORK MUSIC FESTIVAL

CHICAGO / USA

↓
Tame Impala performs at Pitchfork festival, Union Park, Chicago, July 2018.

→→
Erykah Badu performs at Pitchfork festival, Chicago, July 2021.

Founded in 2006 as the brainchild of Ryan Schreiber's well-known online magazine *Pitchfork*, the festival of the same name focuses on the indie/alternative rock scene. Over time, it has started to tap into the latest trends in contemporary music by opening up to jazz, electronica, and hip-hop. In 2011 the festival inaugurated its own European offshoot, held annually in Paris at the Grande Halle de la Villette.

43° 31′ 54′′ N 5° 26′ 53′′ E

FESTIVAL D'AIX-EN-PROVENCE

AIX-EN-PROVENCE / FRANCE

↓

Iolanta by Pyotr Tchaikovsky, directed by Peter Sellars, Grand Théâtre de Provence, Aix-en-Provence, July 2015.

Between Provence and the French Riviera, the city of Aix-en-Provence has hosted one of Europe's leading opera music festivals since 1948. Founded by stage director Gabriel Dussurget, based on an idea of Countess Lily Pastré, each year the festival presents the best of international classical music and opera in its four venues: the Archevêché theater, the Grande Théâtre de Provence, the Théâtre du Jeu de Paume, and the Hôtel Maynier d'Oppède.

37° 7′ 4″ N -8° 32′ 7″ E

AFRO NATION

PORTIMÃO / PORTUGAL SAN JUAN / PUERTO RICO

↓

Afro Nation festival, San Juan, Puerto Rico, March 2022.

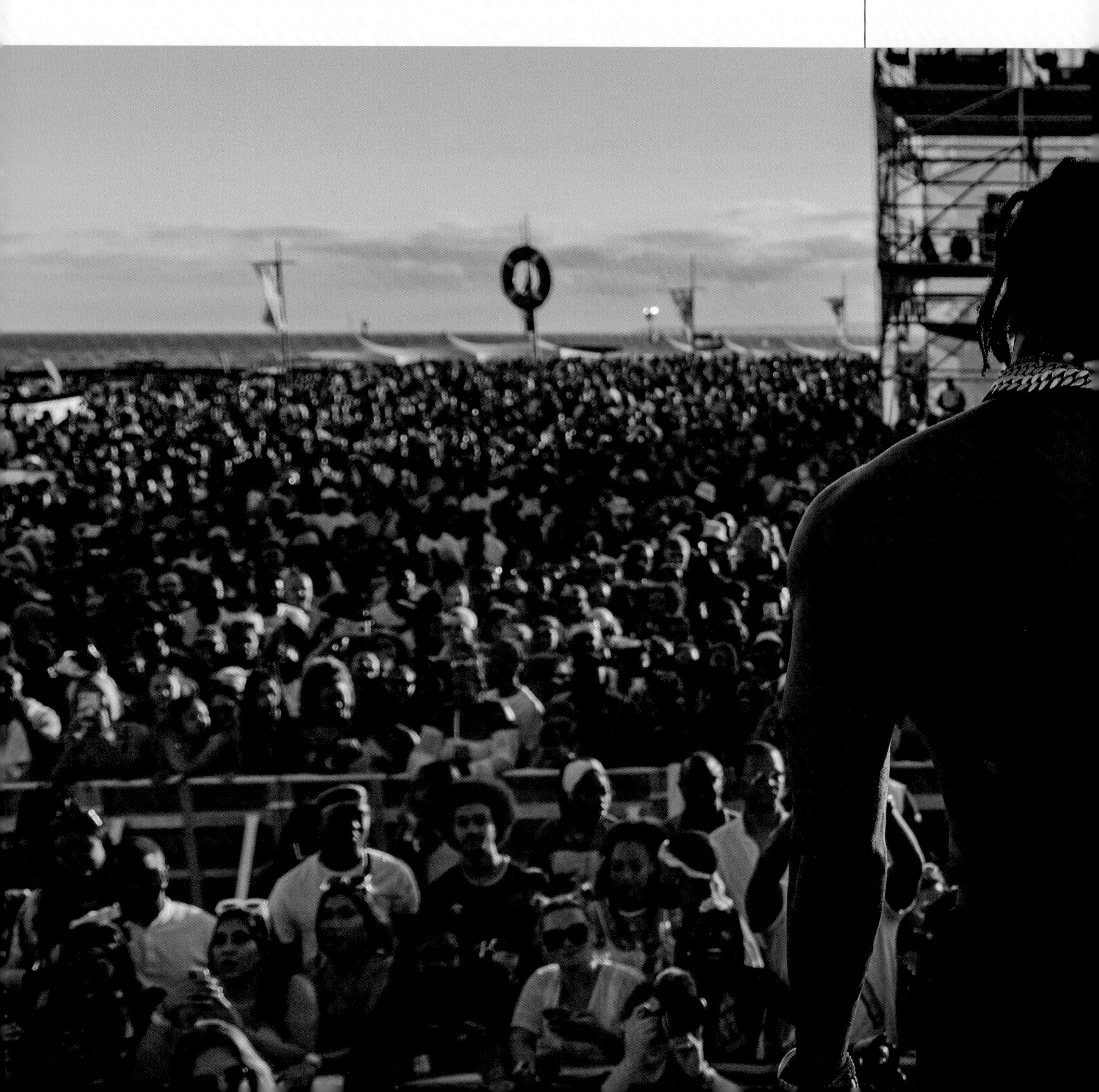

Established in 2019 based on an initiative of two Nigerian entrepreneurs, Smade and Obi Asika, Afro Nation is a music festival dedicated to African music. Afrobeats, hip-hop, R&B, dancehall, and amapiano are just some of the genres that feature at the festival, which was established with the specific intention of bringing together African artists from various parts of the world. The first festival was held in Algarve in Portugal; over time it expanded to add further locations in Puerto Rico and Miami.

40° 38′ 55″ N 14° 36′ 46″ E

RAVELLO FESTIVAL

RAVELLO / ITALY

The brainchild of Paolo Caruso to celebrate the music of German composer Richard Wagner, the Ravello Festival focuses primarily on classical music but is also open to film and literature. Since 1953, the beautiful terrace of Villa Rufolo has hosted the most famous international orchestras, such as the Royal Philharmonic Orchestra, the London Symphony Orchestra, and the St. Petersburg Philharmonic Orchestra.

↓ Piano concert at the Ravello Festival, Summer 1967.

47° 30′ 16″ N 9° 44′ 16″ E

LUCERNE FESTIVAL

LUCERNE / SWITZERLAND

↑
Daniel Harding directs the National Youth Orchestra of the USA, European Tour of August 2022.

Founded in 1938 by Ernest Ansermet and Walter Schulthess, the Lucerne Festival is one of Europe's leading events dedicated to classical music. It currently branches into three annual events—the main one in the summer and the other two in the spring and fall—and is accompanied by the activities of the Lucerne Festival Academy, where participants work with the best-known international composers and orchestra directors on contemporary productions from the twentieth and twenty-first centuries.

30° 1′ 10″ N -89° 59′ 17″ E

NEW ORLEANS JAZZ & HERITAGE FESTIVAL

NEW ORLEANS / USA

↓

BB King shaking hands with fans during the New Orleans Jazz & Heritage Festival, April 1978.

The New Orleans Jazz & Heritage Festival is a celebration of Louisiana's cultural heritage, including its food, crafts, and music. Created in 1970 by George Wein, for many years the festival has offered the best of jazz, gospel, blues, and world music, both traditional and experimental. In over 50 years, its stages have hosted performances by the likes of Mahalia Jackson, Duke Ellington, Miles Davis, Stevie Wonder, Eric Clapton, Santana, Fats Domino, and many others.

28° 17′ 47″ N 75° 16′ 29″ E

MAGNETIC FIELDS

ALSISAR / INDIA

↑ Artists perform during the Magnetic Fields festival, Alsisar, June 2015.

The Magnetic Fields festival has been held every year since 2013 in the abandoned spaces of the Maharaja's old palace in Alsisar, Rajasthan. Underground electronic music, performances by local musicians, and a celebration of traditional Indian culture are the features of a festival that has established itself as one of the most interesting events on the Asian scene.

36° 49′ 32″ N 139° 4′ 33″ E

LABYRINTH

NAEBA GREENLAND / JAPAN

Founded in 2008 and set among the green mountains of Niigata Prefecture, Labyrinth is now one of the most fascinating festivals dedicated to electronic music. Renowned for its secret lineups and the limited number of available tickets, this festival offers the possibility to enjoy the most experimental electronic music in close contact with nature.

↓ Labyrinth festival, Japan, 2022.

41° 24′ 34″ N 2° 13′ 33″ E

PRIMAVERA SOUND

BARCELONA / SPAIN

↓ Primavera Sound avant-garde music festival, Barcelona, June 2022.

Primavera Sound is a multi-genre festival established in 2001 and held annually in Barcelona at the beautiful Parc del Fòrum. Since it started, it has hosted leading groups from the international music scene—from indie to mainstream—offering innovative lineups from rock music through pop to electronic. Its success brought the festival to add further editions in Porto in 2012 and in Buenos Aires, São Paulo, Los Angeles, and Santiago, Chile, in 2022.

41° 52′ 36″ N -87° 37′ 9″ E

LOLLAPALOOZA

CHICAGO / USA

Lollapalooza has been held since 1991 in Grant Park in the very heart of Chicago. Initially dedicated to alternative rock, the festival has expanded to welcome electronic, pop, hip-hop, and heavy metal. Created by Perry Farrell, the front man of Jane's Addiction, it has over time become an internationally renowned festival, hosting the biggest and most acclaimed international musicians on its stage.

↓

Victoria De Angelis and Thomas Raggi of Måneskin perform at Lollapalooza, Chicago, July 2022.

-28° 28′ 53″ N 153° 30′ 57″ E

SPLENDOUR IN THE GRASS

YELGUN / AUSTRALIA

↑ Duke Dumont performs at Splendour in the Grass, Yelgun, July 2022.

Since 2001, Splendour in the Grass has brought the North Byron Parklands location to life. Surrounded by greenery, this site immersed in nature regularly hosts various types of cultural events. The festival is dedicated to rock, hip-hop, and electronica, and welcomes thousands of spectators each year; in previous years, artists such as Kendrick Lamar, The Cure, Coldplay, Tyler The Creator, James Blake, and Ben Harper have performed on its stage.

1° 44′ 59″ N 110° 19′ E

RAINFOREST WORLD MUSIC FESTIVAL (RWMF)

KUCHING / MALAYSIA

↓
Ballet Folclórico de Chile (BAFOCHI) of Rapa Nui performing during the Rainforest World Music Festival at Sarawak Cultural Village, Kuching, July 2019.

Every year since 1998, the region of Sarawak, known for the local ethnic music Sape, has hosted RWMF, a festival dedicated to traditional music and, more generally, world music. Created to celebrate the diversity of world music, the festival seeks to encourage the use of traditional instruments through dedicated workshops and sometimes overlaps into contemporary genres.

47° 32′ 55″ N 19° 3′ 5″ E

SZIGET FESTIVAL

BUDAPEST / HUNGARY

↑ Justin Bieber on stage at Sziget Festival on Óbuda island, Budapest, August 2022.

Sziget Festival has been held every summer since 1993 on the Óbuda island in the middle of the Danube River in Budapest. A brainchild of Hungarian artist Péter Sziámi Müller, the festival is dedicated to music in all its forms. In recent years it has drawn the largest numbers of attendees in the world for an event of this genre. In addition to music—the primary focus of the festival—the island is brought to life with theater, dance, circus performances, and every kind of entertainment imaginable.

41° 21′ 18 N 2° 7′ 57 E

SÓNAR FESTIVAL

BARCELONA / SPAIN

The Sónar Festival was founded in Barcelona in 1994 by the music critic Ricardo Robles and the musicians and visual artists Enric Palau and Sergio Caballero. Born with the title Festival of Advanced Music and Multimedia Art, since its inception Sónar has highlighted the close connection between music, new technologies, and visual arts. This connection is emphasized by the location of this two-part festival, organized in Sónar by Day and Sónar by Night. Over the years, the festival has completed many collaborative projects with the Centre de Cultura Contemporània de Barcelona and Museu d'Art Contemporani de Barcelona. To date, the festival—now joined by Sónar +D, a collaboration dedicated to the relationship between technology and creativity—has achieved impressive numbers, becoming one of the reference points in the European and international music scene.

→ Sónar Festival, Barcelona, Summer 2022.

→→ Sónar Festival, Barcelona, Summer 2022.

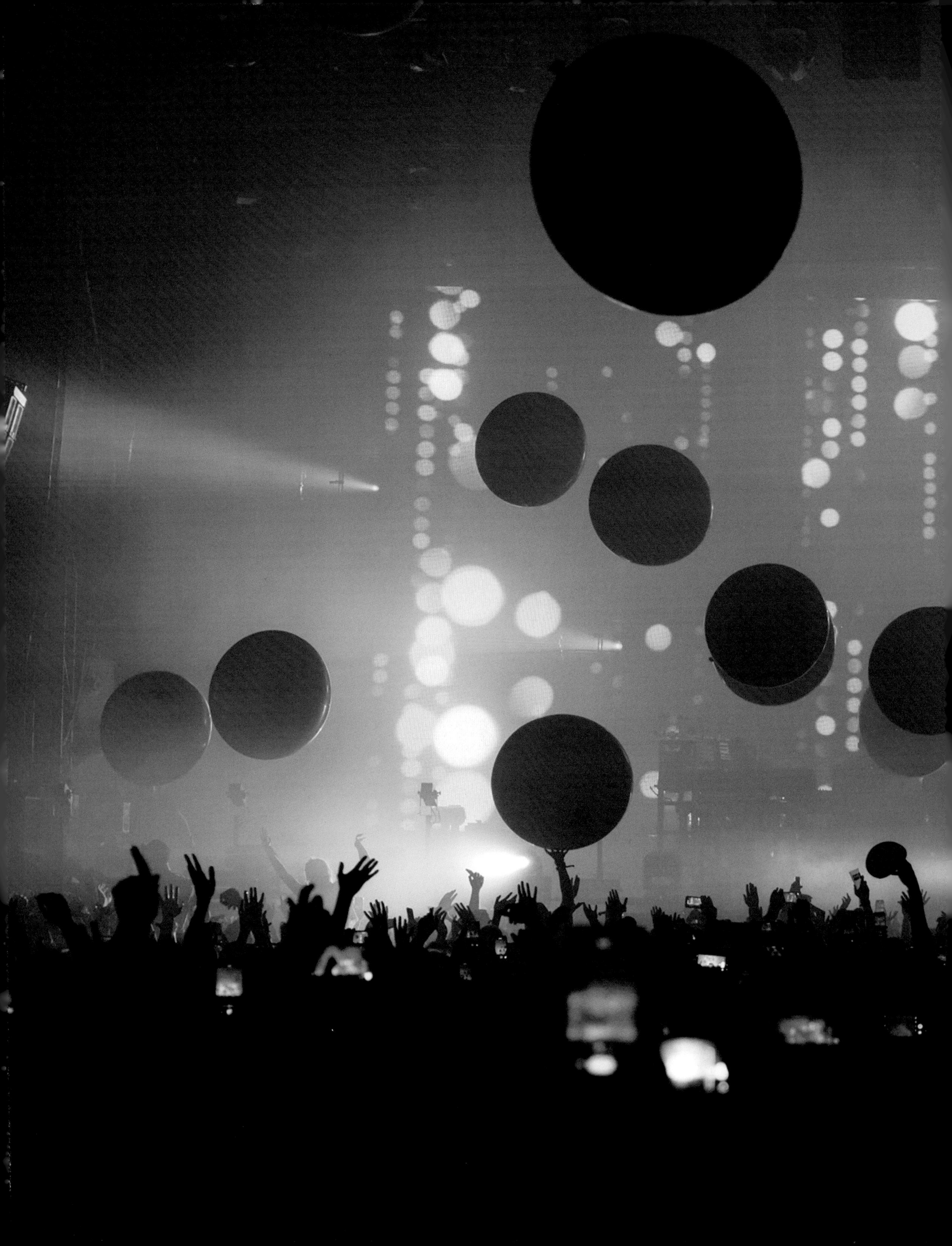

CONCLUSION

On May 10, 2020, in the midst of the pandemic crisis, the rapper Travis Scott unveiled his new single on Fortnite through a ten-minute performance involving some twelve million viewers. Fortnite is one of the most widely played online video games in the world, which *The New York Times* defined as "the Instagram of video games." Distributed over various servers, players could watch through their avatar the show put on by the American rapper who, in the guise of a virtual giant towering over the video game scenarios, interacted with the surrounding world, which took form as the virtual performance progressed. The players/viewers experienced the concert by moving through the scenarios that were being constructed. They increased their participation by interacting autonomously with the world around them, receiving a unique perspective of the performance. The show broadcast on Fortnite was not simply the translation of a live concert into a video game. By taking advantage of the graphic capacities of the platform, the spectacularity of the performance was enhanced by shifting the relationship with the viewers up to a higher level, stimulating their sensory experience instead of relying on the mere passive reception of the visual content witnessed. The experience acquired a personal interpretation, an autonomous construction based on the perspective from which it was enjoyed, while still a collective spectacle consolidated by the shared component of an experience that initially may appear individual, given its digital format.

The concert on Fortnite opened the doors to large-scale performativity in the metaverse, demonstrating how it is possible to act in a completely virtual environment even for artistic initiatives that consider the direct, physical relationship with their audience their raison d'être. Travis Scott's performance marked a turning point for the performing arts, rewriting the notions of live performance and presence. It marked a fundamental shift in the ongoing transformations that have been accelerated (not created) by the pandemic, which only sped up processes that had already been germinating for several years. The social context of today's post-digital age has transformed our relationship with the digital, which is now a *de facto* component of everyday life. This transformation has obviously taken root in all of today's social expressions—whether culture-related or not—and increases our relational capacity. In the world of performing arts, this change has been reflected in different ways, firstly by not distorting the fundamental element represented by the performer-spectator relationship. The pandemic has led artists and cultural institutions to rethink spaces of action by imagining new ones and reinventing existing ones. The potential generated by this process has set the ground for the emergence of new emotional states, but also innovative practices and relational breakthroughs within performance. In a context that has experienced the emergence of a significant crisis in all cultural spheres—especially those in which a live component is a fundamental element—we have witnessed an ongoing process of redefinition that has transported performativity to the next level.

Perhaps the most significant breakthrough that led to a re-discussion of the entire art world was the introduction of the metaverse and, to a lesser degree, of Non-Fungible Tokens (NFTs). The world of performing arts too has had to deal with the metaverse revolution that now pervades the entire performance sector, from dance to music and theater. Obviously, the metaverse dimension is still being defined and experimented with, but there are several cultural centers and theaters that are accompanying more traditional cultural production—now thankfully functioning again following the pandemic—with evolving expressive languages focused not on the total virtualization of content but on a powerful hybridization between physical performance and new digital spaces. It is no coincidence that alongside the diffusion of the metaverse, immersive technologies or XR (eXtended Reality), such as VR (virtual reality) and AR (Augmented Reality), are increasingly central to the Performing Arts, underscoring the "in presence" approach of performative instances that cannot be detached from this *modus operandi*. Thanks to the metaverse, artists are able to create unique performances that combine 3D graphics, human interaction, sound carpets, and powerful immersive storytelling that, when enjoyed through a virtual reality viewer, manifest unprecedented emotional power and capacity to engage. This is complemented by the possibility of reaching wider audiences and participating in story-living modes related to much-loved gaming. This is seen in the GenZ, who are no longer "video-first" but socialize, relate, purchase, and entertain themselves through gaming, interaction, and immersiveness.

Cultural centers, theaters, and multidisciplinary and music festivals are exploring the issue of the metaverse and extended realities with increasing attention. An example is the Matadero in Madrid, which is planning an exhibition entitled *Exhibition Metaverse Until 2023: Realities in Transition*, featuring a selection of different metaverses. The works were created during the pandemic and can be considered as cultural alternatives to the "metaversal" constructs of digital behemoths such as Zuckerberg's Meta. The specifics of each metaverse are different, ranging from virtual landscapes filled with artwork to actual clubs. The goal of the exhibition is not only to experience new virtual spaces, but to analyze how, through the metaverse, new forms of physicality arise and are translated into virtual contexts. Again, hybridization takes center stage in the construction of new expressive languages in which materiality and virtuality merge. The Matadero exhibition also underlines the need to reinforce the relationship between performativity and sociality through the creation of new spaces, in which even the mere presence or choice of one's avatar constitutes a principle of performativity. As part of the main exhibition, the Matadero unveiled in early 2023 a project dedicated to the construction of *e-raves:* "hybrid actions and online exhibitions in metaverses, virtual reality platforms, and streaming platforms (Club Cooee, IMVU, Twitch), where attendees can interact and be part of the experience through 3D avatars juxtaposed with the physical space." Organized by Neuro-Dungeon with the collaboration of several local and international artists and DJs, the project aims to create new urban gathering spaces in parallel with Matadero's goals and activities in the physical dimension. On the music festival front, the next edition of Barcelona's Sónar Festival scheduled for summer 2023, with the subtitle *Music, Creativity & Technology*, has dedicated several slots to performances related to Virtual Reality (VR) and Augmented Reality (AR). This will transform and expand the festival's physical dimension by transcending its physicality and expanding its receptivity. In addition, the entire campaign was managed by AI (Artificial Intelligence), which processed all the images from the previous 29 festivals to celebrate the thirtieth one.

Dance and theater have also moved toward the metaverse, seeking to actualize their expressive languages and increase their audience. Again in contexts of emergency that brought theaters and other cultural institutions to the brink of an unprecedented crisis, the virtual derivations of these performances should not be considered as single episodes but as a collateral evolution of more traditional work. There have been projects in which physical performativity has been hybridized through digital immersion in virtual spaces. One of these—*Dancing in the Metaverse*—is a hybrid online and onsite performance organized by Goldsmiths University in London. Broadcast via live streaming, this performance consists of a "digital dance" in which three performers move together in real time through a remote connection. The intimate interaction between the distant artists, who are physically present in London and New York, takes place within a computer-generated virtual landscape, with their avatars spinning shapes, lights, and particles that intertwine to give a sense of virtual contact and physical connection via motion-capture technology. In addition to the evolution of dance in virtual contexts, another interesting aspect is the phenomenon of delocalization that a certain type of experience can generate. Through virtual reality technologies and the construction of alternative worlds, performers present in different locations can be linked in a single space, multiplying modalities for the performance to be enjoyed.

→→
Eric Prydz presents *Holo*, Sónar Festival, Barcelona, Summer 2022.

pp. → 422 | 423

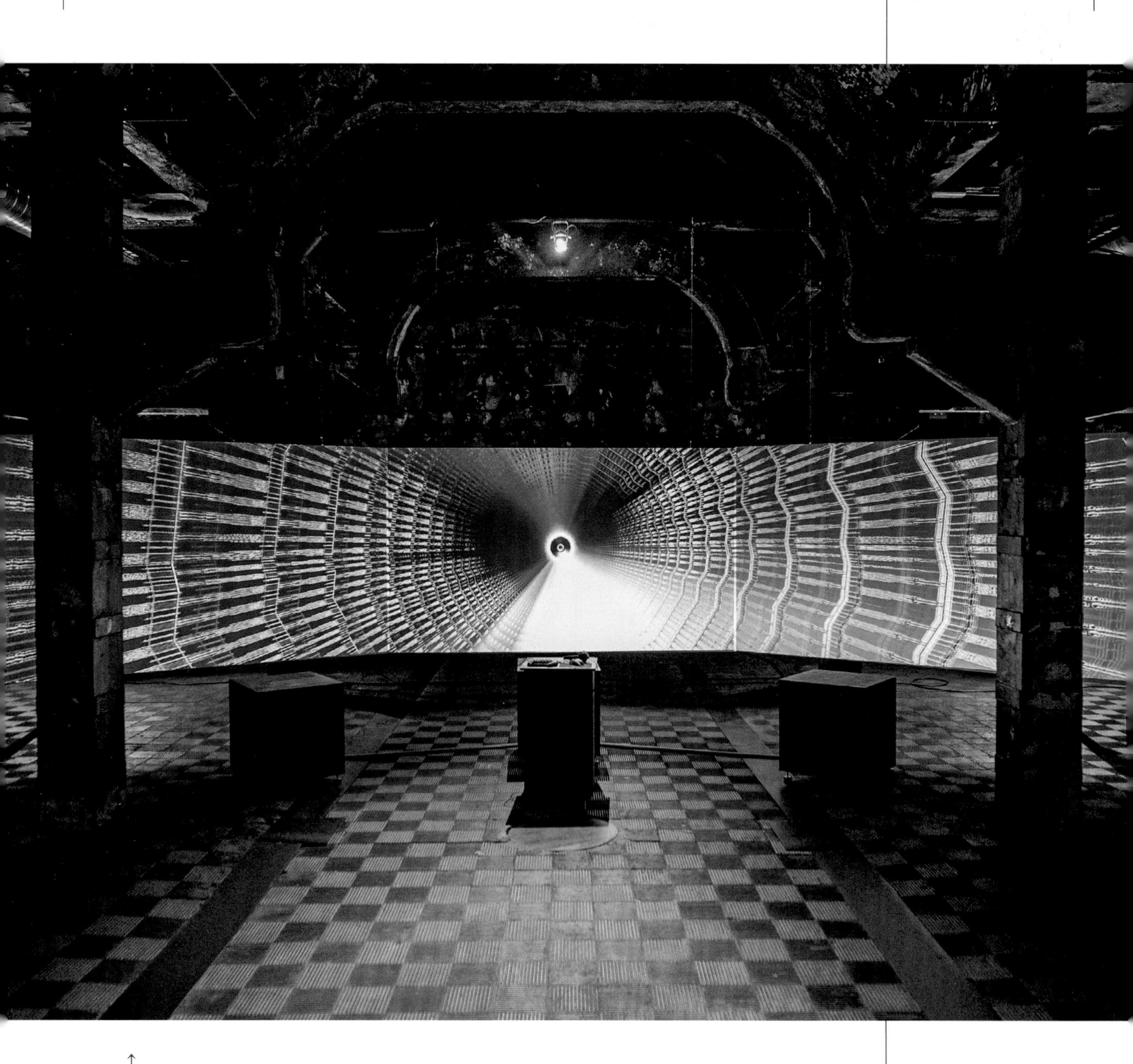

↑
The *Metaversos. Realidades en transición* exhibition, L.E.V. festival, Matadero Madrid, 2023.

Another dance-related project revolving around virtual reality is the work of Spanish choreographer and director Blanca Li entitled *Le Bal de Paris*. Presented at the 78th Venice Film Festival in the section dedicated to VR, it received the "Best Experience" award. *Le Bal de Paris* is an immersive performance that engages the viewers in a total experience while watching through visors. The public watches the performance of the two lead dancers interacting with each other and with the surrounding world that envelops them. The bond between dance and eXtended Reality (XR) is a very powerful combination that many artists take into consideration when creating their own works. The 2022 edition of the ZED festival (the international video dance festival) in Bologna also devoted much of its programming to XR, giving space to the works of French choreographer Fabien Prioville.

While kindred and complementary to the metaverse, the phenomenon of Non-Fungible Tokens (NFTs) is still distant from the performing arts world, even though in recent years there have been some sporadic contacts between the two. Early approaches were simply virtual attestations of the recordings of performance acts, as in the case of Marina Abramović's *The Hero* in 2001. In this case, the artist repurposed her work by adapting it to modern video formats and recording its certification, which was done digitally in the form of an NFT.

Some performance actions, however, have dealt with NFTs differently by reflecting on the processing and the very nature of non-fungible tokens. One example is the performative action of the provocative artist Petr Davydtchenko who, outside the European Parliament, protested against "the depravity of pharmaceutical companies" by eating a live bat. Beyond the aesthetic qualities and sense of performance, what makes this interesting is that the action was disseminated directly through the OpenSea digital marketplace platform solely as a digital artifact. Considered the first experiment in NFT performance, it still falls into the category of an action that ignores the procedural mechanics behind blockchains and NFTs, but focuses primarily on the search for an alternative art market that is more democratic and free from any outdated logic. This primacy, however, is challenged by another Russian activist through a work with aesthetic implications that are far more interesting and complex than a mere protest. The work in question is *The Title*, the artist is named Pak. It all started as a Twitter post in which Pak offered his work to an auction house; it was acquired by Sotheby's in 2020 and resold soon after. *The Title* reflects on the issues of authenticity and artistic value that are generated by NFTs. The work is composed of several versions of the same digital image sold at widely varying prices, from zero up to $1 million for an aptly named edition, *The Unsold*. Consisting of multiple sales and deriving its artistic significance from the participation with buyers has led some media to consider this as the first example of NFT performance art. The performative aspect is reflected in the action itself and in the concept behind the operation, as Melissa Gilmour, a curator specializing in NFT, says: "art is both an object and a process in the NFT space." It is interesting to consider this process as a performative act, and the virtual space of NFTs as fertile territory for experimentation with new forms of performativity. A change of value in art is currently ongoing and this is precisely what the mysterious Pak reflects on: whether the true value of the work is in its data file or whether it is the creative process itself that generates value.

Having established the ever-changing boundaries of the metaverse and NFTs, it is crucial to focus on the primary change we are currently witnessing—that is, the disruption of the paradigms of media liveness, which is the transformation of the very concept of live through its transition into a digital format. The pivotal idea of liveness, the *hic et nunc*, the co-presence of the performer and spectator sharing both space and time has been upturned by the digitization of some artistic content, especially since the rather violent acceleration brought about by the pandemic that revolutionized live performance and its enjoyment. The process that has brought about the greatest evolution is the massive diffusion of live streaming and the affirmation of *digital liveness*. Created primarily for the dissemination of amateur performance content and to consolidate sociality in a digital format, in recent years live streaming has redefined how artistic/performance content is disseminated. The ubiquity of digital live streaming has caused the performer/audience relationship to evolve and follow completely different trajectories. The border that separates them has been eliminated, thus creating a greater amplitude and causing the evolution of new languages by the performer who—aided by new technologies—is the recipient of the spectators' experience, which then becomes an integral part of the performance itself. An example in this regard is the activity of the Venezuelan producer and singer Alejandra Ghersi Rodríguez (aka Arca) through her Twitch account, a pivotal platform of digital live performativity. In 2020, in the midst of the pandemic, Arca started by live broadcasting one of her preview tracks. She did not limit herself, however, to using the platform solely as another channel to distribute her music, but imported her queer accelerationist aesthetics into the creation of live shows in which she alternates between simple conversations with the audience, live composition, and visual research. The shared creative process becomes an opportunity for Arca to produce autonomous contents that are not only inspired by input from her followers but which experiment with new relationships with the audience.

Some artists have taken this new type of digital interaction to even greater extremes, whereas others have transformed the absence of the audience in venues

→
Le Bal de Paris by Blanca Li, immersive performance, 78th Venice Film Festival, Summer 2021.

→→
Il barbiere di Siviglia by W. A. Mozart, musical direction by Daniele Gatti, staging and direction by Mario Martone, 2021/2022 season.

designated for performativity into a tool to enhance the message and potency of their performance. One example is Mario Martone's productions of Verdi's *La Traviata* and Rossini's *Il Barbiere di Siviglia* for the Teatro dell'Opera in Rome. In these two performances Martone transformed the theater spaces, empty of any public by *force majeure*, into a site-specific device. In Rossini's work, the Neapolitan director used the absence of spectators as a fundamental element of the performance, which was emphasized when broadcast and streamed by the Italian national television network RAI. For *La Traviata*, Martone's intervention was even more powerful, creating greater spectacularity by breaking down the boundary between the stage and the space reserved for the audience and transforming the whole theater into a single stage. Martone's operations must obviously be analyzed in the extraordinary context in which they were created; with the return of an audience, they obviously lose that specific significance. This gives us an ideal opportunity to rethink stage spaces, the stage/audience dichotomy, and the forms in which a theatrical performance can be disseminated. The relationship with the audience and its presence—or absence—is central to Martone's productions and, more generally, it is a topical issue in the discussion of the post-pandemic future of performing arts. There is still no clear answer as there is no single way ahead, but much thought has been dedicated to this matter; reflections were born precisely through the performative effort, the practice of and experimentation with a new language, a new performative aesthetic, and a renewed vision of relations. One work that has certainly placed these issues under the spotlight is the performance *DOOU* of the Rome artist Nico Vascellari, which was live-streamed on YouTube on May 2, 2020. Created to present the new channel of CODALUNGA (an experimental platform that commissions content and audiovisual interventions from various international artists), the performance consisted of a live broadcast lasting 24 consecutive hours in which the artist chanted like a mantra the phrase "I trusted you." With a clear reference to Andy Kaufman, one of the most brilliant performers in American history, *DOOU* immediately received attention for the impression it creates, initially onanistic and provocative. By donning the guise of something disturbing, Vascellari reflects on the limitations of the artist/performer and so the performance becomes an important litmus test to analyze the viewer's innovative approach in participating in such an event. The total absence of an audience at the performance venue was substituted by the comments published during the live-stream that triggered a process of shared participation and a powerful feeling of being part of a community. Many and varied reactions were received, from those who commented negatively, not comprehending the utility of such an action, to those who could not help but return to the live broadcast, even after leaving it. This highlights the driving power of a work that carefully reflects on a specific historical moment. Vascellari clearly emphasizes the importance of presence, taking to the next level what RoseLee Goldberg upholds: that performance insists on actual presence, on the very experience of *being there* where the *there* of the viewer is no longer in front of/with the performer in a delimited physical space, but is present in the digital unboundedness

The panorama that has been outlined here delineates just some of the traveled and other still-to-be-traveled paths of the performing arts in an attempt to identify directions for research and experimentation, contemporary trends, and future challenges to be faced when entering the post-digital era. What is increasingly important to understand is that performativity has become central to our everyday lives; the way the new generations relate to one another explains how human "contact" is increasingly filtered in a relentless quest to perform, to showcase, and share every aspect of one's life through a digital filter. Social media platforms, particularly TikTok, have accelerated this process: they have become the ideal filter for externalizing a performativity that we can define as continuous, and that is no longer a necessity but an acquired relational approach. This is a mode of communication that has become the most defining and totalizing aspect of social rituals. This was evident in one of the most powerful events in recent years, Pope Francis's benediction to the faithful in empty St. Peter's Square during the pandemic. Before a sea of faithful worshipers who were not there but at home, watching on television or live streaming by the state television RAI, in an atmosphere of heart-wrenching poignancy the Pope addressed an empty square, his joined hands emphasizing how no physical limits exist in creating performance.

→→

Pope Francis leads the Via Crucis ceremony in front of St. Peter's Basilica, Vatican, April 2020.

CRISTIANO LEONE

Cristiano Leone is a philologist, university lecturer, curator, artistic director, and cultural entrepreneur. He has worked both in the public and private sectors and has collaborated with Sorbonne Universités, Villa Médicis – Académie de France à Rome, the National Roman Museum, the Spanish Embassy in Italy, the INDA Foundation (National Institute of Ancient Drama), the Teatro Due Foundation, the Centre des Monuments Nationaux, and Hermès International. He has taught at University of Namur, Sciences Po Paris, Bocconi University in Milan, and Luiss Guido Carli Business School in Rome. Cristiano has written several volumes for leading publishing houses such as Salerno Editrice, Accademia Nazionale dei Lincei, and Electa. He is based in Rome, Paris, and Capri.

Introduction. Culture that Transforms

PERFORMANCE ART:

– Aubin, Charles, Carlos Mínguez Carrasco (eds.). *Bodybuilding. Architecture and Performance*. New York: Performa, 2020.

– Austin, John L. *How to do Things with Words*, eds. J. O. Urmson and Marina Sbisà. Oxford : Clarendon Press, 1975.

– Bacon, T. J. *An Introduction to Phenomenology of Performance Art: SELF/s*. Chicago: University of Chicago Press, 2022.

– Barilli, Renato. *Prima e dopo il 2000: La ricerca artistica 1970-2005*. Milan: Feltrinelli, 2006.

– Battcock, Gregory, Robert Nickas (eds.). *The Art of Performance: A Critical Anthology*. Boston: E. P. Dutton, 1984.

– Boulle, Catherine, Jay Pather (eds.). *Acts of Transgression: Contemporary Live Art in South Africa*. Johannesburg: Wits University Press, 2019.

– Brimfeld, Mel. *This Is Performance Art*. London: Black Dog Publishing, 2011.

– Cassel Oliver, Valerie (ed.). *Radical Presence: Black Performance in Contemporary Art*. Houston: Contemporary Arts Museum, 2013.

– De Bellis, Vincenzo, *La performance dal tempo sospeso. Il tableau vivant tra realtà e rappresentazione*. Milan: Mousse Publishing, 2015.

– Duberman, Martin. *Black Mountain: An Exploration in Community*. Boston: E. P. Dutton, 1972.

– Fischer-Lichte, Erika. *The Transformative Power of Performance: A New Aesthetics*. London: Routledge, 2008.

– Fontana, Giovanni, Nicola Frangione, and Roberto Rossini (eds.). *Italian Performance Art*. Genoa: Sagep Editori, 2015.

– Gallagher, Shaun. *Performance/Art: The Venetian Lectures*. Sesto San Giovanni: Mimesis, 2021.

– Goldberg, RoseLee. *Performance Art: From Futurism to Present*. London: Thames & Hudson, 1988.

– Goldberg, RoseLee. *Performance: Live Art Since the 60s*. London: Thames & Hudson, 2004.

– Goldberg, RoseLee. *Performance Now: Live Art in the 21st Century*. London: Thames & Hudson, 2018.

– Higgins, Hannah. *Fluxus Experience*. Berkeley: University of California Press, 2002.

– Howell, Anthony. *The Analysis of Performance Art: A Guide to Its Theory and Practice*. London: Routledge, 1999.

– Johnson, Dominic. *The Art of Living: An Oral History of Performance Art*. London: Red Globe Press, 2015.

– Jones, Amelia, Tracey Warr. *The Artist's Body*. New York: Phaidon, 2002.

– Macrì, Teresa. *Il Corpo Postorganico. Sconfinamenti della Performance*. Genoa: Costa & Nolan, 1996.

– Macrì, Teresa. *Slittamenti della Performance. Volume 1, Anni 1960-2000*. Milan: Postmedia Books, 2020.

– Martore, Paolo, Chiara Mu (eds.). *Performance Art. Traiettorie ed Esperienze Internazionali*. Rome: Castelvecchi, 2018.

– McEvilley, Thomas. *The Triumph of Anti-Art. Conceptual and Performance Art in the Formation of Post-Modernism*. New York: McPerson & Company, 2005.

– Miliani, Jacopo. *Performance come Metodologia. Gesti e scritture*. Milan: Postmedia Books, 2021.

– Moten, Fred. *Endless Shout*. Philadelphia: Inventory Press, 2019.

– Orrell, Paula (ed.). *Marina Abramović + the Future of Performance Art*. Munich: Prestel, 2010.

– Philips, Áine (ed.), *Performance Art in Ireland: A History*. Bristol: Intellect, 2015.

– Schimmel, Paul (ed.). *Out of Actions: Between Performance and the Object, 1949-1979*. London: Thames & Hudson, 1998.

– Ward, Frazier. *No Innocent Bystanders: Performance Art and Audience*. Dartmouth: Dartmouth College Press, 2012.

– Wood, Catherine. *Performance in Contemporary Art*. London: Tate Publishing, 2022.

PERFORMING ARTS:
– Alexander, J. C., B. Giesen, and J. L. Mast. *Social Performance: Symbolic Action, Cultural Pragmatics and Ritual*. Cambridge: Cambridge University Press, 2006.
– André, Naomi, Yolanda Covington-Ward, and Hungbo Jendele (eds.). *African Performance Arts and Political Acts*. Ann Arbor: University of Michigan Press, 2021.
– Auslander, Philip. *From Acting to Performance*. London: Routledge, 1997.
– Auslander, Philip. *In Concert; Performing Musical Persona*. Ann Arbor: University of Michigan Press, 2021.
– Auslander, Philip. *Liveness: Performance in Mediatized Culture*. London: Routledge, 1999.
– Auslander, Philip (ed.). *Performance: Critical Concepts in Literary and Cultural Studies*. London: Routledge, 2003.
– Bailes, Sara Jane. *Performance Theatre and the Poetics of Failure*. London: Routledge, 2011.
– Baker, Simon, Fiontan Moran (eds.). *Performing for the Camera*. London: Tate Publishing, 2016.
– Bay-Cheng, Sarah, Chiel Kattenbelt, Andy Lavender, and Nelson Robin (eds.). *Intermediality in Performance*. Amsterdam: Amsterdam University Press, 2010.
– Beasley, Myron. *Performance, Art and Politics in the African Diaspora*. London: Routledge, 2023.
– Blades, Hetty, Emma Mehan (eds.). *Performing Process. Sharing Dance and Choreographic Practice*. Bristol: Intellect, 2018.
– Blanga-Gubbay, Daniel, Lars Kwakkenbos (eds.). *The Time We Share. Reflecting on and through Performing Arts*. New Haven: Yale University Press, 2016.
– Bial, Henry, Sara Brady (eds.). *The Performance Studies Reader*. London: Routledge, 2015.
– Boffone, Trevor, Teresa Marrero, and Chantal Rodriguez. *Encuentro: Latinx Performance for the New American Theater*. Evanston: Northwestern University Press, 2019.
– Bourdieu, Pierre. *La distinction. Critique sociale du jugement*. Paris: Les Editions de Minuit, 1979
– Carr, Cynthia. *On Edge. Performance at the End of the Twentieth Century*. Middletown: Wesleyan University Press, 2008.
– Carlson Marvin. *Performance: A Critical Introduction*. London: Routledge, 1996.
– Chapple Freda, Chiel Kattenbelt (eds.). *Intermediality in Theatre and Performance*. Amsterdam and New York: Rodopi, 2006.
– Cole, M. Catherine. *Performance and the Afterlives of Injustice*. Ann Arbor: University of Michigan Press, 2020.
– Diamond, Elin. *Performance and Cultural Politics*. London: Routledge, 1996.
– Dixon, Steve. *Digital Performance: A History of New Media in Theater, Dance, Performance Art, and Installation*. Cambridge: MIT Press, 2007.
– Fischer-Lichte, Erika. *Estetica del Performativo. Una teoria del teatro e dell'arte*. Rome: Carocci, 2014.
– Heathfield, Adrian (ed.). *LIVE: Art and Performance*. London: Tate Publishing, 2015.
– Hodge, Alison (ed.). *Twentieth-Century Actor Training*. London: Routledge, 1999.
– Hughes-Freeland, Felicia. *Ritual, Performance, Media*. London: Routledge, 1998.
– Huxley, Michael, Noel Wits (eds.). *The Twentieth-Century Performance Reader*. London: Routledge, 1996.
– Jackson, Shannon. *Professing Performance: Theatre in the Academy from Philosophy to Performativity*. Cambridge: Cambridge University Press, 2004.
– Jackson, Shannon, *Social Works. Performing Art, Supporting Publics*. London: Routledge, 2011.
– Janssen, Shauna, Anja Mølle Lindelof (eds.). *Performing Institutions. Contested Sites and Structures of Care*. Bristol: Intellect, 2023.
– Jones, Amelia, Adrian Heathfield (eds.). *Perform, Repeat, Record. Live Art in History*. Bristol: Intellect, 2001.
– Jones, Amelia, Andrew Stephenson (eds.). *Performing the Body / Performing the Text*. London: Routledge, 1999.
– Lepecki, André, *Exhausting Dance. Performance and the Politics of Movement*. London: Routledge, 2006.
– Lepecki, André (ed.). *Of the Presence of the Body: Essays on Dance and Performance Theory*. Middletown: Wesleyan University Press, 2004.
– Loxley, James (ed.). *Performativity*. London: Routledge, 2007.
– Marshall, Alice, *Entertainment in the Performing Arts*. London: Routledge, 2022.
– McAuley, Gay (ed.). *Unstable Ground: Performance and the Politics of Place*. Bristol: P. I. E. Peter Lang, 2007.
– Mock, Roberta. *Performing Processes. Creating Live Performance*. Bristol: Intellect, 2000.

– Monteverdi, Anna Maria, *Nuovi media, nuovo teatro. Teorie e pratiche tra teatro e digitalità*. Milan: Franco Angeli, 2012.
– Mroz, Daniel. *The Dancing Word*. Amsterdam: Brill, 2011.
– Nancy, Jean-Luc. *Corpo Teatro*. Naples: Cronopio, 2010.
– Oddey, Alison. *Devising Theatre: A Practical and Theoretical Handbook*. London: Routledge, 1994.
– Paterson, Mary, Karen Cristopher (eds.). *Entanglements of Two: A Series of Duets*. Bristol: Intellect, 2021.
– Phelan, Peggy. *Unmarked: The Politics of Performance*. London: Routledge, 1996.
– Reinelt, Janelle, J. R. Roach (eds.). *Critical Theory and Performance*. Ann Arbor: Michigan University Press, 1992.
– Ross, Janice. *Anna Halprin: Experience as Dance*. Berkeley: University of California Press, 2009.
– Safir, Margery Arent (ed.). *Robert Wilson from Within*. Paris: Flammarion, 2011.
– Schechner, Richard, *Between Theatre and Anthropology*. Chicago: University of Chicago Press, 1985.
– Schechner, Richard. *Performance Theory*. London: Routledge, 2003.
– Schechner, Richard. *The Future of Ritual: Writings on Culture and Performance*. London: Routledge, 1993.
– Shepherd, Simon, Mick Wallis. *Drama/Theatre/Performance*. London: Routledge, 2004.
– Steinman, Louise. *The Knowing Body: Elements of Contemporary Performance and Dance*. Berkeley: Shambhala, 1986.
– Turner, Victor. *The Anthropology of Performance*. Cambridge: PAJ Publications, 1988.
– Valentini, Valentina. *Mondi, corpi, materie. Teatri del secondo Novecento*. Milano: Bruno Mondadori, 2007.
– Vanden Heuvel, Michael. *Performing Drama / Dramatizing Performance*. Ann Arbor: University of Michigan Press, 1991.
– Vidler, Laura L. *Performance Reconstruction and Spanish Golden Age Drama*. London: Palgrave Macmillan, 2014.
– Wang, Victor (ed.). *Performance Histories from East Asia: 1960s-1990s*. London: David Roberts Art Foundation, 2018.
– Wiles, David. *Mask and Performance in Greek Tragedy: From Ancient Festival to Modern Experimentation*. Cambridge: Cambridge University Press, 2007.
– Youling Deng, Yanjie Zhang (eds.). *Dance Studies in China*. Bristol: Intellect, 2022.

I. Culture that Transforms Space

– Banks, Grace (ed.). *Art Escapes: Hidden Art Experiences Outside the Museum*. Berlin: Gestalten, 2022.
– Bo Bardi, Lina. *Cidadela da Liberdade: Lina Bo Bardi e o Sesc Pompéia*. São Paulo: Edições Sesc, 2013.
– Bo Bardi, Lina. *Il diritto al brutto e il Sesc-Fàbrica da Pompéia*. Naples: Clean, 2012.
– Bo Bardi, Lina. *Sesc Pompéia*. São Paulo: Obra Comunicaçao, 2014.
– Cantarella, Robert, Frédéric Fisbach. *L'anti-musée*. Nouveaux débats publics, 2009.
– Cousin, Jean-Pierre. *104 Paris, l'architecture de l'invisible*. Paris: Archive d'Architecture Moderne, 2009.
– Cupelloni, Luciano. *Il Mattatoio di Testaccio a Roma*. Rome: Gangemi Editore, 2002.
– De Rosa, Agostino (ed.). *James Turrell: Geometrie di Luce Roden Crater*. Milan: Electa, 2007.
– Duràn, Gloria G., Alan W. Moore. "La Tabacalera of Lavapiés: A Social Experiment or a Work of Art?", *Field*, no. 1 (2016): 49–75.
– Fremantle, Gill (ed.). *Deep Mapping. Lough Boora Sculpture Park*. Tullamore: Offaly County Council, 2020.
– Frumkin, Peter, Ana Kolendo. *Building for the Arts. The Strategic Design of Cultural Facilities*. Chicago: University of Chicago Press, 2014.
– Fukutake, Nobuto, Soichiro Fukutake (eds.). *The Chichu Museum. Tadao Ando builds for Walter De Maria, James Turrell and Claude Monet*. Naoshima: Fukutake Foundation, 2005.
– García Dory, Fernanda, Lucia Pietroiusti (eds.). *Matadero Estudios Criticos. Vol. 1. Microhabitable*. Madrid: Madrid Destino, 2021.
– Holm, Michael. *Louisiana Museum of Modern Art: Landscape and Architecture*. Humlebaek: Louisiana Museum of Modern Art, 2017.
– Huang, Wenya, Kaixuan Cui. *798: Inside China's Art Zone*. San Francisco: Long River Press, 2010.
– Ivy, Robert, Alistair Hicks. *Château La Coste: Art and Architecture in Provence*. London: Merrell, 2020.
– Jarvinen, Tomas. *Strategic Cultural Center Management*. London: Routledge, 2021.

– Kaneshiro, Kenjiro (ed.). *Becoming: Benesse Art Site Naoshima*. Naoshima: Fukutake Foundation, 2013.
– Le Feuvre, Lisa (ed.). *The Generous Landscape: Ten Years of Jupiter Artland Foundation*. Edinburgh: Jupiter Artland Foundation, 2018.
– Mazzanti, Anna (ed.). *Niki de Saint Phalle: Il Giardino dei Tarocchi*. Milan: Charta, 1997.
– Messner, Magdalena Maria. *Messner Mountain Museum: Six Places, Six Exhibitions, Six Experiences*. Bolzano: Folio, 2016.
– n/a. *Hakone Open-Air Museum: Utsukushi-Ga-Hara Open-Air Museum 1969-1999*. Tokyo: The Hakone Open-Air Museum, 1999.
– Pedrosa, Adriano, Rodrigo Moura (eds.). *Atraves: Inhotim Centro de Arte Contemporanea*. Brumadinho: Pedrosa, Adriano & Moura, Rodrigo edition, 2008.
– Pommerau, Claude (ed.), *Punta della Dogana / Palazzo Grassi/François Pinault Foundation*. Boulogne–Billancourt: Beaux-Arts Éditions, 2009.
– Rock, Michael. *Prada Book*. Milan: Progetto Prada Arte, 2009.
– Thompson, Jerry L. *Earth, Sky, and Sculpture: Storm King Art Center*. New York: Storm King Art Center, 2009.
– True, Marion, Jorge Silvetti. *The Getty Villa*. Los Angeles: J. Paul Getty Museum Publisher, 2006.
– van Kooten, Toos, Marente Bloemheuvel (eds.). *Sculpture Garden Kröller-Müller Museum*. Rotterdam: Nai Uitgevers Publisher, 2007.

II. Theaters: Matrix Spaces

– Adejemi, Sola, Duro Oni (eds.). *Developments in the Theory and Practice of Contemporary Nigerian Drama and Theatre*. Lagos: Alpha Crownes Publishers, 2017.
– Affron, Charles, Jona Mirella Affron. *Grand Opera: The Story of the Met*. Berkeley: University of California Press, 2014.
– Ahuja, Chaman. *Contemporary Theatre of India: An Overview*. New Delhi: National Book Trust India, 2012.
– Beard, Alex, Cory Wright (eds.). *Royal Opera House*. London: Thames & Hudson, 2020.
– Bame, Kwabena N. *Come to Laugh: African Traditional Theatre in Ghana*. New York: Lilian Barber Press, 1985.
– Brandon, James R. *Theatre in Southeast Asia*. Cambridge: Harvard University Press, 1967.
– Brett, Richard, John Offord. *Copenhagen Opera House*. Great Shelford: Entertainment Technology Press, 2006.
– Cavaglieri, Livia (ed.). *Il Piccolo Teatro di Milano*. Rome: Bulzoni Editore, 2002.
– Cho, Ho-Kon. *Korean Theatre: From Rituals to the Avant-Garde*. Fremont: Jain Publishing Company, 2015.
– Cole, Catherine M. *Ghana's Concert Party Theatre*. Bloomington: Indiana University Press, 2001.
– Coulibaly, Fanta. *Theater in Mali*. Chişinău: ScienciaScripts, 2022.
– Delgado, Maria M., David T. Gies. *A History of Theatre in Spain*. Cambridge: Cambridge University Press, 2012.
– Fuchs, Anne. *Playing the Market. The Market Theatre*. Johannesburg and Amsterdam: Brill, 2002.
– Holdsworth, Nadine. *English Theatre and Social Abjection. A Divided Nation*. London: Palgrave Macmillan, 2020.
– Hoss de le Comte, Monica G. *El Teatro Colón / The Colón Theatre*. Buenos Aires: Maizal Ediciones, 2014.
– Jacobs, Reginald. *Covent Garden: Its Romance and History*. Dublin: Nonsuch Publishing, 2007.
– Lanfossi, Carlo (ed.). *Teatro alla Scala*. Milan: Skira, 2014.
– Lecoq, Jacques. *Theatre of Movement and Gesture*. London: Routledge, 2006.
– Lehmann, Hans-Thies. *Postdramatic Theatre*. London: Routledge, 2006.
– Mancini, Franco (ed.). *Il Teatro di San Carlo, 1737-1987*. Naples: Electa Napoli, 1987.
– Marañón, Gregorio, Ignacio García-Belenguer, Rubén Amón, and Joan Matabosch. *The Book of the Teatro Real*. Madrid: La Fábrica, 2018.
– Mead, Cristopher. *Charles Garnier's Paris Opera: Architectural Empathy and the Renaissance of French Classicism*. Cambridge: MIT Press, 1991.
– Mioli, Piero. *Teatro di San Carlo di Napoli*. Bologna: Scripta Maneant, 2020.
– Muhumuza, Michael. *The Nature of Theatre in Uganda*. Chişinău: Lambert Academic Publishing, 2018.
– Mujica, Bárbara (ed.). *Staging and Stage Décor: Early Modern Spanish Theater*. Malaga: Vernon Press, 2022.
– Ning, Wang. *National Centre for the Performing Arts*. Moscow: Foreign Languages Publishing House, 2022.

– Pitt, Helen. *The House*. Sydney: Allen & Unwin, 2018.
– Plastow, Jane. *A History of East African Theatre, Volume 1*. London: Palgrave Macmillan, 2020.
– Plastow, Jane. *A History of East African Theatre, Volume 2*. London: Palgrave Macmillan, 2021.
– Polisi, Joseph W. *Beacon of the World. A History of Lincoln Center*. New Haven: Yale University Press, 2022.
– Porcheddu, Andrea. "Riforma: ecco i nuovi teatri nazionali," *Gli Stati Generali*, February 24, 2005.
– Richmond, Farley P., Darius L. Swann, and Phillip B. Zarrilli. *Indian Theatre. Traditions of Performance*. New Delhi: Motilal Banarsidass Publisher, 1993.
– Sachs, Edwin O. *Modern Opera Houses and Theatres*. New York: Benjamin Blom, 1968.
– Salloukh, Tarek. *Theater in Lebanon. Production, Reception and Confessionalism*. Bielefield: Transcript, 2005.
– Seebohm, Andrea (ed.). *The Vienna Opera*. New York: Rizzoli, 1987.
– Shank, Theodore (ed.). *Contemporary British Theatre*. London: Palgrave Macmillan, 1996.
– Slonimsky, Yuri. *The Bolshoi Ballet*. Moscow: Foreign Languages Publishing House, 1960.
– Staples, David. *Modern Theatres 1950–2020*. London: Routledge, 2021.
– Young, Edgar B. *Lincoln Center: The Building of an Institution*. New York: New York University Press, 1980.
– Weiss, Judith A. *Colombian Theatre in the Vortex: Seven Plays*. Lewisburg: Bucknell University Press, 2004.

III. Multidisciplinary Festivals

– Campbell, Leon. *The Adelaide Festival Centre Story*. Adelaide: Wakefield Press, 1998.
– Cestelli Guidi, Anna. *La "Documenta" di Kassel. Percorsi dell'Arte Contemporanea*. Genoa: Costa & Nolan, 1997.
– Courtet, Catherine. *Traversées des Mondes. Rencontres Recherche et Création du Festival d'Avignon*. Paris: CNRS éditions, 2020.
– d'Adamo, Ada. *25 Romaeuropa Festival. 1986-2010*. Milan: Electa, 2010.
– De Baecque, Antoine, Emmanuelle Loyer. *Histoire du Festival d'Avignon*. Paris: Gallimard, 2016.
– Delanty, Gerard, Liana Giorgi, and Monica Sassatelli. *Festivals and the Cultural Public Sphere*. London: Routledge, 2011.
– Cabanis, Anne-Françoise, Philippe Choulet, and Nathalie Diot. *20 Éditions d'un Festival d'exception: Festival Mondial des Théâtres de Marionnettes*. Bouvellemont: Noires Terres, 2020.
– Everist, Mark. *Opera in Paris from the Empire to the Commune*. London: Routledge, 2020.
– Eyre, Richard, Nicholas Wright. *Changing Stages: A View of British Theatre in the Twentieth Century*. London: Bloomsbury Publishing, 2001.
– Ferraresi, Roberta et al. *Santarcangelo 50 festival*. Bologna: Corraini, 2021.
– Fenton, Lucy, Lucy Neal. *The Turning World: Stories from the London International Festival of Theatre*. Lisbon: Calouste Gulbenkian Foundation, 2005.
– Fisher, Mark. *The Edinburgh Fringe Survival Guide: How to Make Your Show a Success*. London: Methuen Drama, 2012.
– Goldberg, RoseLee. *On the Town. A Performa Compendium 2016–2021*. New York: Performa, 2021.
– Goldberg, RoseLee. *Performa: New Visual Art Performance*. New York: Performa, 2007.
– Gross, Raphael. *Documenta: Politics and Art*. Munich: Prestel, 2021.
– Kidwell, Jeremy H., Maria Nita (eds.). *Festival Cultures. Mapping New Fields in the Arts and Social Sciences*. London: Palgrave Macmillan, 2022.
– Meuli, Andrea. *Die Bregenzer Festspiele*. Vienna: Residenz Verlag, 1995.
– Mulazzani, Marco. *Guida ai Padiglioni della Biennale di Venezia dal 1887*. Milan: Electa, 2022.
– Palau, Pierre. *Il était une fois le festival d'Avignon*. Grenoble: Dauphiné Libéré, 2014.
– Pasqualino, Antonio. *L'Opera dei Pupi*. Palermo: Sellerio, 1977.
– Patterson, Tom. *First Stage: The Making of Stratford Festival*. Richmond Hill: Firefly Books, 1999.
– Pederson, Jesper Strandgaard, Elisa Salvador (eds.). *Managing Cultural Festivals. Tradition and Innovation in Europe*. London: Routledge, 2022.
– Portinari, Stefania, Nico Stringa. *Storie della Biennale di Venezia*. Venice: Edizioni Ca' Foscari, 2019.

– Scarpetta, Guy. *Le Festival d'Automne de Michel Guy*. Paris: Les Éditions du Regard, 1992.
– Thomasson, Sarah. *The Festival Cities of Edinburgh and Adelaide*. London: Palgrave Macmillan, 2022.
– Vollerin, Alain. *Histoire des Biennales d'art contemporain de Lyon*. Lyon: Mémoire des Arts, 2005.
– Whitelock, Derek A. *Festival! The Story of the Adelaide Festival of Arts*. Adelaide: Derek A. Whitelock, 1980.

IV. Music Festivals

– Arnaud, Robert. *Montreux Jazz Festival: Fifty Summers of Music*. Paris: Textuel, 2016.
– Aubrey, Crispin, John Shearlow. *Glastonbury Festival Tales*. London: Ebury Publishing, 2004.
– Becker, Cynthia J. *Blackness in Morocco: Gnawa Identity through Music and Visual Culture*. Minneapolis: Minnesota University Press, 2020.
– Bowditch, Rachel. *On the Edge of Utopia. Performance and Ritual at Burning Man*. Chicago: Chicago University Press, 2008.
– Bowman, Edith. *Edith Bowman's Great British Music Festivals*. London: Blink Publishing, 2015.
– Carneiro, Felipe Luiz. *Rock in Rio: a história do maior festival de música do mundo.* Rio de Janeiro: Globo, 2010.
– Chaudhuri, Amit. *Finding the Raga: An Improvisation on Indian Music*. New York: New York Review Books, 2021.
– Chen, Katherine K. *Enabling Creative Chaos. The Organization Behind the Burning Man Event.* Chicago: Chicago University Press, 2009.
– Clupper, Wendy. "Burning Man: Festival Culture in the United States – Festival Culture in a Global Perspective," in *Festivalising! Theatrical Events, Politics and Culture*. Leiden: Brill, 2007.
– Daniélou, Alain. *Sacred Music. Its Origins, Powers, and Future*. Varanasi: Indica Books, 2003.
– Eavis, Emily, Michael Eavis. *Glastonbury 50: The Official Story of Glastonbury Festival*. Edinburgh: Trapeze, 2019.
– Gallup, Stephen. *A History of the Salzburg Festival*. Salem: Salem House Press, 1988.
– Gilmore, Lee. *Theatre in a Crowded Fire: Ritual and Spirituality at Burning Man*. Berkeley: University of California Press, 2010.
– Heiser, Jörg, Mateo Kries, and Catherine Rossi (eds.). *Night Fever. Designing Club Culture. 1960–Today*. Weil am Rhein: Vitra Design Museum, 2018.
– Harsløf, Olav, *The Great Festival. A Theoretical Performance Narrative of Antiquity's Feasts and the Modern Rock Festival*. London: Routledge, 2020.
– Jones, Steve T. *The Tribes of Burning Man*. San Francisco: CCC Publishing, 2011.
– Kapchan, Deborah. *Traveling Spirit Masters. Moroccan Gnawa Trance and Music in the Global Marketplace*. Middletown: Wesleyan University Press, 2007.
– Keens, Oliver, *Festivals: A Music Lover's Guide to the Festivals You Need To Know*. London: Frances Lincoln, 2021.
– McCaffrey, Kevin (ed.). *The Incomplete, Year-by-Year Selectively Quirky, Prime Facts Edition of the History of The New Orleans Jazz & Heritage Festival*. E/Prime Publications, 2005.
– n/a. *Time Warp. The Truth is on the Dancefloor*. Mannheim: Time Warp, 2016.
– Négrier, Emmanuel, Lluís Bonet, and Michel Guérin (eds.). *Music Festivals: A Changing World*. Paris: Éditions Michel De Maule, 2013.
– Odell, Michael. *The Festival Book*. London: Bantam Press, 2017.
– Patey-Ferguson, Phoebe. *LIFT and the GLC versus Thatcher: London's Cultural Battleground in 1981*. Cambridge University Press, 2020.
– Pruett, John. *The Music Festival Guide: For Music Lovers and Musicians*. Chicago: Chicago Review Press, 2004.
– Raiser, Jennifer. *Burning Man: Art on Fire*. New York: Race Point Publishing, 2014.
– Reynold, Simon. *Energy Flash: A Journey Through Rave Music and Dance Culture*. New York: Soft Skull, 2012.
– Robinson, Greg. *Coachella (Monster Music Festivals)*. New York: Rosen Publishing, 2008.
– Sabine, Nicole (ed.). *Montreux Jazz Festival: On Stage Backstage*. Zurich: L'Illustré, 1986.
– Shister, Neil. *Radical Ritual: How Burning Man Changed the World*. Berkeley: Counterpoint, 2019.
– Steinberg, Michael P. *Austria as Theater and Ideology. The Meaning of the Salzburg Festival*. New York: Cornell University Press, 2000.
– Wall, Jennifer. *The Coachella Valley Music and Arts Festival Handbook*. Brisbane: Emereo Publishing, 2016.

Photo credits

Cover: © BertSternTrust photograph by Bert Stern
p. 10: Stunk-Kender @ J. Paul Getty Trust © Succession Yves Klein 2023
p. 14: Luciano Romano © Marina Abramović, by SIAE 2023
p. 16: Arnold Genthe, Courtesy Library of Congress
p. 17: Carl Van Vechten Estate, 1966, Courtesy Library of Congress
p. 19: Batard Patrick/ABACA/Shutterstock
pp. 20–21: GRAGNON François/Paris Match via Getty Images
pp. 22–23: AP Photo/LaPresse
p. 24: Courtesy NASA Archive
p. 25: Alan Welner/AP Photo/LaPresse
p. 27: Klaus Lefebvre, Courtesy Romeo Castellucci
p. 30: Photo by Sukita
p. 31: Gary Gershoff/Getty Images
p. 32: Robbie Jack/Corbis via Getty Images
p. 33: Courtesy Zhang Huan Studio
p. 35: Courtesy of the artist
pp. 40–49: Quentin Chevrier
pp. 50, 55, 57, 58–59: Courtesy Matadero Madrid
pp. 52–53: Eugenio Ampudia
pp. 62, 67: Courtesy Istituto Bardi Archive
pp. 64, 69, 70: Nelson Kon
p. 72: Eden Breitz/Alamy Foto Stock/Ipa Agency
pp. 74–75: Alejo Maria Corsiglia, Courtesy Radialsystem
p. 77: Courtesy Radialsystem
p. 81: Lieberenz/ullstein bild/Getty Images
p. 82: Seiichi Ohsawa, Courtesy of Fukutake Foundation
pp. 84–85: View Picturs/SuperStock
p. 87: Mitsuo Matsuoka, Courtesy of Fukutake Foundation
p. 88: Tadasu Yamamoto, Courtesy of Fukutake Foundation
p. 91: Tadasu Yamamoto, Courtesy of Fukutake Foundation
p. 92: Naoya Hatakeyama, Courtesy of Fukutake Foundation
p. 96: Mauro Pimentel/AFP via Getty Images
pp. 98–99: Eduardo Rodrigues/Getty Images
pp. 102–103, 107: Nelson Almeida/AFP via Getty Images
p. 104: Cmanuel Photography – Portugal/Getty Images
p. 108: Cristian Vinatea/Getty Images
pp. 112–113: Courtesy Mona
p. 114 : Felix Lipov/Shutterstock
p. 115: Jan Willem van Hofwegen/ Shutterstock
pp. 116–117: Andrew Pattman. Louise Bourgeois © The Easton Foundation/Licensed by VAGA, New York and SIAE
pp. 118–119: Topimages/Shutterstock
p. 120: China Photos/Getty Images
p. 121: Gideon Mendel/Corbis via Getty Images
pp. 122–123: Invictus SARL/Alamy Stock Photo/ Ipa Agency
p. 124: Bas Princen, Courtesy Fondazione Prada
p. 125: Oli Scarff/Getty Images
pp. 126–127: Pablo Blazquez Dominguez/Getty Images
pp. 128, 129: Hufton+Crow/View Pictures/Universal Images Group via Getty Images
p. 130: Lewis Mulatero/Moment Mobile/Getty Images – © Anish Kapoor. All Rights Reserved, DACS/SIAE
p. 131: Aly Wight, Courtesy Jupiter-Artland
pp. 132–133: Allan Pollok-Morris, Courtesy Jupiter-Artland © Christian Boltansky, by SIAE 2023
pp. 134–135: Taller Mauricio Rocha, Courtesy Fábrica de San Pedro
p. 136: Eye Ubiquitous/Alamy Stock Photo/Ipa Agency
pp. 137, 138–139: Lunatikai, Courtesy www.lukiskiukalejmas.it
p. 140: Tahnee L. Cracchiola, Courtesy Getty Villas
p. 141: Morteza Nikoubazl/NurPhoto via Getty Images
p. 142: Pinault Collection, Courtesy the Felix Gonzalez-Torres Foundation. Installation View *Luogo e Segni* at

Punta della Dogana, 2019 © Palazzo Grassi, © Delfino Sisto Legnani and Marco Cappelletti
p. 143: Dirk Renckhoff/Alamy Stock Photo/Ipa Agency © Calder Foundation, New York
pp. 144–145: Ruediger Glatz
pp. 150–151, 152, 157, 158–159: Javier del Real, Courtesy Teatro Real
p. 154: Monika Rittershaus, Courtesy Teatro Real
pp. 160–161: Buren, Courtesy Khaaitheater
pp. 162–163, 170: Christophe Raynaud de Lage, Courtesy Khaaitheater
p. 165: Wonge Bergmann, Courtesy Khaaitheater
p. 166: Raoul Gilibert, Courtesy Khaaitheater
p. 169: Kristof Vrancken, Courtesy Khaaitheater
p. 172: Stefano Triggiani, Courtesy ERT
pp. 174–175: Luca Del Pia, Courtesy ERT
p. 176 : Brunella Giolivo, Courtesy ERT
p. 179: Nairí Aharonián, Courtesy ERT
p. 180: May Zircus TNC, Courtesy ERT
p. 184: Marcell Rév, Courtesy ERT
p. 187: Tommaso Le Pera, Courtesy ERT
p. 190: Nikolai Ignatiev/Alamy Stock Photo/Ipa Agency
p. 191: Mondadori Portfolio
pp. 192–193: Luciano Romano 2008
p. 194: Masahiko Terashi, Courtesy NNTT
p. 195: Masiar Pasquali, Courtesy Piccolo Teatro di Milano – Teatro d'Europa
p. 196: Bridgemanart/Mondadori Portfolio
p. 197: Hulton-Deutsch/Hulton-Deutsch Collection/ Corbis via Getty Images
pp. 198-199: Bridgemanart/Mondadori Portfolio
p. 200: Gisele Freund/Photo Researchers History/ Getty Images
p. 201: Salvatore Laporta/KONTROLAB /LightRocket via Getty Images
pp. 202–203: David Gray/Getty Images
p. 204: Viktor Pazemin/Alamy Stock Photo/Ipa Agency
p. 205: Daniel Tchetchik, Courtesy Suzanne Dellal Centre
pp. 206–207: Independent Picture Service/Universal Images Group via Getty Images
p. 208 : PJPHOTO/Alamy Stock Photo/Ipa Agency © Chagall ®
p. 209: Eileen_10/Shuttestock
pp. 210–211: Frank Lee/Moment Unreleased/Getty Images
p. 212: Courtesy The Walt Disney Hall
p. 213: camw@kglteater.dk
pp. 214–215: YuanYuan Yan/Alamy Stock Photo/ Ipa Agency
p. 221: Enrico Nawrath, Courtesy Bayreuther Festspiele/
p. 222: © Jean-Claude Carbonne/ArtComPress via opale. photo/Mondadori Portfolio
pp. 224–225: © Jean-Claude Carbonne/ArtComPress via opale. photo/ Mondadori Portfolio
p. 228: Bertrand Langlois/AFP via Getty Images
p. 232: Boris Horvat/AFP via Getty Images
p. 236: Jeff J. Mitchell/Getty Images
pp. 238–239: Andrew Downie, Courtesy Edinburgh Festival Fringe Society
p. 241: David Montieth-Hodge 2019, Courtesy Edinburgh Festival Fringe Society
p. 243: Jane Barlow/PA Images via Getty Images
p. 247: Robbie Jack-Corbis/Corbis via Getty Images
p. 250: Camera Press/1080 Media/ED/CE/Contrasto
pp. 254–255: Samir Hussein, Courtesy LIFT
p. 256: Tristam Kenton
p. 259: Ray Tang/Shutterstock
pp. 262, 264–265, 267, 270–271, 274–275: Mihaela Marin
pp. 276, 278–279, 281, 284: Courtesy Santarcangelo Festival
p. 288: NnoMan, Courtesy Festival d'Automne
p. 289: Erwan Fichou, Courtesy Festival d'Automne
pp. 290–291: Renato Mangolin, Courtesy Festival d'Automne
p. 292: Daniel Garzon Herazo/NurPhoto via Getty Images
p. 293: Guillermo Legaria/AFP via Getty Images
p. 294: Marcello Norberth/Piccolo Teatro di Milano – Teatro d'Europa
p. 285: Karl Forster
pp. 296–297: Nicolas Wefers, Courtesy Documenta
p. 298: Julia Ga, Courtesy Berliner Festspiele
p. 299: Oleksii Karpovych, Courtesy Berliner Festspiele
pp. 300–301: Francesco Bellina, Courtesy Manifesta 12 Palermo
pp: 302–303 : Francesco Galli/Archivio Storico della Biennale di Venezia, ASAC
pp. 304, 305: © Anna Van Waeg RHoK, Courtesy KFDA
pp. 306–307: Luciano Romano
p. 308: Giacomo Bordonaro
p. 309: Allan Titmuss/ArenaPAL/ArenaPal/Mondadori Portfolio

p. 310 : Paula Court, Courtesy Performa
pp. 316–317: Brian Rasic/Getty Images
pp. 318, 329: Andy Buchanan/AFP via Getty Images
pp. 322–323: Leon Neal/Getty Images
p. 325: Ian Tyas/Keystone Features/Getty Images
p. 332: Joseph Okpako/WireImage/ Getty Images
p. 334: Delio Nijmeijer, Courtesy Tomorrowland
pp. 336–337, 349: Courtesy Tomorrowland
p. 339: Fille Roelants Photography, Courtesy Tomorrowland
p. 342: Jonas Roosens/Belga/Sipa USA
pp. 344–345: David Pintens/AFP via Getty Images
p. 350: Jeff Kravitz/FilmMagic/Getty Images
pp. 352–353: Karl Walter/Getty Images
p. 355: USA Today Network/Sipa USA/Mondadori Portfolio
p. 359: Larry Busacca/Getty Images for Coachella
p. 360: USA Today Network/Sipa USA/Mondadori Portfolio
pp. 362–363: Matt Masin/The Orange County Register via ZUMA Wire/Mondadori Portfolio
p. 366: Lionel Flusin/Gamma-Rapho via Getty Images
pp. 370–371: Lionel Flusin
p. 372: © Jean-Marie Périer/Photo12/Contrasto
pp. 374–375: Lionel Flusin/Gamma-Rapho via Getty Images
pp. 376–377: From left: Courtesy Montreux Jazz Festival, © Jean Tinguely, by SIAE 2023, Courtesy Montreux Jazz Festival
p. 378: Lionel Flusin/Gamma-Rapho via Getty Images
p. 380: Lact Atkins/The Chronicle/AP Photo/LaPresse
pp: 382–383: Erik Pendzich/Shutterstock
p. 385: Brad Horn/AP Photo/LaPresse
p. 386: Debra Reid/AP Photo/ LaPresse
pp: 388–389: Neale Haynes/Shutterstock
p. 390: Carlos Avila Gonzalez/The San Francisco Chronicle via Getty Images
p. 394: Courtesy Rick in Rio
p. 395: @ anendfor, Courtesy Rick in Rio. Photo Wesley Allen
p. 396: Mark Horton/Getty Images
p. 397: Michael Hickey/Getty Images
pp. 398–399: Barry Brecheisen/Getty Images
pp. 400–401: Pascal Victor/ArtComPress via opale. photo/ Mondadori Portfolio
pp. 402–403: Courtesy Afro Nation
p. 404: Courtesy Festival di Ravello/Fondo Parisio e Troncone
p. 405: Manuela Jans, Courtesty Lucerne Festival
pp. 406–407: Chuck Fishman/Getty Images
p. 408: Rebecca Conway/AFP via Getty Images
p. 409: Courtesy Labyrinth Festival
pp. 410–411: Eric Pamies, Courtesy Primavera Sound
p. 412: Tim Mosenfelder/Getty Images
p. 413: Marc Grimwade/WireImage
pp. 414–415: Robertus Pudyanto/Getty Images
p. 416: Joseph Okpako/WireImage/Getty Images
p. 417: Ariel Martini, Courtesy Sónar
pp. 418–419: NereaColl, Courtesy Sónar
pp. 424–425 : Courtesy Sónar
p. 426: Courtesy Matadero Madrid
pp. 428–428: Courtesy Le Bal de Paris de Blanca Li
pp. 430–431: Yasuko Kageyama, Courtesy Teatro dell'Opera di Roma
pp. 434–435: Massimo Valicchia/NurPhoto via Getty Images
p. 443: Sebastiano Luciano

The Publisher may be contacted by entitled parties for any iconographic sources that have not been identified.

Distributed in English throughout the World
by Rizzoli International Publications Inc.
300 Park Avenue South
New York, NY 10010, USA
ISBN: 978-88-918380-1-8
2023 2024 2025 2026/ 10 9 8 7 6 5 4 3 2 1
First edition: September 2023

Author: Cristiano Leone
Project and Book Management: Maddalena d'Alfonso
with Md'A Design Agency
Graphic Design and Layout: Stefano Mandato
with Silvia Casavola
Picture Research and Photo Editing: Simona Girella
Translation: Alan Daniel Taylor
Cover: *The Life and Times of Sigmund Freud*,
a scene from the play by Robert Wilson
(*Vogue*, August 1970). Photo by Bert Stern

This volume was printed at O.G.M. SpA
Via 1ª Strada, 87 – 35129 Padova
Printed in Italy

Visit us online:
Facebook.com/RizzoliNewYork
Twitter: @Rizzoli_Books
Instagram.com/RizzoliBooks
Pinterest.com/RizzoliBooks
Youtube.com/user/RizzoliNY
Issuu.com/Rizzoli